THE
AMERICAN
COMMUNIST MOVEMENT

Storming Heaven Itself

SOCIAL MOVEMENTS PAST AND PRESENT

Irwin T. Sanders, Editor

THE
AMERICAN
COMMUNIST MOVEMENT

Storming Heaven Itself

Harvey Klehr and John Earl Haynes

Twayne Publishers • New York
Maxwell Macmillan Canada • Toronto
Maxwell Macmillan International • New York Oxford Singapore Sydney

The American Communist Movement: Storming Heaven Itself
Harvey Klehr and John Earl Haynes

Copyright 1992 by Twayne Publishers.

Twayne Publishers
Macmillan Publishing Company
866 Third Avenue
New York, New York 10022

Maxwell Macmillan Canada, Inc.
1200 Eglinton Avenue East
Suite 200
Don Mills, Ontario M3C 3N1

Macmillan Publishing Company is part of the Maxwell Communications
Group of Companies.

10 9 8 7 6 5 4 3 2 1 (hc)
10 9 8 7 6 5 4 3 2 1 (pb)

The paper used in this publication meets the minimum requirements
of American National Standard for Information Sciences—Permanence
of Paper for Printed Library Materials. ANSI Z3948-1984. ∞™

Library of Congress Cataloging-in-Publication Data

Klehr, Harvey.
The American communist movement : storming heaven itself / Harvey
Klehr and John Earl Haynes.
p.   cm.—(Social movements past and present)
Includes bibliographical references and index.
ISBN 0-8057-3855-X (hc)—ISBN 0-8057-3856-8 (pb)
1. Communism—United States—History.   I. Haynes, John Earl.
II. Title.   III. Series.
HX83.K549   1992
324.273′7′09—dc20   92-1081
CIP

To my sons Benjamin, Gabriel, and Joshua and my brother Lenny
H.K.

To my wife Janette, who has tolerated my interest in this subject.
J.H.

For mortal daring nothing is too high.
In our blind folly we storm heaven itself

–Horace, Odes, Book I

Contents

Acknowledgments

We are grateful to Lowell Dyson for his reading of the manuscript and useful suggestions. We also wish to thank Irwin Sanders (general editor) and John Martin (editor) of this series for their support and advice on the preparation of this volume.

Abbreviations

ADA	Americans for Democratic Action
AFL	American Federation of Labor
ALP	American Labor party
APM	American Peace Mobilization
ASU	American Student Union
AWU	Auto Workers Union
AYC	American Youth Congress
AYD	American Youth for Democracy
BLA	Black Liberation Army
CAWIU	Cannery and Agricultural Workers Industrial Union
CCE	Central Cooperative Exchange
CEC	Central Executive Committee
CIO	Committee for (Congress of) Industrial Organizations
CIO-PAC	CIO Political Action Committee
CLP	Communist Labor party
C.P.	Communist party
CPA	Communist Political Association
CPML	Communist Party Marxist-Leninist
CPPA	Conference for Progressive Political Action

CPUSA	Communist Party USA
CWP	Communist Workers party
DFL	Democratic-Farmer-Labor party
EPIC	End Poverty in California
ERAP	Economic Research and Action Project
FBI	Federal Bureau of Investigation
F.E.	Farm Equipment Workers Union
HUAC	House Un-American Activities Committee
ICCASP	Independent Citizens Committee of the Arts, Sciences, and Professions
ILGWU	International Ladies' Garment Workers Union
ILWU	International Longshoremen's and Warehousemen's Union
InCar	International Committee against Racism
IPP	Independent Progressive party
IWO	International Workers Order
IWW	Industrial Workers of the World
LAW	League of American Writers
LID	League for Industrial Democracy
M2M	May 2nd Movement
NAACP	National Association for the Advancement of Colored People
NCLC	National Caucus of Labor Committees
NCPAC	National Citizens Political Action Committee
NLRB	National Labor Relations Board
NMU	National Miners Union
NTWU	National Textile Workers Union
PCA	Progressive Citizens of America
P.L.	Progressive Labor

RAM	Revolutionary Action Movement
RCP	Revolutionary Communist party
RYM	Revolutionary Youth Movement
SACB	Subversive Activities Control Board
SANE	Committee for a Sane Nuclear Policy
SDS	Students for a Democratic Society
S.I.	Socialist International
SISS	Senate Internal Security Subcommittee
SLP	Socialist Labor party
SNCC	Student Non-Violent Coordinating Committee
S.P.	Socialist party
SWOC	Steel Workers Organizing Committee
SWP	Socialist Workers party
TUEL	Trade Union Educational League
TUUL	Trade Union Unity League
TWU	Transport Workers Union
UCP	United Communist party
UDA	Union for Democratic Action
U.E.	United Electrical, Radio, and Machine Workers Union
UMW	United Mine Workers
UTW	United Textile Workers
VDC	Vietnam Day Committee
WCF	Washington Commonwealth Federation
WPA	Works Progress (Work Projects) Administration
WUO	Weather Underground Organization
WWP	Workers World party
YSA	Young Socialist Alliance

Chapter One

The Nature of the American Communist Movement

At its height in 1939 the American Communist party had only 100,000 members. For much of its 70-year history its membership has been a mere fraction of that number. Communist splinter groups, meanwhile, have never enrolled more than a sliver of that total. Communist movements in virtually every industrial nation in the world have been far larger and far more powerful. Nonetheless, this relatively small social movement has had an impact on American life far out of proportion to its size or, indeed, to its accomplishments.

In recent years there has been an explosion of academic interest in American communism. Historians, political scientists, and sociologists, to say nothing of students of literature, art, and popular culture, have churned out a seemingly endless parade of studies of aspects of the American Communist experience. It sometimes appears that never have so many studied so much about so few.

The latest fascination with American communism has been stimulated by the increasing availability of research material, including files of intelligence agencies (notably the FBI), private papers and files now open to scholars, and the willingness of Communists and ex-Communists to discuss the past more frankly. The lack of primary research material, however, has never hampered interest in the subject. Almost from the moment it came into existence in 1919, the American Communist movement has been the subject of the fascinated interest and scrutiny not only of scholars but also of the mass media, the public, and official government bodies.

Karl Marx had confidently believed that socialism would first emerge in the most advanced capitalist nations, since their working classes would most quickly be taught the harsh lesson that only a fundamental alteration in the nature of their societies could improve their lot. In books such as *Imperialism*, Vladimir Lenin had offered a theoretical explanation for the slow pace of the revolutionary impulse in the developed capitalist world. But even the Russian Bolsheviks, who at first linked the survival of their revolution to the onset of Socialist upheavals in Western Europe, continued to believe that it was only a matter of time before the working classes of advanced capitalist nations seized power.

For Communists, American and foreign, the United States has been the symbol of the doomed capitalist world. For most of the last 70 years they have regarded America as the most potent intellectual, military, and diplomatic enemy faced by communism. As the citadel of capitalism, the United States embodied those values and institutions to which Communists were irrevocably opposed. The progress of America's Communists has, therefore, received more attention from foreign Communists than it might otherwise deserve.

A healthy American Communist movement might symbolize the growing weakness of American capitalism. If communism could thrive in the United States, the very center of world reaction, its prognosis would be encouraging. Moreover, the stronger American communism and its allies, the less able the United States would be to combat Communist and other "progressive" movements abroad. Since few Communists were so optimistic as to envisage the triumph of their movement in the United States in the short term, they placed great stress on the crucial role it could play in ensuring that American imperialism not have a free hand abroad, but be constrained by domestic opposition.

The American Communist movement was unusual among American social movements insofar as it regarded itself as a junior partner of a worldwide movement whose leadership was intimately tied to the foreign policy of a foreign state. The Russian Revolution had led to the formation of the Union of Soviet Socialist Republics, hailed by many radicals around the world as the first workers' state. The revolution had also called into being the Communist movement, distinguished from the Socialists, who also claimed a commitment to Marxism, by its insistence that the transition to socialism required the leadership of a disciplined party of professional revolutionaries. That movement, formalized in the Communist

International, headquartered in Moscow and entranced by the success of the Russian Revolution, was naturally dominated by the Russians.

Throughout its history the Comintern faithfully reflected the wishes of Soviet foreign policy. It was not merely that the organizational reins of the Comintern were held by the Russians or that so many of the foreign Communists who staffed it were political exiles whose very lives it held forfeit, although both were true. The tremendous moral authority held by the Russians, as the architects of the first and, for many years, only successful Socialist revolution predisposed thousands of radicals around the world to accept Soviet pronouncements on revolutionary strategy, tactics, and leadership as definitive.

The peculiar relationship between American Communists and the Soviet Union had a major impact on the course of the Communist movement. Unlike those European or Asian nations whose native Communists could, however plausibly, claim that there was no inherent conflict between their country and the Soviet Union, American Communists lived and worked within a nation that, whatever temporary community of interests it might share with the USSR, was its major foe on the international scene, particularly after World War II. As the strongest capitalist nation on earth, America was, by definition, in conflict with a Soviet Union that saw itself as the harbinger of a future, noncapitalist world.

When American and Soviet foreign policies were in rough congruence, as for example during the late 1930s and World War II, American Communists enjoyed some moderate successes. When the United States and the Soviet Union confronted each other as enemies, American Communists found themselves in the unpopular and uncomfortable position of seeming to defend the interests of their country's most determined and dangerous foe.

American Communists did not consider themselves martyrs, however. For the first half of their existence, they held to an optimistic vision of their future success. While recognizing the magnitude inherent in challenging the largest, most powerful, most successful capitalist democracy on earth from the inside, they were armed with the faith provided by Marxist-Leninist theory, the shining example of the Soviet Union, which they regarded as a potent model of the society they wished to construct, and the support of several distinct and vibrant subcultures in the United States, from which they obtained the bulk of their recruits.

In later years, when the cold war had ended its dreams of success, the American Communist movement retained an importance in American political life even more out of proportion to its numbers. As an object of political attack, domestic communism became one of the key, if not the major, issues on the American agenda of the late 1940s and early 1950s. For nearly a decade American Communists spent much of their time defending themselves and their movement from a variety of attacks and legal charges. Government efforts to destroy the Communist party and impose restrictions and penalties on party members raised serious constitutional issues and provoked bitter and far-ranging debates about the nature of a democratic society.

Every era in the history of the American Communist movement has been inaugurated by developments in the Communist world abroad. The Russian Revolution led to the formation of the first American Communist party. Soviet pressure led to the abandonment of an underground Communist party. Comintern directives led American Communists to adopt an ultrarevolutionary posture during the late 1920s. Soviet foreign policy needs midwifed the birth of the Popular Front in the mid-1930s. The Nazi-Soviet Pact destroyed the Popular Front in 1939, and the German attack on the Soviet Union reconstituted it in 1941. The onset of the cold war cast American Communists into political purgatory after World War II, and Nikita Khrushchev's devastating exposé of Joseph Stalin's crimes in 1957 tore the American Communists apart.

By the late 1950s the disarray in the Communist world, with Stalinism under attack in the Soviet Union and a rift between the Chinese and the Soviets, the American Communist movement lost its bearings. As the "Communist Party USA," to use its formal name, dwindled in size, splinter groups loyal to other sectors of the Communist world made their appearance. Although Communist sects had been in existence since the earliest days of the movement, their attachment to new Communist governments and the disarray of the Communist party gave them a legitimacy among radicals and an opportunity they had long lacked.

During the late 1960s and early 1970s, the American Communist movement was a bewildering array of tiny groups, each professing loyalty to one or another of the trends in world communism. Tiny sects upholding the wisdom of Albania's Enver Hoxha or North Korea's Kim Il Sung competed with larger groupings insisting they held the key to applying the insights of China's Mao Zedong to the United States. Although the Communist Party USA remained the largest of these small Communist groups, it seemed old, tired, and increasingly irrelevant even on the American radical left.

As the revolutionary wave of the 1960s receded, however, many of the exotic Communist groups it had carried with it vanished. By the

1980s the Communist party had once again become the dominant force in the American Communist movement. Encouraged by a more flexible Soviet policy, revisionist accounts of its history, and a reflexive societal recoil from anything that could remotely be described as McCarthyism, the Communist party was once again attempting, with some modest success, to build a Popular Front, an effort that was once again endangered by the collapse of Communist regimes in Eastern Europe and the Soviet Union's greater willingness to examine self-critically its own ideology.

American communism has worn a number of different hats in its 70 years of existence. At times it has appeared as the defender of American democratic traditions; at other moments it has stridently called for the destruction of that system. Its tactics have ranged from clandestine organizing in revolutionary cells to coalitions with the Democratic party. Its membership has fluctuated wildly, and it has altered its organizational structure numerous times. Its ethnic and social base has shifted over the years, as has its leadership.

This book offers an analysis of the membership, leadership, ethnic appeal, organizational structure, social strategy, and intellectual stance of American communism, through a historical discussion of the movement from its origins to the 1980s. Precisely because it has changed so much, the essence of American communism cannot be captured by a static description of it at one point in time. Its leaders today may be denounced as archenemies tomorrow. Today's members may be expelled or resign next year. This moment's tactics may be tossed overboard on a signal from abroad.

In the past decade some students of American communism have complained about "institutional" histories that focus on the party elite and ignore the activities of the rank and file. The Communist party, however, was not merely a collection of people who shared membership in a social organization. It was a Leninist party with certain goals, visions, and plans, however perfectly or imperfectly these were realized or carried out by the membership. Party turnover was so large precisely because many people, once in the party, learned that they could not meet its requirements or discovered aspects of party life they could not tolerate. That the experiences of rank-and-file Communists differed from that of party cadres or party leaders is undeniable. But it was the latter two groups that set the tone of the party, not only because as a Leninist organization the Communist party gave decisive decision-making power to "professional revolutionaries," but also because ordinary party members rarely lasted for lengthy periods of time. In each chapter, we have tried to indicate the tensions and stresses within the party itself caused by such incongruence.

The chapters that follow discuss the American Communist movement in four different historical periods. Until 1930 American communism was at the margins of American society. Nonetheless, these early years were a crucial period in the development of the movement. Not only were some basic organizational principles decided on, but the relationship between American Communists and the Soviet Union was set and a cadre of party leaders molded who were to play a significant role for the next 30 years. From 1930 to 1945 the Communist movement enjoyed its greatest success in American life. The postwar era saw the party on the defensive. Beginning in 1960, the breakdown in the Communist consensus in the world inaugurated a new era in the American Communist movement.

Within each chapter we have included a discussion of the appropriate Communist splinter groups. Not every such group has been included; many of these tiny sects were too insignificant to warrant discussion. Where these groups played an important role in the larger world or where they significantly affected the tone or structure of the American Communist movement, they have been included.

This is a study of the American Communist movement; it does not include radical, non-Communist groups such as the Socialist party or the anarchists. Communists believe in the tenets of Marxism-Leninism, identify with the states based on such visions, and profess allegiance to the views of self-identified revolutionary internationals such as that founded by Leon Trotsky.

To American Communists capitalism was an outmoded, irrational, and exploitive system that benefited a small minority of wealthy people at the expense of the vast majority of Americans. Whatever tactical concessions they made to its strength or to their own weaknesses, American Communists fervently believed that it would someday be replaced by a more humane, rational, and democratic society modeled on the Soviet Union.

As part of their critique of capitalism, American Communists believed that it rested on the exploitation of underdeveloped countries around the globe. Imperialism, Lenin had taught them, was an inevitable concomitant of a developed capitalist society. Therefore, not only were Communists obliged to oppose capitalism's depredations against its own working class, but they also needed to combat its rapacious foreign policies, which led to economic and political repression in colonies and armed conflicts with its capitalist competitors over foreign markets.

American Communists were not militant liberals or "liberals in a hurry." The ideological system to which they gave their adherence, Marxism-Leninism, was not a variant of traditional American liberalism or progressivism. Indeed, it regarded those views as fundamentally flawed, just as it refused to accept the legitimacy of any other set of views. Marxism-Leninism claimed to offer a scientific interpretation of history; to its adherents it was true and other interpretations were false.

Because they believed their party to be in possession of scientific truth, American Communists had not only an arrogance peculiar to true believers but also a fierce commitment to the Soviet Union as the fount of that truth. They considered themselves revolutionaries, marching inevitably along the path of human liberation. What made them such formidable political organizers and activists was their deep faith in their cause and its ultimate triumph. That same idealism—and its ability to attract tens of thousands of men and women committed to peace, civil rights, and the alleviation of human suffering—made their movement such a challenge to American democracy.

Chapter Two

Origins and First Decade, 1919–1929

"It was the Russian Revolution—the Bolshevik Revolution of November 7, 1917—which created the American Communist movement," said Charles E. Ruthenberg, one of the movement's chief founders. To understand why this was so is an essential step in understanding American communism.[1]

Before Bolshevism

In 1912 the Socialist party of America (S.P.) was at the height of its power. At its birth in 1901 the S.P. had claimed 10,000 members; most likely the actual figure was half of that. Even so, by 1912 its dues-paying membership reached 118,045 members, and in that year the S.P.'s presidential candidate, Eugene Debs, received 897,011 votes, 6 percent of the total vote (over 10 percent in seven states). Over 1,000 Socialists held elected office, including more than 300 city council members, over 50 mayors, and a number of state legislators. Wisconsin voters sent the first Socialist, Victor Berger, to Congress in 1910. Although most unions of the American Federation of Labor (AFL) were non-Socialist, S.P. support was growing; in 1912 a Socialist won one-third of the votes for the AFL presidency.

Debs's vote and the S.P.'s other gains were only modestly significant and look large only in comparison to socialism's marginal past and more marginal future. Nevertheless, this electoral progress represented real growth and appeared to presage a mass movement. Giving strength to the prospect of a mass movement was the Socialist press: 5 English- and 8 foreign-language daily newspapers, 262 English- and 36 foreign-language weekly papers, and 12 monthly journals as well. Prior to the formation of the S.P., socialism in America had been very nearly the exclusive property of a small band of immigrants, chiefly German Marxists. The Socialist Labor party (SLP), founded in 1877, embodied this immigrant socialism and had rarely had a native-born constituency that exceeds 10 percent of its membership. Although the S.P. contained a sizable immigrant membership, most members were American-born and English-speaking.

The years of the Socialist party's flourishing were years of rapid change in America. The nation was in the full flush of industrial growth, with its heavy industries approaching world leadership. Millions of Americans were leaving the farms for the growing cities. This era also saw an extraordinary foreign migration. In the period from 1900 to 1914 more than 13 million persons came to the United States. America's middle class expanded, and its growing nonfarm work force experienced a rising standard of living. Annual real wages (1914 dollars) averaged $503 in 1885–89, rose to $606 in 1901–5 (up 20.4 percent), and increased further to $685 in 1911–15 (up 13 percent).[2] Yet rapid growth also extracted a heavy cost. In heavy industry employment was insecure, and little relief existed to cushion joblessness. Although most workers experienced a decline in working hours along with rising real wages, in the steel industry 12-hour days and a seven-day work week were standard. Although the new industrial cities provided conveniences undreamt of by many immigrants from rural poverty, the cities also contained slums of almost unimaginable degradation. In sharp contrast, rapid growth delivered enormous power and ostentatious wealth into the hands of newly enriched capitalists.

In time the American economy would become based on the mass consumption of consumer goods and deliver to most of its citizens one of the highest standards of living in the world. Much of the American working class would become incorporated into the nation's enormous middle class. In time a welfare system would cushion the shocks of economic change and public regulation and a strong union movement would reign in private corporate power. What is clear in retrospect was not clear at the time, however. As one historian noted, most radicals "mistook the birth pangs of large-scale industrial society for the death throes of the capitalist system."[3] Radicals looked at the growth of the industrial work force and saw the creation of a class that, as it grew conscious of its interests, would assume the direction of society. How the working class would do this was a matter of dispute.

Milwaukee's Socialists exemplified the moderate socialism that brought the Socialist party electoral victories in dozens of cities. Victor Berger's Milwaukee Socialists established a firm base within the city's influential AFL trade unions. Although expressing a firmly class-conscious socialism, Wisconsin Socialist candidates emphasized practical reform goals. These included municipal ownership or regulation of privately owned public services, public health regulations, an end to rampant political corruption, and improved benefits and working conditions for municipal workers. Berger and his colleagues displaced the Socialist future to a distant day and placed in the forefront reforms that did not differ dramatically from those of non-Socialist progressives.

The Socialist left was amorphous and partly outside the S.P. What set it off from more moderate sectors of American radicalism was not so much ideology as attitude. The left tended to exemplify impatience, hostility toward electoral activity, contempt for half measures, and support of revolutionary violence. The leftist Socialist Labor party countered the S.P.'s moderate agenda with a strident advocacy of uncompromised Marxism. Daniel De Leon, the SLP's leader since 1890, rejected all reforms short of total socialism, but, to the dissatisfaction of most on the revolutionary left, insisted that the only path to socialism was electoral politics. De Leon avoided insurrectionary violence and regarded unions as a subordinate arm of the Socialist political movement. Most of the revolutionary left were as impatient with De Leon's futile preaching of Marxism as they were with Berger's immersion in the humdrum of gradual reform.

The Industrial Workers of the World (IWW) was the nearest thing to a center of the revolutionary left outside the S.P. In 1905, at its first convention, William Haywood, its leading figure, thundered, "This organization will be formed, based and founded on the class struggle, having in view no compromise and no surrender, and but one object and one purpose and that is to bring the workers of this country into the possession of the full value of the product of their toil."[4] Unlike the AFL, the IWW championed industrial rather than craft unionism, tried to organize unskilled workers, and, unlike many AFL affiliates, welcomed black, Asian, and immigrant workers. The IWW found its most long-lasting constituency among workers on the fringe of the evolving industrial society. These included lumberjacks, whose work was seasonal and isolated, migratory agricultural workers, and maritime workers, many of whom lacked stable social ties. Wobblies (as IWW members were known) offered these disinherited a primitive millenarian vision of a society were the last shall be first. An appropriately millennial event, the "general strike," would usher in the new society when all workers would spontaneously rise in revolt. Wobbly ideology resembled and was often equated with that of the syndicalists. Syndicalism (the name derives from a French word for labor unions) was a powerful radical movement in Europe, particularly France, Italy, and Spain. Syndicalists saw labor unions, not political parties, as the instrument of revolution. Further, syndicalists envisioned the postrevolutionary society as one in which workers' unions, not the government or a political party, would control society. In the envisioned syndicalist society the government would be little more than the agent of the all-powerful unions or, in the case of anarcho-syndicalism, the political state would fade away entirely. Syndicalist attitudes permeated much of the revolutionary left in America.

IWW rhetoric rang with violent images and fire-breathing talk of dynamite. *"I despise the law,"* said Haywood, "and I am not a law-abiding citizen."[5] Wobblies also endorsed, hinted at, or suggested that industrial sabotage was a preferred tactic. All of this gave Wobblies an image not much different from that of bomb-throwing anarchists. Yet the perception was in large part myth, although a myth to which the IWW's own rhetoric contributed. IWW strikes were not noticeably more violent than strikes by the nonrevolutionary AFL. By rhetorically invoking violence, however, Wobblies generated fears (often real, sometimes feigned) in the rest of society that brought down on them the coercive power of the state anyway.

The Forward March of Socialism

Marxist-led movements grew rapidly throughout Europe in the early years of the twentieth century. In Germany Socialists received 4.25 million votes in 1912, about one-third of the total, and their 110 members of parliament was the largest single party bloc in the Reichstag. The German Social Democratic party maintained a mass membership of hundreds of thousands, led a powerful trade union movement with millions of members, and ran thousands of Socialist schools, youth groups, cultural societies, and newspapers. Social Democratic confidence that their movement was destined to rule Germany seemed justified by the steady growth of the Socialist institutions. Although less formidable than the German movement, Socialist parties and unions showed impressive growth in France, Italy, Belgium, the Netherlands, the Austro-Hungarian Empire, the Scandinavian states, and Great Britain.

Up to 1914, it was easy to see how many radicals developed a triumphalist confidence in the victory of socialism. Many even believed that the Socialist movement's power would prevent a general European war. The Socialist International (S.I.), the federation of the world's Socialist parties, in 1912 called for a revolt of the working class of all belligerents to stop "the monstrosity of a world war." As tensions in Europe in 1914 built toward war, *New Times,* Minnesota's leading Socialist newspaper, said, "It becomes evident that a general European war is almost an impossibility," explaining that "growing class-consciousness and solidarity among the workers of all lands" was such that workers would overthrow their governments before going to war. On 4 August 1914, however, Social Democrats in Germany's Reichstag voted unanimously for war, Socialist members of the French Chamber of Deputies announced their support for war, and in Belgium Emile Vandevelde, head of the S.I. itself, entered the government war cabinet. Initially, *New Times* did not believe it, asserting, "Censored reports from Russia, Germany, France, and Austria are giving out the impression that the Socialists have succumbed to the war fever and are supporting their respective governments. That these reports are absolutely false is indicated." When it became clear that Germany's Socialists had voted for war, *New Times* published reports—false ones, as it turned out—that the Kaiser had executed several Socialist Reichstag deputies and coerced the rest as the only reasonable explanation. [6]

There were, of course, Socialists who opposed the war. Many were simply pacifists who opposed violence. At the other extreme was the little-known Lenin, the exiled leader of the Bolshevik wing of the Russian Social Democratic Workers party. Lenin urged revolutionaries to work for the defeat of their own nation and "turn the imperialist war into a civil war" of proletarian revolution. Antiwar socialism gained strength as war weariness and disgust with the mass butchery of the prolonged conflict grew. Still, it remained a minority position, subject to suppression in the belligerent nations, with limited support, and without consensus about ideology.

The shattering of expectations that the Socialist movement could prevent world war was not the only source of frustration for American radicals. As it turned out, 1912 was the high point of the Socialist party's political appeal. Although a reformist spirit dominated American politics in the era, the S.P.'s electoral victories, vote totals, and party membership fell after 1912. As for the radical Industrial Workers of the World, it never seriously challenged the moderate AFL. Wobblies involved themselves in hundreds of strikes and even took over major strikes by immigrant workers ignored by the AFL. Most of these strikes were lost, and even those won did not redound to the IWW's permanent benefit. Institutional staying power was not a Wobbly attribute.

America's entrance into the war in 1917 threatened to finish off radicalism. For years the IWW had denounced the government as a tyrannical leviathan, but the government generally had not acted the part. Although Wobblies had faced harassment, beatings, and jailing from local authorities, until 1917 official intolerance was sporadic. For the most part the IWW had gone about organizing the revolutionary destruction of the capitalist state without the state responding. Nevertheless, few nations fighting a major external enemy will risk tolerating an internal enemy—even one that is more talk than action—working for the government's overthrow and urging sabotage of the war effort. Public authorities, empowered by Congress's passage in 1918 of the Sedition Act and with enthusiastic public support, jailed the IWW's officials, suppressed its newspapers, closed its offices, and infiltrated it with secret agents.

Although the Socialist party opposed the war, it was not a revolutionary organization, and authorities did not suppress it as they did the IWW. Even so, its antiwar stance resulted in the suspension of the postal mailing privileges of many of its newspapers. Authorities jailed dozens of individual S.P. activists for antiwar agitation. A fervent popular war spirit supported this suppression, and America was not a belligerent for enough time for war weariness to allow the S.P.'s antiwar stance to strike a responsive chord with the public. The slide of party influence also affected the internal alignment of the radical movement. The S.P. reached the peak of its influence under the leadership of its moderate sectors. The decline of the party's influence after 1912 could not but weaken Socialist moderates and embolden radicals. In late 1915 the S.P.'s left wing, from which the Communist movement grew, began to take an organized form. The first explicitly left-wing organization was the Socialist Propaganda League of Boston, which called for a new international organization of antiwar, revolutionary Socialist parties to replace the moderate S.I.

Although the leaders of the league were native-born, its financing came chiefly from the Lettish (Latvian) Workers' Society of Boston, an S.P. affiliate. The role of Lettish Socialists foreshadowed a return of immigrants to the center of the radical stage. When the Socialist party formed in 1901 it emphasized the leading role of its American-born element as it sought to influence the mass of American voters. Still, these were years of heavy immigration. In 1910 over a quarter of America's nonfarm labor force was foreign-born; the S.P. needed to appeal to immigrant workers. There was also the practical problem of how the party could include immigrants who spoke little English. The solution was the creation of S.P. branches for each language and the linking of these branches together as semiautonomous federations. By 1915 the S.P. had 14 such federations. As warweariness fed radicalism within European Socialist parties, a parallel turn toward radicalism appeared among immigrant Socialists in the United States. Membership in the language federations began to grow even as the S.P.'s total membership declined.

Although never large, the Socialist Propaganda League created a factional press for the Socialist party's evolving left. *The Internationalist* appeared in January of 1916, became *The New International* in 1917, and was succeeded in 1918 by *The Revolutionary Age*. Louis C. Fraina edited the latter two journals. *The Class Struggle,* a theoretical magazine edited by Fraina, Ludwig Lore (a leader of the S.P.'s German language federation), and Louis Boudin (a Russian Jewish immigrant and leading Marxist theoretician), also appeared in 1917. Louis Fraina was born in Italy in 1892 and came to the United States in 1895. He left school at the age of 14 and embarked on a career as a radical journalist. After joining the Socialist party, he shifted first to the SLP then to the IWW, before returning to the S.P. in 1917. The revolutionary socialism espoused by Fraina's journals had a syndicalist cast. The engine of revolutionary action was "mass action," a vaguely defined concept of "instinctive group action" by workers.[7] As explained by Fraina, mass action combined mass industrial revolt through industrial unions with extralegal political agitation. The merging of syndicalist and political Socialist concepts appealed strongly to American leftists who identified syndicalism as embodied in the IWW with the revolutionary tradition. The enthusiasm for mass action also reflects the influence of the views of Dutch anarcho-syndicalists. S. J. Rutgers, a representative of the Dutch syndicalist left living in America, played a key role in organizing and raising funds for the Socialist Propaganda League.

Nor was Rutgers the only foreign influence on the left wing. On 14 January 1917 leaders of the Boston-based Socialist Propaganda League met with New York left-wing leaders. The New Yorkers present included Fraina, Lore, Boudin, Sen Katayama (an exiled Japanese Marxist), and five Russians, also political exiles rather than immigrants. The Russian presence reflects the importance of the Socialist party's Russian federation to the left wing. Although founded only in 1915, that federation's rapid growth and radicalism made it a source of left-wing strength. Among the five were Nikolai Bukharin and Leon Trotsky, both soon to be major figures in the Russian Revolution. Bukharin, a Bolshevik, arrived in the United States late in 1916 and served for a few months as editor of *Novy Mir*, the Russian federation's newspaper. Trotsky, then an independent revolutionary not as yet aligned with Lenin's Bolsheviks, arrived early in 1917 and also wrote for *Novy Mir*. This meeting decided upon the conversion of *The Internationalist* into *The New International* under Fraina's leadership.

In April 1917 the Socialist party met in convention to decide upon an attitude toward America's entrance into World War I. S.P. leaders presented a militantly worded resolution that stated "unalterable opposition to the war just declared by the Government of the United States."[8] The left found it was difficult to find a point of principle to argue about, aside from complaining that the S.P.'s incumbent leaders were not sincere. The leadership's resolution passed with 140 votes, as opposed to 31 for a left-wing alternative authored by Boudin and 5 for a prowar alternative. The left wing's charge had a great deal of truth to it. Victor Berger, leader of the S.P. right, supported the resolution but later explained it in such a way as to deprive it of a militant interpretation. Although these tactics frustrated the left wing, the S.P.'s moderates paid a price. Prowar Socialists, including the S.P.'s 1916 presidential candidate, left the party and thereby weakened its right. The government also did not see the resolution as a tactical maneuver. The government's restriction on S.P. newspapers and its prosecution of party spokesmen (those arrested included both Berger on the right and Fraina on the left) were based in part on the antiwar resolution.

Red Dawn

In November 1917 revolutionary workers, sailors, and soldiers under Bolshevik leadership proclaimed a Marxist republic in Russia. The Bolsheviks shot the Czar and his family, pulled out of the war against the German empire, and abolished capitalism. Utopia was in arms and in power. After the postponement of earlier Socialist expectations, here was a living Marxist state. One dazzled radical newspaper in America wrote:

Russia turned all barracks, jails, palaces and churches into national homes, libraries, universities and healthy dwellings for the working masses. Russia gave land to peasants, factories and shops to workers, all accumulated wealth to the whole people. Russia revolutionized science, art, thought and morale. Russia hastened to mend the new life of communes, soviets, and the vigorous human personality. . . . Russia began the revolution. She will carry this fire over all the countries and nations and will consume all the scum of historic evils and untruths, will destroy all governments which have shattered human individuality and will install a new, yet unknown, complete freedom, beauty, care free and happy order of life.[9]

Communism, as Bolsheviks named their variant of Marxism, offered a way out of the dilemmas that bedeviled revolutionary Socialists. Prewar Socialists had built an impressive structure of unions, parties, cultural societies, and other institutions that had won the membership of millions of workers. However, becoming institutionalized also changed socialism into a moderate movement that sought socialism through legislative action. Moderate Socialists were content to allow socialism to grow piecemeal and postponed complete socialism to a distant future. The Russian Revolution proved to many radicals that those who understood Marxism-Leninism and who had the ruthless will to carry out its requirements could leapfrog whole eras of human development. American radicals knew little about Russia or the conditions that brought about the collapse of the Czarist state in March and the Bolshevik triumph in November 1917. They knew, however, that the Bolshevik party had been tiny— about 11,000 members—early in 1917 and ruled one-sixth of the earth by the end of the year.

In Lenin's revision of Marxism, revolution became not the product of inexorable social forces but the willful act of the revolutionary vanguard, a small group of disciplined men and women who knew how to command those forces. As one American leftist spokesman commented, "Though we are a minority, if we are revolutionary Socialists, if we know what the working class wants, we are going to establish the dictatorship of the proletariat in spite of the ignorance of the majority. We shall do it now,— not wait until we get the majority." For those who loathed the evils they saw around them and longed for a world where man did not exploit man, Leninism showed how they could save humanity. If Red revolution could succeed in Russia, the most backward society in Europe, then all things were possible. *The Ohio Socialist,* a leading left-wing paper, said, "You can quit thinking small thoughts and acting small acts and you can embrace mankind and consecrate your life to its emancipation. . . . You can be everything if you will join the hosts of revolutionary labor in the joyous labor of making labor supreme."[10]

Nor did these nascent Communists believe that their road to power would be a long one. After the failure of its 1918 offensive in the West, an exhausted Germany faced external military and internal social collapse. The Kaiser fled Berlin, and a period of disorder followed that many felt would end with the creation of a Red Germany. Surely, it seemed, the old world of capitalism was dying. "The call to action of the proletarian revolution in Russia will soon—*now, perhaps*—marshal the iron of battalions of the international proletariat," wrote Fraina in 1918. Indeed, Lenin and Trotsky proclaimed, "Comrades! Greetings from the first proletarian republic of the world. We call you to arms for the international social revolution."[11]

In January 1918 the pro-Bolshevik wing of the Finnish Social Democratic party seized the government and proclaimed a Finnish Red republic. In Latvia, Ukraine, and Georgia, formerly subject nations of the Czarist empire, revolutionaries established workers' republics. In November 1918 soldiers and sailors mutinied and joined workers in forming revolutionary councils in the German port of Kiel. In January 1919 Spartacists (German revolutionary Socialists) seized control of Berlin and proclaimed a workers' republic. In March 1919 revolutionaries took control of the southern German state of Bavaria and proclaimed a Communist republic, and in Hungary Communists established yet another Red republic. One can understand the confidence with which Charles Ruthenberg, the left-wing leader of the Ohio Socialist party, wrote, "New Soviet governments will arise as the months go by and it will not be long until the . . . boundary of Soviet Europe is the Rhine. . . . The Soviet movement will sweep forward and onward until the Soviet Republic of the World comes into being."[12]

Nor was America immune from strife. The sudden collapse of the German army caught America in the full flush of war mobilization. The government canceled war contracts, and the economy went through a painful, although brief, transition from war to consumer goods production. Prices, no longer controlled, shot up, and by 1920 the cost of living was more than double the prewar level of 1914. Workers, no longer constrained by wartime restrictions, struck in numbers unprecedented before or since. The year 1919 was, in fact, the peak of the largest strike wave in American history, extending from 1915 to 1922. The year opened with more than 30,000 Seattle shipyard workers walking out for higher wages. The strike escalated when the Seattle Central Labor Union, representing all AFL unions, voted to conduct a general strike, and another 30,000 workers left their jobs. The leading proponent of the

Seattle general strike was a vocal admirer of the Bolshevik revolution. The strike paralyzed Seattle for five days. (A citywide general strike also immobilized Winnipeg, Manitoba.) In September AFL policemen in Boston walked off the job. Vandalism and looting followed within a day. In September an AFL-led strike shut down most of the nation's steel production as 365,000 men walked out. Strikers and steel company men fought it out in the streets; 20 men died. Shortly after the steel strike began, 394,000 soft-coal miners (soft coal was then a vital industrial fuel) walked out under the banner of the AFL's United Mine Workers.

In 1919 a new world was in birth (a much better one, radicals presumed). The example of revolution in Europe reversed the loss of membership in the American Socialist party. Party membership stood at 80,379 in 1917 and rose to 108,504 in 1919. Much of the growth came from the S.P.'s language federations of the nationalities of the Czarist empire. The Russian federation grew from 2,373 members in December 1918 to 7,824 in April 1919, the Ukrainian from 2,400 to 3,836, and the Lithuanian from 4,760 to 6,049. By April 1919 the membership of the federations formed a majority of the Socialist party.

In late 1918 in New York, a center of S.P. membership, Socialist city aldermen voted to support the sale of U.S. war bonds. The left wing denounced the votes, and in January 1919 S.P. locals in New York met to consider charges against the officials. Moderate party leaders blocked any action. Left-wing delegates bolted and formed a left-wing council, which quickly became an alternative S.P. organization rivaling the regular organization and publishing the *New York Communist,* edited by John Reed.

Reed was born in 1887 in Oregon to parents of upper-class, old-stock American background. After graduating from Harvard in 1910, Reed became part of the cultural bohemianism of Greenwich Village. He interested himself in radical causes, publicized the IWW's 1913 Paterson, New Jersey, silk strike, and reported on labor unrest and the Mexican Revolution for a variety of journals. He reported on World War I for a time, but his antiwar views estranged him from most publishers. After the fall of the Czar, he hurried to Russia in time to see the Bolshevik seizure of power. The Bolshevik vision captivated him, and he joined the Bolshevik party's Bureau of International Revolutionary Propaganda. He returned to the United States in 1918 to write *Ten Days That Shook the World,* describing the Bolshevik coup. The book was an immediately popular success. In addition to being one of the first English-language accounts of the revolution by an eye witness, Reed wrote in vivid images and infused the book with his own romantic enthusiasm. He wrote of the Bolshevik insurrection: "Adventure it was, and one of the most marvelous mankind ever embarked upon, sweeping into history at the head of the toiling masses, and staking everything on their vast and simple desires."[13]

In January 1919 Lenin invited revolutionaries all over the world to join Russian Bolsheviks in forming the Communist International (Comintern) to replace the prewar Socialist International. His manifesto invited 39 organizations to send delegates to the first Comintern convention. Four of these were American: the left wing of the S.P., the Socialist Labor party, the SLP's tiny labor affiliate, and the IWW. The invitation tempted the SLP and the IWW, but the temptation rested on a misunderstanding. At first both believed that Bolshevism was essentially a Russian form of their own doctrines. The SLP, however, adhered rigidly to De Leon's program of achieving Marxist socialism through America's electoral system. Once the SLP discovered that the Bolsheviks wanted to overturn that system rather than seek socialism through it, the SLP turned away from communism. Nor did the IWW's syndicalism have much in common with the politicized state collectivism of communism. By the early 1920s the IWW realized this and rejected communism. Communists, however, did win over William Haywood, the IWW's leader and the nation's best-known radical. Haywood had been convicted of conspiracy to violate wartime federal statutes. In 1921, while out on bail, Haywood fled to Russia.

American communism also won the allegiance of a large segment of the IWW's membership, particularly its Finnish-American constituency. Radicalism attracted proportionately more Finns than members of any other immigrant group; 20–30 percent of Finnish Americans had some association with the Socialist, Wobbly, or Communist movements. The Finnish Socialist Federation was the S.P.'s oldest and largest language affiliate. When the S.P. disavowed the IWW's violence and syndicalism in 1912, the Finnish federation split into two feuding wings, one of which supported the IWW. Most Finnish Wobblies turned Communist after the Bolshevik Revolution. Among them was Carl Päiviö, editor of *Luokkataistelu* (Class Struggle), a Finnish-language syndicalist journal published in New York. Päiviö received a jail term under New York's antisubversive law for a 1919 *Luokkataistelu* editorial stating: "a rioting mob is the one and only possible means for organizing a fight in the every day as well as in these last open and decisive blood-battles between the capitalists and the working class. . . . To hell with the teachings of peaceful revolution. The bloody seizure of power by the working classes is the only possible way."[14] The establishment of the Red Finnish government in 1918 also radicalized many Finns who had sided with the Socialist party in 1912. Santeri Nuorteva, editor of *Raivaaja* (Pioneer), a Finnish-language Socialist newspaper published in Fitchburg, Massachusetts, became the ambassador to the United States of the Finnish Red republic. After "White" Finnish nationalists crushed the Red government in a bloody civil war, Nuorteva joined the Russian Soviet Government Information Bureau. (The United States and the new Soviet state did not have formal diplomatic ties, and the bureau acted as the Soviet government's unofficial embassy in the United States.)

Factionalism and Founding Conventions

In the spring of 1919 the pro-Bolshevik left wing prepared to take control of the S.P. Seven of the language federations—the Russian, Polish, Hungarian, South Slavic (Yugoslav), Lettish, Lithuanian, and Ukrainian—endorsed the left. In New York 20 S.P. branches with 4,000 members joined the left-wing council, while dozens of other locals around the nation announced left-wing loyalties. A party referendum to join the Comintern passed with a vote of more than 10 to 1. A referendum for the party's National Executive Committee gave the left 12 of 15 seats. Fraina, one of the left's candidates, received the highest vote in the referendum.

The left wing drew from the Bolshevik example the lesson of no compromise with moderate socialism. *The Revolutionary Age* referred to moderates as "Social-Gangsters and traitors to Socialism," and a Russian federation leader demanded that Socialists "clean our ranks from that mire."[15] The S.P.'s moderates could see no future in the party should the left take control, and in May 1919 incumbent leaders expelled the S.P.'s left wing, including the entire Michigan, Massachusetts, and Ohio state organizations, seven language federations, and dozens of S.P. locals—in all, about two-thirds of the party's membership. Incumbent leaders also called an emergency Socialist party convention for Chicago on 30 August 1919.

Left-wing leaders called a June "National Conference of the Left Wing" to decide upon a response to the expulsions. Some advocated abandoning the party and creating an American Communist party. Those supporting a new party attempted to preempt the conference by having the expelled Michigan Socialist party issue a call for a national convention to form a new party. The leaders of the Michigan S.P., oddly enough, were not Bolsheviks. They opposed the reformism of the old S.P. but believed that American capitalism was too strong for immediate revolution. Instead, they called for a long period of education carried out by a revolutionary party free of the S.P.'s compromised right wing. Still, the Michigan program of forming a new party coincided for the moment with the strategy of the pro-Bolshevik foreign-language federations.

Most delegates at the June conference, however, followed the lead of the left's English-speaking leaders: Louis Fraina (head of the expelled Boston S.P.), John Reed and Benjamin Gitlow of New York, Charles Ruthenberg of Ohio, and James P. Cannon, editor of the Socialist *Workers' World* in Kansas. They argued for mounting a last effort at taking over the Socialist party with an eye to winning control of its considerable financial assets, newspapers, and property. Those favoring capturing the S.P. carried the vote, but the language federations had taken the lessons of Lenin's history to heart: no compromise. With the Russian federation in the lead, they walked out. The remaining delegates, about two-thirds of the total, elected a National Council of the Left Wing, named Fraina's *The Revolutionary Age* as its official organ, and adopted a manifesto written by Fraina. The conference called for an attempt to take control of the S.P. at its August 30 convention. If this failed, then the conference provided for a convention to form a new Communist party on 1 September 1919.

Meanwhile, the language federations and the Michigan Socialist party set about founding a new Communist party. They also scheduled a convention in Chicago on September 1. They had no spokesmen with the talent or prestige to match that of Fraina or Reed. The Russian federation itself had existed only since 1915, and its membership was new to American radicalism. Even so, the Russian federation had something of greater worth: the moral ascendancy of the Bolshevik Revolution. As *The Revolutionary Age* commented, the Bolsheviks were "architects of the new structure of society, the seers and heralds of the new age."[16] Distance and the chaos of revolution blocked communications with the new Soviet state, however, and the Western Allies, attempting to prevent Bolshevism's spread, censored what information did get out of Russia. Few Americans had read the writings (chiefly in Russian and as yet largely untranslated) of Lenin, Trotsky, or other Bolsheviks. The Russian Socialist federation was the nearest most radicals could get to real Bolsheviks.

The left wing's English-speaking leaders could not withstand the Russian federation's taunts that only it understood Bolshevism. When in July the language federations spurned a delegation from the Left Wing Council that pleaded for cooperation, the council collapsed. A majority, including Fraina and Ruthenberg, voted to join the language federations and go straight to a Communist convention. A minority that included John Reed and Benjamin Gitlow persisted in the attempt to take over the Socialist party.

The Reed-Gitlow plan for taking control of the S.P. convention was simple. There were some delegates to the convention who sympathized with the left wing. There were other leftist delegates whose credentials had been challenged but who had a right to have their challenges heard by the convention. To these, Reed and Gitlow added a bloc of militants who would arrive early, seize seats, and claim delegate status in the name of their various expelled S.P. bodies. Unfortunately, the Gitlow-Reed caucus discussed these plans in a Chicago barroom where the bartender was a friend of Adolph Germer, the S.P.'s right-wing executive secretary. Germer arrived early at Chicago's Machinists' Hall on August 30 and ordered the left-wing activists out. They refused, daring him to call in the capitalist police. Germer had no scruples about using the police; he had the left wingers tossed out.

Later, those left-wing sympathizers seated at the S.P. convention walked out to join their ousted comrades. The next evening the Reed-Gitlow group, 82 strong, met on the ground floor of the Machinists' Hall while the S.P. continued its convention on the second floor. Alfred Wagenknecht, editor of *The Ohio Socialist,* gaveled the convention to order, and the delegates rose to sing the "Internationale," the anthem of the world Socialist movement. The convention founded the Communist Labor party (CLP) with Wagenknecht as its executive secretary and John Reed as one of its international delegates.

The CLP proclaimed undeviating loyalty to the Comintern and its policies, although the delegates only partly understood what those were. The CLP said it had "only one demand: the establishment of the Dictatorship of the Proletariat." The convention reflected its unfamiliarity with the nature of bolshevism in its continued use of syndicalist concepts. It declared "the most important means of capturing state power for the workers is the *action of the masses,* proceeding from the place where the workers are gathered together—in the shop and factories." Not surprisingly, the Communist Labor party denounced the Socialist party as corrupt and unrevolutionary. The CLP directed much of its fire, however, at its fellow left wingers of the language federations. Ruthenberg, now aligned with the federations, attended the CLP convention and urged its delegates to join the Communist convention sponsored by the federations. The CLP rejected the offer after an angry debate in which John Reed said the CLP would never accept an American Communist party dominated by foreigners. The CLP did, however, create a committee to negotiate with the other Communist convention. As a rebuke to the language federations, the CLP's platform pointedly stated "no autonomous groups of federations independent of the will of the entire Party shall be permitted."[17]

The other Communist convention got under way on September 1 at the headquarters of the Russian federation in Chicago. Having planned to hold a separate convention from the start, red streamers, red rose floral arrangements, and huge pictures of Marx, Trotsky, and Lenin decorated the federations's convention. The decorations were almost for naught, however, as the Chicago police arrived to arrest a Michigan Socialist party leader for an earlier speech that violated the state's anti-radical laws. In the process the policemen ripped down the decorations and roughed up objecting delegates. Even so, the convention got underway with a band leading the 128 delegates in the "Internationale." The convention, which adopted the name Communist Party of America (C.P.), immediately divided into three blocs. The language federations, under the leadership of the Russian federation, made up the largest faction. An English-speaking bloc from the Left Wing Council followed in size. The smallest group was the Michigan S.P. organization. The immediate point at issue was the attitude toward the rival Communist Labor party. The Fraina-Ruthenberg Left Wing Council group wanted the Communist party to negotiate a merger with the CLP. The other factions rejected this by a vote of 75 to 31. The council group then resigned from the convention's governing committee and threatened a boycott. Faced with the loss of its most talented English-speaking allies, the federations backed down and appointed a committee to meet with the CLP, but nothing came of the negotiations. The three blocs split again over the C.P.'s manifesto. The Michigan group backed one reflecting its view that the revolution would be a long time coming. The federations and the council group backed a draft prepared by Fraina. When the Fraina draft won, 20 Michigan delegates announced a boycott. The other two factions ignored the threat. (Within a year the Michigan group moved outside the Communist movement. It formed the Proletarian party, which lingered on for decades.)

The C.P.'s manifesto stated: "The world is on the verge of a new era. Europe is in revolt. The masses of Asia are stirring uneasily. Capitalism is in collapse. The workers of the world are seeing a new life and securing new courage. Out of the night of war is coming a new day." It went on to denounce moderate socialism, saying, "Communism does not propose to 'capture' the bourgeoisie parliamentary state, but to conquer and destroy it." Lest anyone think that Communists were gentle, democratic idealists, the Communist party platform put in italic type the message "it is necessary that the proletariat organize its own state *for the coercion and suppression of the bourgeoisie.*" While the CLP had championed "action of the masses," the C.P. called for "mass action." It stated: "Mass action develops as the spontaneous activity of unorganized workers in the basic industry; its initial form is the mass strike of the unskilled. In these strikes large masses of workers are unified by the impulse of the struggle, developing a new tactic and a new ideology." Unlike IWW-style syndicalism, Communists explained, "mass action is industrial in its origin, but it acquires political character as it develops fuller forms" and results in "the conquest of the power of the state."[18] No matter how defined, however, the C.P.'s "mass action" bore little relationship to what it eventually learned was real bolshevism. Nonetheless, what was important to these new American Communists was not a particular principle but the example of bolshevism. When it discovered that communism was not syndicalism with a political twist, it jettisoned "mass action" without a second look.

Unlike the Communist Labor party, the Communist party did not clip the wings of the language federations. The C.P. proclaimed its internationalism and charged the CLP with "this treacherous ideology of 'Americanism'" by questioning the role of foreigners in the American Communist movement.[19] Still, the language federations knew it would be folly to choose persons who spoke little English as the leaders of the American Communist party. Consequently, the Left Wing Council faction picked up many of the party's leading positions. The convention chose Ruthenberg as its national secretary, while Fraina received the post of international secretary and editor of the party's journal, *The Communist.* Charles Ruthenberg, unlike other prominent Communist founders, was an organization man rather than a journalist, orator, or ideologue. He was born in Ohio in 1882, the son of German immigrant parents. He completed high school, enrolled in a business college, and worked at a variety of white-collar jobs. In 1909 he joined the Socialist party and was a Socialist candidate for numerous Ohio public offices. World War I radicalized Ruthenberg, who was jailed for antidraft agitation, and he became the leader of the left wing of the Ohio S.P.

Neither of the new Communist parties was very large. The CP claimed

50,000 members, while the CLP avowed 30,000. Each exaggerated and based their numbers on the membership of their affiliates before the split in the S.P. Dues-paying membership for the C.P. toward the end of 1919 averaged about 24,000. Ten foreign-language federations dominated the C.P.; the Russian federation, with 7,000 members, was the largest, followed by the Lithuanian (4,400), Ukrainian (4,000), South Slavic (2,200), Polish (1,750), Lettish (1,200), Jewish (Yiddish-speaking: 1,000), Hungarian (1,000), German (850), Estonian (280), and 1,100 unaffiliated non-English speakers. The C.P.'s English-speaking membership of 1,900 included 800 in the Michigan organization that left the C.P. in 1920.[20] The Communist Labor party's membership was much less, probably about 10,000, although it was stronger than the C.P. on the West Coast. The CLP also had a higher proportion of English speakers, but even in the CLP they were probably less than one-fifth.

By September 1919 America had two Communist parties. These parties were born at the peak of revolutionary expectation. Bolshevism seemed on the verge of sweeping out of Russia and through Central Europe. America was in the midst of the biggest strike wave of its history. *The Ohio Socialist,* soon to become the CLP's *The Toiler,* attributed the strike wave to bolshevism, commenting that American labor was "setting its face toward the rising sun, toward the east where the crimson of the new day greets mankind with the new message. Labor has thundered its ultimatum in foreign lands and its lightning has blasted the chains of wage slavery."[21] In retrospect there was little revolutionary potential in the strikes. A desire to catch up with inflation and the opportunity for success offered by the tight labor market motivated most of the strikes. At the time, though, the hopes of radicals that the United States teetered on the edge of revolution seemed plausible.

No strike was more central to the continued growth of organized labor than that of the steel industry in 1919. If the labor movement could organize this industry, with its hundred of thousands of unskilled immigrant workers, the heartland of industrial America lay open. Both Communist parties denounced the AFL unions that sponsored the strike and ridiculed William Z. Foster, the syndicalist who headed the strike committee. Communists demanded that strike leaders put aside demands for union recognition, higher wages, and better working conditions. Instead, Communists wanted the strike transformed into "the general political strike that will break the power of Capitalism and initiate the dictatorship of the proletariat—all power to the workers!"[22] Both the CLP and the C.P. declared that they wished the destruction of the American Federation of

Labor; since AFL unions led the strike wave, this assured Communist exclusion from any meaningful role in the strike movement.

Considerable political turmoil accompanied the strike wave. The election of 1920 produced a brief resurgence of Socialist party electoral success. Wisconsin elected ten Socialist state legislators and one congressman. New York elected one Socialist congressman and five legislators. The "progressive" wing of the AFL, led by the Chicago Federation of Labor, organized first a local Labor party and then a national Farmer-Labor party in hopes of breaking the two-party system. Both Communist parties ridiculed these efforts, and the C.P. dismissed the Labor party movement as "a minor phase of proletarian unrest," essentially an effort of the reactionary AFL unions to "conserve what they have secured as a privileged caste."[23] The Communist ultrarevolutionary stance also produced one peculiar campaign slogan. Some left-wing activists had, before the formation of the C.P. and CLP, entered and won Socialist primaries for local offices in New York. They were thus on the official general election ballot. Because the Communists meanwhile had decided that the path to power was not through the ballot, these candidates adopted the slogan "Boycott the elections!"

Looking back on it, these actions appear frivolous, as if these newborn American Communists were playing at revolution. They were, however, serious. The reality of their own tiny size, of the underlying stability of American society, and the unrevolutionary content of the strike wave was not apparent to Communists. Communists lived in a mental universe constructed from their vision of the Bolshevik Revolution and the belief that all things were possible. In that universe, American workers were ready to storm heaven itself and proclaim a Soviet America.

The Red Scare

Some government officials and a segment of the public shared a portion of the Communist dream, although to them it was a nightmare. They, too, saw bolshevism sweeping through Europe. They, too, saw revolutionary potential in the great strike wave; in addition, a series of political terrorist acts frighted them. In 1919 and 1920 terrorists murdered 35 persons and badly injured more than 200 in a series of bombings in every region of the country. Even more would have died had not 16 mail bombs been put aside by the post office due to insufficient postage. No one was ever convicted for these murders, although the evidence pointed to left-wing anarchists.

Communists had nothing to do with the bombings and little to do with the massive strikes of 1919 and 1920. A good portion of the public, however, cared little for the ideological distinctions between anarchists, syndicalists, Socialists, and Communists. Adding to public panic was propaganda from business sectors threatened by the strike wave. Much of this propaganda deliberately, and often mendaciously, attributed revolutionary motivation to the strikers and their AFL unions. The "Red Scare" that followed was also a continuation of government suppression of those who had opposed the American war effort. Further, many Americans were under the impression that bolshevism was a plot by the hated German empire. The German military, after the fall of the Czar early in 1917, had transported Lenin into Russia to disrupt the tottering Russian government, a ploy that proved to be an immense success. Lenin and his Bolsheviks used Russian war weariness to destroy the post-Czarist government and bring themselves to power in November 1917. The Germans then forced the weak Bolshevik regime to sign the Treaty of Brest-Litovsk, which gave Germany most of what it desired in eastern Europe. The treaty also freed scores of thousands of German troops that had been fighting Russians in the East to meet American soldiers just reaching the Western Front. The relationship between the German military and the Bolsheviks had been a temporary marriage of convenience for both parties. At the time, nonetheless, much of the American press treated the Bolsheviks as little more than hirelings of the German Kaiser. The wartime image of bolshevism as a German covert operation lingered for years.

In the fall of 1919 U.S. Attorney General A. Mitchell Palmer launched a series of raids to round up alien radicals. His initial targets were only incidentally Communists; the heaviest blows fell on the IWW and immigrant radicals, particularly syndicalists and anarchists. On 7 November Palmer-ordered raids in a dozen cities resulted in the arrest of several hundred members of the syndicalist Union of Russian Workers, a group that furnished many recruits for the Communist movement. Turning to the Communists themselves, a series of raids in January 1920 netted more than 5,000 suspected C.P. and CLP members. If those arrested were aliens, the U.S. government moved to deport them. State authorities prosecuted citizen Communists under state antisubversive laws. (Thirty-five states outlawed revolutionary activity and, in some cases, speech advocating revolution.) In November 1919 New York police raided dozens of radical clubs, confiscated tons of literature, and arrested hundreds. New York authorities later prosecuted 75 of those arrested in the raids, included Communist leaders Benjamin Gitlow and Charles Ruthenberg. The two received sentences of 5–10 years, but actually served less than 3. Illinois sent 20 Communists to jail; California arrested 500 and sent more than half to prison.

Police and federal officials paid minimal regard to civil liberties in the Palmer raids. Officials often failed to obtain search warrants, held those arrested incommunicado, or subjected them to abuse. The raids produced much evidence of revolutionary advocacy but very little of bomb making, arms, or other terrorist activity. In its early stages few public figures complained of the abuses of the Palmer raids. Later, over Palmer's protests, the U.S. Labor Department ruled that the government could not deport an alien without a hearing. This forced the release of many of those arrested, although the U.S. deported about 600 alien radicals after hearings in addition to the several hundred deported before the hearing requirement.

By 1921 the Red Scare was over. The international trends that had engendered fears of revolution receded. The Spartacist revolt in Berlin failed, and anti-Communist forces overthrew the Communist regimes in Bavaria, Hungary, Latvia, and Finland. Estonia and Lithuania emerged from the Czarist empire as independent anti-Communist nations on Russia's Baltic flank. In 1920 the new Polish republic threw back a Bolshevik invasion that had threatened to incorporate Poland into the Soviet Union. In 1921 a Communist uprising in the German Ruhr failed badly. The Soviet Union survived and even reconquered much of the old Czarist empire, including the briefly independent nations of Ukraine, Georgia, and Azerbaijan. The Soviet state, however, was isolated and exhausted. The American public decided that the threat of revolution had been exaggerated or, in any case, was over. President Warren G. Harding announced that "too much has been said about Bolshevism in America."[24] Harding released early most of those imprisoned on federal charges during the Red Scare. Many states followed Harding's precedent.

As brief as it was, the Red Scare drove both Communist parties underground. Communists destroyed their membership cards, broke their branches into small groups of less than a dozen members, changed meeting places, and used the names of innocuous organizations. Communist leaders adopted pseudonyms when writing in the party press. The Communist press continued to publish but without proclaiming an official connection to the party. Party members unwilling to risk arrest left the movement. Party leaders investigated those who remained to weed out government informers, of whom there were many; often entirely loyal

Communists were expelled on mere suspicion of a government link. Within a year Communist membership fell by 80 percent. Some Communists liked the underground; after all, bolshevism had been an underground conspiracy subjected to the oppression of the Czar's political police, and it had come to power. The underground experience would, they thought, get rid of the summer soldiers of revolution and leave a hard core of Leninist revolutionaries.

Further Factionalism

Meanwhile, the CLP and the C.P. still had to settle the question of who was the American Communist party. The Communist Labor party was the most eager for unity; the Palmer raids had reduced it to almost nothing. Within the Communist party, the English-speaking group under Ruthenberg also wanted unity, as it needed allies against the overbearing language federations. Ruthenberg denounced the Russian federation's exclusiveness for making the C.P. into "an institution for the holding of ritualistic incantations to the Russian Revolution."[25] The federations, however, opposed any significant concessions to the CLP. Meanwhile the Soviet regime was beginning to establish its suzerainty over the Communist movements that had sprung up in imitation of the Bolshevik Revolution. The first direct messages to American Communists from the Comintern came in 1919 and early 1920. Latvian authorities intercepted the messages when they captured Soviet couriers on the way west. Consequently, the messages reached American authorities and the American press before they reached American Communists. One of the messages, signed by Grigory Yevseyevich Zinovyev, head of the Comintern, urged unity between the C.P. and the CLP, reduced autonomy for the language federations, Communist participation in strikes and other mass protests, and the adoption of the name United Communist Party.

In April 1920 the C.P. split into two organizations, both claiming the name Communist Party of America and publishing newspapers identically entitled *The Communist*. This briefly put three Communist parties into the field (two C.P.'s and the Communist Labor party). Ruthenberg and Jay Lovestone led the smaller of the two C.P. organizations, which attracted most of the party's English-speaking members. The larger C.P., led by Nicholas Hourwich of the Russian federation and Alexander Bittelman of the Jewish federation, consisted almost entirely of non-English speakers. So much as there was a principle involved in the split, it was over the relative emphasis on insurrectionary violence. The Hourwich-

Bittelman C.P. favored an uncompromising advocacy of violent revolution, while the Ruthenberg-Lovestone C.P. favored moderating the party's insurrectionary program sufficiently to allow Communists to participate in peaceful strikes and popular political protests. At the end of May 1920 Ruthenberg's C.P. met with the CLP in a secret unity convention. This convention, too, nearly split over the emphasis given armed insurrection. In the end, the convention endorsed insurrection but said an armed revolt was not the party's chief concern. The convention urged Communists to support the IWW, nearly lifeless at this point. As for the AFL, it said, "a Communist who belong to the AFL should seize every opportunity to voice his hostility to this organization, not to reform it but to destroy it."[26] The convention elected a governing board evenly split between the CLP and Ruthenberg's C.P. and, as Zinovyev had suggested, adopted the name United Communist party (UCP).

This still left two Communist parties in the field, the Hourwich-Bittelman C.P. and the UCP. Each was down to less than 10,000 members. Each was predominately foreign. Each lacked contact with the mass of America's workers and played no significant role in the labor movement or in any popular political cause. Shortly after their founding, both the CLP (before its merger into the UCP) and the C.P. dispatched delegates to Moscow in hopes of claiming Moscow's endorsement as the real Communist party. This was the period of a Western boycott, and reaching the Soviet Union was not easy. John Reed, the CLP emissary, worked his way across the Atlantic under an assumed name and slipped into Russia through Finland. Louis Fraina, the C.P.'s representative, followed, also under an assumed name, but unknowingly in the company of a "fellow Communist" who was in fact a secret U.S. government agent. After some delays, however, Fraina separated from his companion and got into Russia by way of Germany and Estonia.

Reed received a cordial reception based on his acquaintance with Bolshevik leaders from his days as a journalist in 1917. Fraina, however, had to go through an investigation of charges that he was a U.S. agent. Earlier, a secret U.S. Justice Department agent had circulated the charges in American Communist circles in hopes of disrupting the C.P. and covering his own tracks. A Communist party trial in America cleared Fraina, but he faced a reexamination when he got to Russia. Santeri Nuorteva, also in Russia at the time, believed the charges and pressed the case against Fraina. Lenin personally cleared Fraina, but the experience weakened Fraina's morale and standing.

The Comintern insisted on unity, and Reed and Fraina became part of a single American delegation to the Second Comintern Congress (July–August 1920). They quickly learned that both the C.P. and the CLP were out of step with the Comintern. By 1920 Lenin realized that continued expectations of world revolution were illusory. He drafted a new program that allowed the Soviet Union to stabilize its regime at home and foreign Communist movements to operate in a nonrevolutionary environment in the West. Lenin's new doctrine, expressed in his pamphlet *Left-Wing Communism: An Infantile Disorder,* set aside ultrarevolutionary purity. In its place Lenin called for pragmatic tactics to advance the Communist cause. Specifically, he urged Communists to participate in elections and work within "reactionary trade unions" to bring them to a progressive stance. The new doctrine blatantly conflicted with the emphasis on revolutionary purity, semisyndicalist suspicion of electoral activity, and pledges to destroy the AFL found in both American parties. The Comintern directed the American delegation to adopt this view. It did, but Reed dissented on the trade union question. He had always admired the IWW's romantic swagger and despised the prosaic AFL. Reed's day in the American Communist movement, however, was over. He contracted typhus and died in Moscow in October 1920. With an honor guard of Red Army soldiers standing by, he was buried beneath the Kremlin Wall.

Zinovyev also decided to reduce factionalism in the American movement by removing Fraina. Comintern leaders sent him to Mexico and instructed him to stay out of American affairs. Distressed by the spy charges and removal from the American movement, Fraina dropped out of the Communist movement and returned to the United States in 1923. He financed his return with $4,200 of Comintern money in his possession. After a few years, Fraina embarked on a new career as a writer on economics under the name of Lewis Corey. His sophisticated Marxist interpretation of American capitalism attracted attention, and by the mid-1930s he was a respected economist. In 1941 Fraina became a professor of economics at Antioch College, where he taught until 1951.

Corey supported Communist political causes in the early 1930s but became more critical when Joseph Stalin began his blood-soaked mass purges. The Nazi-Soviet Pact of 1939 destroyed his remaining faith in communism. By 1940 he opposed communism and was skeptical of Marxist collectivism. While at Antioch, Communists promoted rumors that he had embezzled $50,000 to $500,000 in Comintern funds. At the same time, right-wing organizations attacked him as a disguised Communist. In 1952 the U.S. government began deportation proceedings against Corey, who had never become an American citizen, based on his

Communist membership from 1919 to 1923. He appealed, but died in 1953 two days before the government officially dropped its deportation action.

The Comintern and American Communists

Reed's dissent aside, American Communists did not object to Comintern control. All American Communists viewed their movement as the American branch of a worldwide movement with headquarters in the Soviet Union. The Comintern adopted and the American Communist movement accepted 21 requirements for admission to the Comintern. The sixteenth read, "All resolutions of the congresses of the Communist International, as well as the resolutions of the Executive Committee, are binding upon all parties joining the Communist International." As late as 1925 American Communist membership cards read, "The undersigned declares his adherence to the program and statutes of the Communist International and of the Workers (Communist) Party and agrees to submit to the discipline of the Party and to engage actively in its work."[27] To be sure, American Communists viewed the Soviet Communist party as equally subordinate to the Comintern as the American party, at least in theory. They simply allowed that the Russian party, as the one party to achieve a successful revolution, had a leading role in the Comintern. Nevertheless, from the beginning the Russian party ran, not just led, the Comintern. Over time and particularly under Stalin, the Comintern became little more than the Soviet Union's instrument for directing foreign Communist movements.

In 1920 Zinovyev not only insisted that American Communists adopt the moderate turn of Lenin's *Left-Wing Communism,* he insisted that the two American parties merge. Both the Communist party and the United Communist party agreed, but bickering resulted in months of delay. Finally, the Comintern created a committee to resolve the matter headed by Sen Katayama, once a Japanese Marxist in U.S. exile, now a Japanese Communist in Soviet exile. Katayama's committee had the power to create a wholly new Communist party if the two refused to merge. This threat led to a joint convention at Woodstock, New York, in May 1921. The convention produced a single party that adopted the name of Communist Party of America (C.P.). The UCP and the old C.P. divided all offices in the new party between them. The convention also adopted the Comintern's new policy, although with visible reluctance. The old hedging about participation in electoral politics receded and calls for smashing the AFL disappeared. Instead, the convention urged Communists to enter mainstream labor unions and condemned the IWW for creating dual unions without prospects of success. Even so, the convention pledged itself to the "inevitability of and necessity for violent revolution, and will prepare the workers for armed insurrection as the only means of overthrowing the capitalist state."[28] The Communist party remained an underground organization.

All of this pleased the Comintern, but it was not enough. In 1921 Lenin told the Third Comintern Congress that a period of capitalist stabilization lay ahead and ordered Communists to abandon plans for immediate revolution and turn to creating mass Communist parties. Lenin's guidance stunned many Western Communists who had renounced the mass Social Democratic parties of the old Socialist International and modeled themselves on the Bolshevik example of a small revolutionary vanguard. In line with Lenin's new perspective, Comintern leaders demanded that the American party end its underground existence. The American delegation did not like it, but there was no open dissent. The Americans announced, "The delegation of the Communist Party of America declared its agreement with the proposed Theses on Tactics of the Bureau of the Russian delegation. We approve everything unconditionally with respect to the fundamental points and accept the principles under consideration without reservations."[29] Privately, one of the American delegates, Nicholas Hourwich, expressed unhappiness with the new line. Hourwich, however, was a Russian immigrant to America who lacked U.S. citizenship, and the Soviet government took care of his opposition by refusing to allow him to return to the United States.

One product of Lenin's new approach was the emergence of William Z. Foster as a factor in American communism. Foster was a genuine native-born American proletarian, born near Boston in 1881. His father was an Irish immigrant and his mother of old-stock American descent. He left school at age 10 and during the next 26 years roamed the country taking a variety of blue-collar jobs. He spend some years in the Socialist party, but two trips to Europe converted him to syndicalism. He joined the IWW but left and founded his own organization to promote syndicalism within the AFL. In 1917 he convinced John Fitzpatrick of the Chicago Federation of Labor to back a joint organizing drive among meat-packing workers. The campaign, with Foster as chief organizer, was a huge success. Several hundred thousand workers joined the various AFL unions that were part of the drive. The AFL then backed a similar Foster-led joint campaign to organize the steel industry. Again, he proved himself an exceptionally able trade unionist. In 1919, 365,000 steelworkers struck in support of the organizing campaign. This time, however, employers were more intransigent and public temper had changed. The strike failed.

Although Foster's personal prestige was high, he was at loose ends after the steel strike. An employers' "open shop" counterattack put the AFL on the defensive. Prospects faded for massive organizing campaigns such as those Foster had led. His quasi-syndicalist Trade Union Educational League (TUEL) promoted industrial unionism within the AFL, but with limited success. American Communists, who wanted to destroy the AFL, not reform it, scorned him. Lenin's turn toward mass organization, however, changed Communist attitudes. In 1921 the Comintern formed the Red International of Labor Unions as its trade union auxiliary. The Profintern, as it was known from its Russian acronym, reflected Lenin's new stance. Rather than sponsoring new Communist unions, the Profintern tried to win the allegiance of numerous large syndicalist-oriented unions of Europe. In America it sought out representatives from the IWW and AFL activists of a radical inclination. Foster, initially skeptical, agreed to attend the Profintern's congress as an observer.

The first Profintern congress (July 1921, in Moscow) adopted Lenin's new line by directing that revolutionaries enter the mainstream labor movement. This infuriated the Wobbly delegates at the congress, and the IWW consequently refused to join the Profintern. Foster, on the other hand, was delighted; he, after all, had been practicing this strategy for a decade. Further, there were other similarities between Foster's views and Bolshevik practices. Most syndicalists held that after the overthrow of capitalism, worker-controlled industrial unions would govern society. Foster, however, saw a postrevolutionary society controlled by "scientific" principles. He said, "The ordinary unscientific custom of majority rule will be just about eliminated. It will be superseded by the rule of facts and figures." Foster came to believe that Marxism-Leninism was "scientific socialism" and saw in the supervision of every aspect of Soviet society by the Bolshevik party the realization of his vision of a society governed by scientific principles. Foster had never accepted the traditional syndicalist faith in the mass of common workers. He assigned to a "militant minority" the duty of arousing workers and bringing about revolution. Foster decided that his militant minority and Lenin's revolutionary vanguard were the same. Foster stayed in Russia for more than three months; when he left he was a Communist. In return, the Profintern made Foster's TUEL its American affiliate and inserted him into the leadership of the American Communist movement.[30]

Communism Moves Aboveground

The new Comintern line pointed American Communists toward active engagement in mass organizing. The American Communist party, however, was still an underground party. How could a secret conspiracy get in contact with the masses? A segment of the party's leadership, led by Jay Lovestone and Max Bedacht, argued that it could not. They supported forming an aboveground party to engage in popular agitation while maintaining the underground party as well. Most Communists, however, opposed creating an aboveground party at all. In particular, the C.P.'s language federations continued to regard an underground conspiracy as the natural mode for a revolutionary body.

Still, Moscow wanted an aboveground organization, and grudgingly the C.P. created the aboveground American Labor Alliance. The alliance was little more than a coordinating committee for such aboveground Communist-run organizations as the Friends of Soviet Russia, the Irish American Labor League, the Hungarian Workers Federation, and the like. The Comintern signaled that this was not enough. Party leaders then agreed to set up an aboveground party through a merger of the alliance with the Workers' Council, a radical offshoot of the Socialist party that supported the Comintern. Alarmed, Communist enthusiasts for the underground demanded a special convention of the underground party to debate the plan. There was little doubt that a party convention, given a free choice, would reject forming an aboveground party. The leadership, however, was more concerned about Moscow than its own rank and file. It refused to call a convention and suspended those leaders who resisted creating an aboveground party.

The founding convention of the Workers Party of America met in New York in December 1921. The Workers party was not, however, an independent organization. The underground Communist party continued in existence and controlled the aboveground Workers party. The Workers party brought the movement immediate gains in membership when the large Finnish and Jewish Socialist federations, which had before held back from formal Communist affiliation, joined the Workers party.

Militant supporters for the underground party rebelled at what they regarded as revolutionary apostasy. Leaders of several of the language

federations and other underground enthusiasts held a convention (a secret one, naturally) in January 1922 that proclaimed itself to be the legitimate underground Communist party. It denounced the Workers party
as an "aggregation of Compromisers, opportunists and centrists."[31] This
faction, however, faced the problem of the Comintern. The Comintern
wanted a legal organization and, despite having denounced the aboveground Workers party, the pro-underground faction created its own
aboveground organization, the United Toilers of America. Thus, not only
were there once again two Communist parties, both underground with
the same name, there were two aboveground entities, the Workers party
and the United Toilers. Moscow held a hearing on this farcical situation
in March 1922. The Comintern brushed aside the claim, probably accurate, of a spokesman for the United Toilers/C.P., that his organization
had the support of most American Communists. Comintern leaders told
him that the Comintern, not the rank and file of the American party,
decided who were the legitimate leaders of American communism. The
Comintern gave the United Toilers/C.P. faction two months to turn over
all of its records and property to the Workers party/C.P. The only solace
given was an instruction to the Workers party/C.P. to reinstate those
who had taken part in the United Toilers/C.P.

This was not, however, the end to factionalism about an underground
party. Looking at the implications of the new Comintern line, Ruthenberg, Bedacht, and Lovestone (known as the "Liquidators") pushed for
the complete abolition of the underground party. The other side, led by
Gitlow and Wagenknecht, saw liquidation as too much of a concession to
moderation and wanted the underground party continued indefinitely.
This group picked up the name of the "Goose" faction after their opponents complained that they cackled like geese. The Goose faction accepted the name after pointing out that the cackling of geese had once
saved Rome. Moscow sent a three-man delegation to settle the matter.
A unity convention met on a farm near Bridgman, Michigan, in August
1922 to settle the dispute. Only a minority of the convention favored a
wholly aboveground stance for the party; the Comintern representatives, nonetheless, insisted. In the end, the delegates voted to continue
the underground Communist party but shift the organization's emphasis
to the aboveground Workers party. The presence of a federal government agent as one of the delegates brought the convention to a premature end. He notified his superiors of the convention, but because of the
convention's security arrangements, could not get the exact location to
the Justice Department. A Justice Department investigator pinpointed

the location but was himself spotted. By the time police arrived, all but 17 of the 45 delegates had fled. The Comintern representatives escaped, but authorities arrested Ruthenberg and Foster. (Foster's trial resulted in a hung jury, but Ruthenberg was convicted; he was free on appeal when he died in 1927.)

The Bridgman convention was a major step toward legalization, but not a complete one. The Goose faction, reluctant supporters of an above-ground party, remained the dominant group in the C.P. Faced with continued foot dragging on legality, the Comintern intervened again. In the fall of 1922 the Fourth Comintern Congress in Moscow convened a special commission to hear representatives of the two factions and consider Communist strategy in America. The commission came out flatly for legalization. It ordered American Communists to emphasize the above-ground Workers party and keep an underground only as a temporary auxiliary. The Fourth Comintern Congress also enunciated the "united front" policy, an elaboration of Lenin's 1921 directive that Western Communists work within nonrevolutionary mass movements. In line with the policy the Comintern instructed American Communists to join the movement to create a moderate Labor party based on mainstream AFL trade unions. The underground Communist party dissolved in April 1923 and notified the Workers party that the latter was the Communist party in America. In 1925 the Workers party would change its name to the "Workers (Communist) Party of America" and in 1929 to Communist Party USA or CPUSA.

The chief figure in the new Communist party was John Pepper, a Hungarian who under the name Joseph Pogany had served as commissar of war in the short-lived Hungarian Communist republic. The survivors of the Hungarian Red regime, exiles in Moscow, were a fractious lot, and, perhaps to get him out of the way, the Comintern had sent Pepper to America in 1922 as part of the three-member Comintern delegation. The intense rivalry at the Bridgman convention between the Liquidator and Goose caucuses had prompted the Comintern delegation to insist on a compromise slate for the key Central Executive Committee. Pepper became a member of the CEC and held the balance of power between the two factions. After his colleagues returned to Moscow, Pepper used his prestige as a Comintern representative and bloodied revolutionary to make himself the de facto head of American communism. He learned English and lectured his comrades on the need to become more assimilated, complaining "the Workers Party is not enough American."[32] He supervised implementing the Comintern program of full legalization and extinguishing the Goose caucus. Rather than disgracing Goose caucus leaders, however, he welcomed many of them, Benjamin Gitlow for example, as his personal supporters. He brought Jay Lovestone, one of the leading lights of the Liquidator faction, into his circle as well. In 1923 Pepper became secretary of the CEC and exercised more influence than Charles Ruthenberg, the party's general secretary, or James Cannon, its chairman.

The Communist movement that emerged from the underground in 1923 was very different in style from the party of 1919–22. The new party called itself revolutionary, but its tone was strikingly different. It avoided calls for violent insurrection, and immediate reforms, once scorned, came to the fore. Jay Lovestone explained, "We might talk ourselves blue in the face about our holy cause, about the wonders of Communism, about the necessity for shouldering guns against capitalism and yet not enhance the revolution by an iota. But let us talk to the workers about their long hours, their disemployment, their hardships and the why and wherefore of these, and they will be ready listeners and doers."[33] One could easily mistake this as a quote from Victor Berger. On the surface American Communists had come full circle and repudiated the principles that had led them to break with the Socialist party. Such was not the case. American communism as transformed in 1923 was significantly different from either the Social Democratic moderation of the old Socialist party or the openly revolutionary stance of left-wing Socialists and the syndicalist IWW.

The new Communist program envisioned using immediate demands as stepping stones to the overthrow of capitalism. Berger could have said that as well, but the difference was in the process. The old Socialist party had believed that fighting for immediate demands would gradually change society and gradually raise worker consciousness. Socialism would come by an evolutionary process. The new Communist tactic of immediate demands was different. Immediate demands would win support for Communists from the masses of workers. This support would give Communists power: power in trade unions and power in politics. Communists would then use this power to advance the revolutionary cause by whatever means were expedient. This tactic inherently had a large element of subterfuge. It was not conspiratorial in the traditional sense, but neither was it honest. The old Socialist left wing and the IWW had been candidly revolutionary. The new communism was different. Only the initiated Communist party members knew the ultimate intentions. Alexander Bittelman explained: "The whole truth does not mean telling the workers, at every turn of the game, that the seizure of power will have to be accomplished by force of arms. . . . *Telling the workers the whole truth about a given situation does not mean giving the workers the full Communist program.* A Communist program is not a Bible to be brought to the workers always in full, with all its implications. It is a guide to action for the advanced guard of the working class—The Communist Party."[34]

Although the Communist movement's program had changed, its guiding principle had not. American communism had been born in emulation of the Bolshevik Revolution, not as the embodiment of a specific set of principles. The movement's initial policies had reflected what American radicals thought bolshevism was. As they learned more, they had adjusted their principles to more closely reflect Russian bolshevism. The Comintern had demanded, and American Communists had willing granted, control over American communism. They did so because of their conviction that Russia's Communists had discovered the method to make utopian dreams into concrete reality. In 1919 the American journalist Lincoln Steffens visited the new Bolshevik state and came back a supporter of communism. He said, "I have been over into the future, and it works."[35] This was not a mere witticism; it reflected the fundamental attitude of those who stayed with the movement. This set them apart from other radicals. Other radicals could only dream of a Socialist future; Communists had already built a country "where dreams come true," as one American Communist put it.[36] The particulars of the American Communist program changed when Moscow indicated; this was not inconsistency, but dogged adherence to its central vision that the Soviet Union embodied that dream.

American Communism's First Venture into Mass Politics

The aboveground Workers party made its first venture into mass politics through the Farmer-Labor movement. John Fitzpatrick, of the AFL's Chicago Federation of Labor, was the most influential figure in the movement. Fitzpatrick, who already had the skeleton of a Farmer-Labor party in existence, called a convention for July 1923 to found an enlarged national movement of left-of-center but nonrevolutionary trade unionists, reformers, and agrarian radicals. Fitzpatrick initially welcomed Communist interest in his plans and treated the Workers party as a junior partner in his move for a new party.

In addition to the existing Chicago-based Farmer-Labor party, dele-

gates to the convention came from the Workers party, Michigan's Proletarian party, four state farmers' organizations, four national unions (the
Amalgamated Clothing Workers was the largest) and several hundred
local unions, fraternal clubs, and farmers organizations. The delegates
claimed to represent 600,000 people. Many of the delegates, however,
represented only paper organizations. Pepper and the C.P., viewing the
convention as a quick path into the political mainstream, packed the convention. Although the Workers party itself had only 10 delegates,
hundreds of delegates were secret Communists claiming to represent
local unions or such bodies as the Lithuanian Workers' Literature Society. The resulting Communist majority was a tribute to the party's prodigious energy and its utter lack of scruples. The Communist majority
flattened all opposition. Over Fitzpatrick's anguished protests, the convention created a new Federated Farmer-Labor party with Communist
leadership.

Initially, Communists felt they had won a huge victory. Only a year
before they had emerged from the underground as a tiny movement without influence in public life. Now they stood at the head of a movement
with ties to unions and farm organizations all over the nation. In reality,
the Communists had captured a largely paper organization and made a
bitter enemy in John Fitzpatrick. Fitzpatrick took out his anger on the
Communist's Trade Union Educational League. The TUEL under Foster's leadership had made significant bridgeheads on AFL central union
councils in Chicago, Minneapolis, and a few other cities. In several national unions progressive unionists welcomed the TUEL as an ally in their
campaigns against incumbent leaders. The TUEL's campaign for merging
craft unions into broader industrial unions and for American recognition
of the Soviet state had won a measure of support in the AFL. Fitzpatrick
had been the TUEL's most prominent ally among AFL progressives, and
his humiliation caused many progressives to rethink their alliance with
the TUEL's Communists. As progressive unionists made common cause
with the AFL's established leaders, a wave of expulsion of Communists
swept through state and city labor bodies, erasing many of the TUEL's
gains.

Foster and Cannon blamed these reverses on Pepper's overreaching.
Communists, they argued, should build a base within the progressive
wing of the AFL and not seek a leading role in a mass political movement.
Pepper, backed by Ruthenberg, was unrepentant. Despite the evidence,
he insisted, that the Federated Farmer-Labor party was a real mass
party; further, Pepper wanted Communists to throw themselves into the

presidential campaign of Robert La Follette, who in the fall of 1923 appeared to stand an outside chance of winning the election in 1924. A senator from Wisconsin, La Follette had enormous personal prestige as an uncompromised progressive. The Conference for Progressive Political Action (CPPA), the political agency of several major national unions, along with a large segment of independent reformers and the Socialist party, appeared ready to endorse his candidacy.

The two C.P. factions thrashed out their differences at the third Workers party convention (Chicago, December 1923). With the help of a small faction led by Ludwig Lore, Foster and Cannon carried the day. (Lore's faction, the most leftist of the three, sought more caution in adventuring into mainstream American politics.) Ruthenberg remained as the party's executive secretary, but control of the Central Executive Committee shifted to the Foster-Cannon faction. Foster became party chairman, and Pepper's influence declined sharply. Despite their differences over the Fitzpatrick episode, Foster and Cannon agreed with the Ruthenberg-Pepper wing over the desirability of entering the La Follette movement. The chosen vehicle was the Minnesota Farmer-Labor Federation.

In 1922 Minnesota's Farmer-Labor party elected both of the state's U.S. senators and two U.S. representatives, an achievement that gave that party and its head, William Mahoney, significant influence in the national Farmer-Labor movement. Mahoney genuinely supported La Follette, but wanted to make him the candidate of a national Farmer-Labor party with a left-of-center ideology. Communists convinced Mahoney that they and their Federated Farmer-Labor party could assist Mahoney's plans. Mahoney proposed to create a new national party at a convention in St. Paul, Minnesota, prior to the CPPA's launching of La Follette's candidacy. The St. Paul convention would unite the Minnesota Farmer-Labor Federation, the Federated Farmer-Labor party, and several score smaller Farmer-Labor bodies scattered throughout the Midwest and West. The new party, Mahoney thought, would endorse La Follette and negotiate with the CPPA for a role in shaping La Follette's campaign.

At this point Moscow intervened. In May 1924 Foster, Pepper, and Moissaye Olgin (a Lore ally) traveled to Moscow for advice. Lenin had died in January, and the Soviet Communist party was in the throes of a succession struggle between Trotsky and a combined opposition of Zinovyev, Lev Kamenev, and Stalin. Trotsky attacked his opponents by taking a militant revolutionary stance. He condemned the Comintern's united-front policies as opportunistic and denounced its backing for

American Communists taking part in the La Follette candidacy. Zinovyev covered his left flank by temporarily dropping the united front. The Comintern not only censured any support for La Follette's campaign but also denounced Lore because his leftist position resembled Trotsky's. Olgin promptly disavowed the leader of his faction, and the American party expelled Lore from its ranks.

Foster brought back the Comintern decision to America on 1 June 1924, and the C.P. immediately set about reversing its policy toward La Follette's candidacy. Meanwhile, La Follette himself acted. He announced that Communists were the enemies of democracy and forbade their association with his campaign. C.P. participation in the St. Paul convention was known, and La Follette's denunciation dashed Mahoney's hopes that any major unions and prominent politicians would attend. Communists flooded the St. Paul convention (17 June 1924) with hundreds of delegates of bogus Farmer-Labor organizations, although there was significant attendance from genuine Farmer-Labor bodies. After much angry debate, the convention adopted a stance acceptable to the Communists. As a concession to Mahoney, the convention deferred forming a new Farmer-Labor party. It did, however, nominate a presidential ticket, which, Communists assured Mahoney, was simply standing in for La Follette, awaiting the actions of the CPPA convention. When the CPPA convention nominated La Follette, however, the stand-in Farmer-Labor ticket stepped aside not for La Follette, but for William Foster and Benjamin Gitlow. Meanwhile, the Workers party formally nominated Foster and Gitlow as well. The Farmer-Labor organization created at St. Paul was dead. As for Mahoney, he reacted much as Fitzpatrick had. He became an ardent anti-Communist.

In the following presidential campaign Communists spent more time attacking La Follette than they did criticizing the Republican or Democratic candidates. In the election, the Republican candidate, Calvin Coolidge, won with 15 million votes, Democrat John W. Davis was a poor second with 8 million, and La Follette a distant third with 4 million. The Foster-Gitlow ticket received about 33,000 votes, fewer than the Prohibitionist candidate (over 57,000) or the Socialist Labor party candidate (almost 39,000).

In the wake of the La Follette fiasco the Comintern in March 1925 reconsidered its American strategy. The American delegation represented the two major factions: Foster and Cannon for the majority and Ruthenberg and Lovestone for the minority. Once again, factional alignments in the Soviet party shifted and thereby shifted Comintern policy.

Stalin, who had been allied with Zinovyev and Kamenev of the Soviet party's left in order to discredit Trotsky, shifted to an alliance with Nikolai Bukharin, leader of the Soviet party's right, against Trotsky, Zinovyev, and Kamenev. The Comintern, which had insisted on the break with La Follette, looked back and decided that La Follette had represented a forward step for politics in America. Moscow ordered American Communists to pursue a reformist labor party strategy. Both American factions embraced the new line without qualification. The Comintern also ordered the American party to hold a convention and that a neutral chairman, a Russian Comintern agent named Sergei Gusev, settle any disputes.

The Workers party fourth convention opened in August 1925 in Chicago. Foster's faction had a clear majority, perhaps two to one, over Ruthenberg's. Then Gusev intervened to show that majorities at an American party convention meant little. He produced a cable from Moscow that named Ruthenberg's faction as the more loyal to the Comintern. Moscow's intervention enraged Foster, but he submitted. He commented, "I am for the Comintern from start to finish. I want to work with the Comintern, and if the Comintern finds itself criss-cross with my opinions, there is only one thing to do and that is to change my opinions to fit the policy of the Comintern."[37] The two factions split the Central Executive Committee with Gusev as a neutral chairman. As Gusev regularly supported Ruthenberg and Ruthenberg retained the position of party secretary, control passed to Ruthenberg's faction.

With the Comintern encouraging entry into the mainstream, American Communists undertook several initiatives in the union field. In 1925 Communists in alliance with progressive unionists put Ben Gold, a party member, into the leadership of the largest local of the Fur Workers Union. Communists might have taken control of the entire union, but anti-Communists intercepted a Ruthenberg telegram instructing Communists on how to manage the union's convention. This blatant intervention into union matters disconcerted the Communists' allies and prevented a Communist takeover. In 1926, however, Gold led a highly successful strike, and despite desperate efforts by the AFL, Gold and the Communists took command of the Fur Workers Union. The Communists also led the left wing of the International Ladies' Garment Workers Union (ILGWU) in New York. For several years in the mid-1920s the left wing and the ILGWU right wing (fiercely anti-Communist and aligned with the Socialist party) warred for control of the union's largest locals. On several occasions the left won control, only to see the right use its superior power in the ILGWU national organization to thwart them. A 1926 strike started by Communist-led ILGWU locals went badly, and the right regained control of the New York locals.

In 1925 textile mills in Passaic, New Jersey, announced a 10 percent cut in wages already near poverty levels. The workers, largely immigrant and perhaps half female, were angry but unorganized and ignored by the AFL. Under the leadership of a dynamic young Communist, Albert Weisbord, a "United Front Committee" organized the rebellious workers and took on the form of a union. Weisbord soon led a strike of 16,000 workers. The mill owners and police reacted with violence, brutal harassment, and an adamant refusal to negotiate. The strike gained much notoriety and a large measure of public sympathy despite its Communist leadership. The Comintern, however, disliked the dual-union implications of Weisbord's United Front Committee. Over Weisbord's protests, Communists turned the strike over to the AFL's weak United Textile Workers (UTW). The UTW settled the strike under what amounted to an honorable surrender; workers got their jobs back but almost nothing else.

Leadership Struggles at Home and in Moscow

Charles Ruthenberg died in March 1927 after an emergency appendectomy, and his ashes were buried beneath the Kremlin wall while regiments of the Red Army stood at attention. His death reignited factional warfare in the American party. Foster and Cannon teamed up with William Weinstone, a leader of the Ruthenberg faction, to back Weinstone as Ruthenberg's replacement. Gitlow and Bedacht backed Jay Lovestone, Ruthenberg's chief lieutenant, for the post. The party's Political Committee named Lovestone as acting party secretary, though he was only 29 years old. Lovestone, a Lithuanian Jew who had come to the United States at the age of nine, had become a Socialist while in high school. After graduation from City College of New York, he moved through several jobs and briefly attended law school and accountancy school. He spent much of his time agitating for the Socialist party's left wing and was a delegate at the founding of the Communist party in 1919. He got his first full-time party job in 1921 when party leaders selected him to edit *The Communist*.

Although outvoted on the Political Committee, Foster, Cannon, and Weinstone felt they had a majority on the larger Central Executive Committee. They demanded that it act on Lovestone's appointment. Lovestone responded with a threat to call a party convention. Both sides appealed to Moscow. Lovestone had traveled frequently to Moscow and had a close relationship with Bukharin, and in 1927 Bukharin ran the Comintern. The Comintern decision, although keeping Foster in the leadership, went to Lovestone's faction. The Comintern left the final composition of the American party's leaders to a convention, but sent a Comintern agent to oversee the convention. Moscow also directed the American party press to publish Comintern cables making clear its preference for Lovestone and restricting Foster to the union sphere. The convention, held in New York in August 1927, confirmed Lovestone as party secretary, and his faction gained overwhelming majorities on the Political Committee and the CEC.

Lovestone is sometimes linked with the doctrine of "American exceptionalism." In full flower, American exceptionalism holds that America's lack of a feudal past, early achievement of democracy, and abundant natural resources make it an exception to Marxist principles that explain European history. Lovestone, Leninist that he was, never held such a view. He did, however, hold that American capitalism had characteristics that required tactics different from those appropriate to Europe. Before Lovestone, American Communists described America's economy as either in dire crisis or about to enter a crisis. Lovestone recognized the 1920s as a time of extraordinary economic growth and that large sectors of the working class shared in the growing consumer prosperity. He defined American capitalism as in a period of stabilization "on an upward path." Lovestone relied on Lenin's doctrine that imperialism was the final stage of capitalism to explain this phenomenon. He characterized American imperialism in the 1920s as "youthful, vigorous, and growing" in contrast to the decaying colonial empires of Europe.[38] Lovestone predicted that American capitalism faced an unavoidable crisis, but he put the crisis in the future. Lovestone's exceptionalism, then, was little more than an argument over the timing of the inevitable revolution.

Lovestone's view had been in harmony with the Comintern under Bukharin. Bukharin's star, however, was fading. In 1927, having destroyed the leftist opposition of Trotsky and Zinovyev with the aid of Bukharin, Stalin turned on his ally. Stalin's agents began to denounce the "Right Danger" and called for a sharp left turn in Soviet policy. Stalinists announced that the world was entering the "third period" of the struggle between communism and capitalism. The first period, from the Bolshevik Revolution to the failed German Communist insurrection in the Ruhr, had been one of revolutionary crisis. The second period of stabilized capitalism and a decline in revolutionary potential had lasted through 1927. The third period, starting in 1928, signaled a new crisis in capitalism and resurgence of the revolutionary tide. Third Period communism inside the Soviet Union expressed itself in the bloody collectivization of agriculture (3 million to 7 million peasants killed) and hyperexploitation of labor to produce rapid industrialization (the five-year plans). The Comintern reflected Soviet policy and formally adopted a left turn at its Sixth Congress (July to September 1928). After the Sixth Congress, Moscow directed Communists to break ties with nonrevolutionary groups and create revolutionary institutions to take power in the coming crisis.

In America the first sign of the turn came when the Profintern denounced the TUEL for emphasizing work within the AFL. This upset a major Communist effort among coal miners. The United Mine Workers (UMW) was one of the few industrial unions in the largely craft-union AFL. Its battles with mine owners had won it a fiercely loyal following among miners and for a time it had been one of the largest unions in the United States. A series of strike losses in the early 1920s, however, put the union on the verge of extinction. John L. Lewis dominated what remained of the UMW through a union political machine renowned for its brutal intolerance.

John Brophy, along with Communist Pat Toohey, led a strong body of UMW dissidents in the "Save the Union" movement, which sought internal reform and the end to Lewis's leadership. The Profintern's instructions killed the anti-Lewis alliance when Communists shifted toward creating a rival to the UMW rather than reforming it. In September 1928 Communists founded the National Miners Union with Toohey as its leader. Brophy drew the appropriate lessons about Communist reliability as allies. The National Miners Union was only the first of a series of dual unions. Following quickly were the National Textile Workers Union under Albert Weisbord and the Needle Trades Workers Industrial Union under Ben Gold. In 1929 the Trade Union Educational League converted itself into an explicit revolutionary rival of the AFL and became the Trade Union Unity League (TUUL).

The Sixth Comintern Congress also infected the American party with a slight case of Trotskyism. At the congress Trotsky was an object of scorn, and Communists from every nation joined in savage denunciations of Trotsky's views. Trotsky was in internal exile, and Soviet authorities allowed him to reply only in writing and with limited circulation. Yet what he wrote caused a crisis of conscience for James Cannon, one of the American party's delegates. Cannon decided that Trotsky's views were the authentic voice of Marxism-Leninism. He smuggled Trotsky's document out of the Soviet Union and surreptitious gathered a small group who shared his views. When C.P. leaders learned of Cannon's heresy, they immediately expelled him and his chief allies from the party. Communists also burglarized Cannon's apartment to get letters documenting his Trotskyist treason. Cannon tried to reach out to the party rank and file, but Communist strong-arm squads physically broke up meetings organized by Cannon's followers. Only 100 party members followed Cannon out of the C.P. into the "Communist League of America (Opposition)."

In response to the Sixth Congress, Foster and Gitlow, the party's 1928 presidential ticket, campaigned on a platform suffused with fire-breathing rhetoric. Foster told cheering Communists: "When a Communist heads a government in the United States—and that day will come just as surely as the sun rises (Applause)—that government will not be a capitalistic government but a Soviet government and behind the government will stand the Red Army to enforce the Dictatorship of the Proletariat."[39] The Communist ticket received just over 48,000 votes compared to about 268,000 for Socialist Norman Thomas, 15 million for Democrat Al Smith, and 21.4 million for Republican Herbert Hoover.

Lovestone shifted left with the Comintern, but not fast enough for his factional enemies. His opponents accused him of reluctantly embracing Third Period communism and harboring the "American exceptionalism" errors. The opposition was, however, somewhat confused because its leader, Foster, agonized over dual unionism. Dual unionism rejected everything he had stood for as a union organizer. Foster, after all, had come into the Communist movement as the exponent of radicals working within the mainstream AFL union movement. He would within a year become a vocal advocate of revolutionary dual unionism. In the meantime he was crippled as the leader of a faction using Third Period communism to bludgeon its opponents. Leadership of the anti-Lovestone forces fell to Alexander Bittelman.

Most American Communists were not aware as yet of the sharpness of Moscow's left turn. Bukharin was still officially head of the Comintern when it adjourned its Sixth Congress. The "Right Danger" that Stalin denounced did not appear to include Bukharin or Bukharin's friends, such as Lovestone. When the American Communist party met in convention in March 1929, Lovestone's caucus included 95 of the 104 delegates. Even so, Lovestone nearly lost control of the convention. Stalin no longer concealed his assault on Bukharin. Anyone associated with the man who came to personify the "Right Danger" faced destruction. Two Comintern representatives arrived with guidance that Lovestone's shift was not enough in Moscow's eyes. Lovestone maneuvered brilliantly; he promised total loyalty to the new line and introduced a resolution denouncing Bukharin. Lovestone balked only at Moscow's proposal that he and Bittelman accept overseas Comintern posts and that Foster became general secretary. After a flurry of telegrams, Moscow deferred the proposal. The convention's final actions were a Lovestone triumph, given the Comintern's attitude. Lovestone's chief ally, Benjamin Gitlow, became general secretary, and Lovestone majorities dominated the new CEC and Political Committee.

Still, Lovestone was out as general secretary and knew that the Comintern was displeased. He, Gitlow, and Bedacht went to Moscow in April 1929 to argue their case. Another leading Lovestoneite, Bertram Wolfe, was already in Moscow as the American representative to the Comintern. Lovestone and Gitlow left Robert Minor as acting general secretary and Jack Stachel as organization secretary, both staunch Lovestone supporters. Lovestone instructed them to transfer ownership of the party's property to Lovestone supporters should the Comintern turn the party over to the opposition. Foster, Bittelman, and William Weinstone went to Moscow to speak for the opposition.

In Moscow Stalin was at this point in complete control and chose to sit on the Comintern's commission to review the American party's convention. Stalin accused the American party of shaping its strategy in response to particular American events. He labeled this a right-wing ideological error because Communists should act in accordance with the underlying nature of capitalism on an international basis. In other words, Communist tactics were uniform and there was no exception for America. The commission called for reorganizing the American party's leadership and demanded that Lovestone and Bittelman accept Comintern assignments. In May 1929, in a confrontation before the ruling Presidium of the Comintern, Gitlow, asserting that the Lovestone caucus represented an overwhelming majority of the American party, read a statement for the Lovestone delegation rejecting the commission's recommendations. Stalin replied:

You declare you have a certain majority in the American Communist Party and that you will retain that majority under all circumstances. This is untrue, comrades of the American delegation, absolutely untrue. You had a majority because the American Communist Party until now regarded you as the determined supporters of the Communist International. And it was only because the Party regarded you as the friends of the Comintern that you had a majority in the ranks of the American Communist Party. But what will happen if the American workers learn that you intend to break the unity of the ranks of the Comintern and are thinking of conducting a fight against its executive bodies—that is the question, dear comrades? Do you think that the American workers will follow your lead against the Comintern, that they will prefer the interests of your factional group to the interests of the Comintern? . . . A poor hope, comrades! At present you still have a formal majority. But tomorrow you will have no majority and you will find yourselves completely isolated if you attempt to start a fight against the decisions of the Presidium of the Executive Committee of the Comintern. [40]

Gitlow still refused to give way, but Lovestone and Wolfe gave way in part. They said that although they disagreed, they would accept the Comintern's recommendations as a matter of discipline. Stalin expected unequivocal acceptance and treated Lovestone's and Wolfe's position as no better than Gitlow's open defiance. On the other hand, Bedacht surrendered on all points, saying, "We not only accept the decision as a matter of discipline but we accept the correctness of the decision as a matter of recognizing the international and ideological superiority of the Comintern over ourselves. . . . The formal acceptance of a CI decision must be complete with a conscious analysis of the decisions to which we submit in order to penetrate and absorb the political reasons of the Comintern for making the decision." [41] Bedacht's acceptance of the authority of Moscow to decide his inner beliefs as well as his outward behavior exemplified communism's increasingly totalitarian nature.

Lovestone thought that all was not lost. He cabled Minor and Stachel to transfer party assets to safe hands. The Comintern, however, blocked him on all fronts. It instructed the American party to remove Gitlow, Wolfe, and Lovestone from their positions and sent Foster, Weinstone, and Bedacht back to the United States along with a Comintern representative to enforce the order. Soviet authorities temporarily held Lovestone, Gitlow, and Wolfe in Moscow so they could not interfere with the reorganization of the American party. Meanwhile, Minor and Stachel realized that Lovestone's cable was rebellion against Moscow. They refused to rebel, and neither would the CEC of the American party; its Lovestoneite majority vanished, just as Stalin said it would. In June 1929 the American Communist party expelled Lovestone, Gitlow, and Wolfe. Another 200 Communists followed Lovestone out of the party into the

"Communist Party (Majority Group)." Several thousand others also dropped out as a result of the Lovestoneite expulsion without joining his opposition organization.

American Communism after 10 Years

Lovestone's expulsion came only a few months before the tenth anniversary of the founding of American communism. In addition to dizzying political changes, the American Communist movement had undergone major structural changes in its first decade. The two Communist parties founded in 1919 claimed 88,000 adherents, an exaggerated figure; a more realistic one was probably close to 34,000. By the end of 1922 the Workers party claimed a membership of 12,058, increasing to 15,395 in 1923. These claims, too, were exaggerated, likely by a half to a third. Defection, in fact, had begun as early as the founding of American communism. Louis Boudin, a leading Marxist theorist in the Socialist party's left wing, had walked out of the founding convention of the Communist Labor party when it adopted terminology he regarded as doctrinally unorthodox. Eight hundred members left the movement in 1920 when the Michigan Proletarian party split over the readiness of American workers to initiate revolution. Hundreds of others drifted out of the main Communist movement into a variety of tiny ideological sects, while the party itself drove out thousands for the minor sin of "Loreism" and the more significant heresies of Trotskyism and the Lovestoneite "Right Danger."

The early domination of the party by Slavic immigrants passed rapidly. Following the founding of the Communist party and the Communist Labor party, many radical immigrant Russians, Ukrainians, Lithuanians, and Latvians, caught up in the vision of building a workers's society, returned to their homelands. Early in 1921 the Communist party reported that 1,300 members had left for Russia, nearly a fifth of its depleted membership. The U.S. government during the Red Scare of 1919–20 also deported many immigrant Slavic radicals who did not go voluntarily. Starting in 1922, Finnish Americans entered the Communist movement in large numbers and replaced the declining Slavs as the party's most numerous nationality. In 1923 Finns made up 42.6 percent of the party's membership. The next-largest groups were English speakers (including foreign-born speakers of English) with 7.8 percent, South Slavs with 7.0 percent, and Jews with 6.9 percent.

Most Communist Finns were geographically isolated in Finnish enclaves in upper Michigan, northern Wisconsin, northeastern Minnesota, and a few communities in Massachusetts, Oregon, and Washington. Finnish American communism revolved around some 220 radical Finnish cultural clubs with a family membership of about 10,000. Many of the Finnish clubs owned a building (the "Finn hall") with meeting rooms, a library, a stage, a kitchen, and offices. In these halls Finnish immigrants spoke and read Finnish; put on plays, musical events, and sports competitions; arranged outings; socialized and flirted; held marriages; celebrated the birth of children; and held classes for themselves and their children in practical and political subjects, all within an ideologically radical and ethnically Finnish milieu.

Red Finns also controlled a successful Midwestern retail cooperative, the Central Cooperative Exchange (CCE). In 1929 the CCE had 80 stores with 25,000 members and grossed more than $6 million in retail sales. The CCE was explicitly radical, gave funds to a variety of Communist causes, and proudly displayed the Communist hammer-and-sickle emblem on its canned and packaged goods. Red Finns supported such Finnish-language Communist newspapers as *Työmies* (Worker) and the comic *Punikki* (Red) published in Superior, Wisconsin; *Eteenpäin* (Forward) in Worcester, Massachusetts; *Uusi Kotimaa* (New Homeland), a farmers' paper published in New York Mills, Minnesota; and *Toveri* (Comrade) and *Toveritar* (Woman Comrade) of Astoria, Oregon. Circulation of these and other Finnish Communist publications hovered around 50,000 in the 1920s. Despite their numbers, Finnish Americans never dominated American communism in the way Russian immigrants had in the movement's early days. Only four Finns served on the party's central committees in the 1920s, in comparison with 24 natives of Russia.

Red Finns provided generous financial support to the American Communist party as well as to the rebuilding of the Communist movement in Finland after its defeat in the Finnish civil war. Finnish Americans also provided material aid for the development of the Karelian region of the Soviet Union. (Karelia bordered on Finland, and Karelians were ethnically related to the Finns.) In response to a Soviet recruiting campaign, about 6,000 American and Canadian Red Finns also migrated to Karelia in the late 1920s and early 1930s to help build socialism. ("Karelian Fever," as it was known, ended in tragedy. About 1,200, chiefly those who retained American or Canadian citizenship, returned in disillusionment. Most of the rest disappeared into the Gulag labor camps during Stalin's mass terrors of the mid-1930s.)

Membership turnover remained a chronic party problem. For the period 1923 to 1927 the party recruited 23,000 new members and lost

18,000. Official pressure such as the Palmer raids undermined the steadfastness of members in the early years. Membership also rose when the party took a right turn toward mass politics and fell when it turned left toward revolution. It benefited during poor economic times and lost members when the economy expanded. Many people found the party's internal life time-consuming, boring, and stultifying. A typical Communist club meeting consisted of taking up collections for the party's front groups and causes, selling the party press, and dealing with purely organizational matters. The party expected members to put in long hours selling party newspapers on street corners, passing out leaflets, or attending demonstrations and the meetings of party auxiliaries and front groups.

Some people left the movement when they realized that communism in Russia did not meet their expectations. The creation of an all-powerful party state and transformation of the workers' soviets into rubber stamps for the Communist party disenchanted those of a syndicalist inclination. The bloody character of Bolshevik class war appalled others. Between 1917 and 1921 the Cheka (the Soviet secret political and security police created in late 1917 and the predecessor of the modern KGB) had executed a quarter of a million persons for political offenses or for being of the wrong social class. Initially, the Bolshevik regime included as junior partners cooperating Mensheviks (Social Democrats) and the left wing of the peasant-oriented Social Revolutionary party. By 1921 the Bolsheviks had exiled, executed, or sent their former allies to the newly created forced-labor camps of the Gulag. By 1921 the Soviet state was also an economic wreck. The dislocations of World War I and the subsequent revolution and civil war caused much of this. Even so, Bolshevik economic mismanagement was extraordinary. Industrial production fell to a fraction of its prerevolutionary level and recovered only slowly. Serious food shortages affected large areas of the USSR, and in the early 1920s between 2 million and 3 million persons died of starvation.

The news of what was going on in the Soviet Union appalled many who had expected bolshevism to bring political democracy and economic plenty. Those who remained Communists did not believe the largely negative press reports or found justifications for what had happened. Unreliable Western press coverage also encouraged American Communist disregard of negative news. Language problems, political bias, the chaos of revolution, and incompetence produced much erroneous reporting on the new Communist regime. The Bolsheviks excluded most Western reporters in the regime's early years, and reporters covered the Soviet regime from Riga, the Latvian capital. Latvia was fiercely anti-Communist and full of exiles and White Russian counterrevolutionaries. A good portion of what Western reporters picked up in Riga was White wishful thinking. The magazine *New Republic* noted that the New York *Times* from 1917 to 1919 reported that the Bolshevik regime had or was about to fall 91 times, that Lenin and Trotsky were about to flee Russia four times, that they had fled three times, that they had been arrested three times, and that Lenin was dead once. Even so, mixed with this misinformation was a good deal of truth about the totalitarianism of the new Soviet Regime.

The Communist party's small membership understates the party's influence. A large group of sympathizers surrounded the party's small core membership, read its publications, belonged to its front groups, and cooperated with it while avoiding the sacrifices of membership. In 1926 the party's claimed membership was less than 16,000, but it published 27 journals in 19 languages with a total circulation of 177,000. The party surrounded itself with an impressive array of front organizations. International Labor Defense provided legal aid to "class war prisoners," not all of them Communists. The Anti-Fascist Alliance of North America united Italian immigrants and exiles hostile to the Italian Fascist dictator Benito Mussolini and his influence among Italian Americans. The Labor Sports Union promoted working-class athletic competitions. The Friends of Soviet Russia raised money for Russian famine relief. The United Farmers Educational League and its newspaper, *The United Farmer,* spread the Communist message to a few thousand farmers in the upper Midwest and Pacific Northwest. The National Council for Protection of Foreign Born protested mistreatment of immigrants. Most members of these and other front organizations were non-Communists. Communists, however, were the most active members and controlled the key offices.

The most dramatic change in Communist party structure came in 1925 when the party went through "Bolshevization." In 1925 the Comintern issued a set of statutes for all Communist parties based on the structure of the Soviet Communist party. The Workers party adopted the statutes with minor modifications. The chief executive post in the party became the general secretary. A secretariat, generally of three members, shared executive authority. Chief formal authority rested with the Central Executive Committee (later termed the Central Committee or National Board). Between meetings of the CEC a smaller Political Committee (Political Bureau or Politburo) acted in its stead. Party departments consisted of Agitation-Propaganda, Trade Union, Organization, Women,

Agriculture, Negro, and Sport. A Central Control Commission supervised the party's finances and member discipline. From time to time nomenclature changed and the number of departments expanded or
contracted.

Below these central offices existed district organizations that generally
encompassed one or more states (New York had two districts). Subdis-
trict organizations covered several cities, a "section" covered part of a
city, "subsections" sometimes existed in large cities, and a city organization existed for small cities. The lowest unit of organization were shop
"nuclei" (later called branches, clubs, or cells) based on the place of work
and the neighborhood nuclei based on the residence. In addition, party
members operating in a nonparty organization formed C.P. "fractions" to
coordinate their actions. Bolshevization aimed at rooting the party in industry by changing the basic party unit from foreign-language branches
to ones based on the place of work. It also sought to Americanize the
party by destroying the language federations as intermediaries between
members and the party. Although Bolshevization destroyed the autonomy of the old language federations, to deal with the practical problems
of members speaking different languages "language fractions" organized
within a single party unit. Further, most members remained in neighborhood clubs rather than in shop clubs. Although in a formal sense the new
clubs were no longer language units, in a practical sense many neighborhood clubs tended to be foreign-language clubs in all but name.

Bolshevization's effect on membership was severe. Membership stood
at 16,325 early in 1925 and dropped to 7,213 in October after Bolshevization began in earnest. Although some of the loss was regained, the
Bolshevized party was a third smaller, averaging between 9,000 and
10,000 from 1927 until 1930. Membership fell from about 6,000 in the
pre-Bolshevized Finnish federation to a mere 1,500, Finns who joined
the party as individuals. Most Red Finns were more attracted to the
ethnic fraternal life of the Communist "Finn halls" than to a Communist
party stripped of its ethnic enclaves. Bolshevization also destroyed party
ties to the Central Cooperative Exchange. In 1930 the Finns who controlled the CCE rejected demands for increases in the CCE's cash sub-
sidy of party activity and subsequently cut all ties with the C.P., dropping
the hammer-and-sickle trademark.

Despite Bolshevization, the C.P.'s immigrant character changed only
slowly. In 1929 the party recorded two-thirds of its members as non-
English speakers. Even this overstates the proportion of native-born

members, as the English-speaking portion included foreign-born who spoke English as a second language. One young native-born Communist said of his first meeting of an English-speaking party branch in 1925, "There were several nationalities, but broken English, Greek and Yiddish seemed to be the prevailing languages. . . . It was called English-speaking . . . to indicate that the business of the meeting would be conducted in English, however broken."[42]

Although Communists had trouble recruiting native-born members, they gave those they had influence out of proportion to their numbers. Native-born representation on the party's central committees from 1921 to 1929 was never below 25 percent and went as high as 58.3 percent— this when the native-born membership was probably never above 10 percent. One former Communist commented that Earl Browder, who came to prominence after Lovestone's ouster, owed his rise in the party in part to his having "an authentic Kansas twang. He didn't speak with a Russian accent: he didn't speak with a Jewish accent."[43]

The latter comment referred to the prominent role of Jews in the C.P. Although fewer than the Finns, Jewish Communists were more active and took major leadership roles. Jewish Communists were concentrated in New York, a center of party activity, and had a major presence in the largely Jewish clothing unions in New York. The C.P.'s Yiddish-language newspaper *Freiheit* had a larger circulation in the 1920s than did the party's flagship paper, the English-language *Daily Worker.* Jewish membership on central committees in the 1920s was never below one-third and was as high as 44.7 percent. Among the few areas of success for party recruiting among native-born Americans in the 1920s was among Jews, particularly those with immigrant parents. In 1929 Jews made up over 40 percent of the Young Communist League's membership.

There were no black delegates at the founding conventions of the Communist Labor party and the Communist party. The CLP did not mention black Americans in its founding manifesto, while the C.P. briefly defined the black question as simply a particular aspect of the plight of unskilled workers in general. (The Socialist party had a similar view.) Despite this, communism attracted a few black radicals at an early date. Otto Huiswoud, a Caribbean immigrant, may have been the party's earliest black recruit. The C.P. also won the allegiance of Cyril Briggs, another Caribbean immigrant and editor of *The Crusader,* the journal of the African Blood Brotherhood. Under Brigg's influence the brotherhood combined communism with its prior program of black nationalism and became the party's first black front group. Uncomfortable with racial nationalism, in 1925 the C.P. abandoned the brotherhood and replaced it with the more class-oriented American Negro Labor Congress. The number of black Communists in the 1920s is hard to determine, but the highest estimate is a few hundred and the low estimate is about 50 for the late 1920s. There were no black members of the party's central committee until 1929, when Briggs, Huiswoud, and Otto Hall were added.

The initial attitude of American communism toward women's issues also resembled that of the old Socialist party. Women's issues did not fit easily into a class struggle analysis and received little emphasis. Women made up 15–20 percent of the party's membership in the 1920s, but most were members as a consequence of husbands' taking out family memberships. The Communist movement had a few influential women organizers. Juliet Stuart Poyntz was a prominent Socialist party figure when she joined the nascent Communist movement. Poyntz came from a middle-class family, received an advanced education, and taught at Columbia University before she devoted herself to radical activity. She joined the Communist party in 1921, directed its Women's Department, headed the C.P.'s party school in New York, and served the Friends of the Soviet Union and the International Labor Defense in various posts. In 1934 she dropped visible party activity to do intelligence work for the Soviet NKVD (the KGB of that era). She disappeared in 1937 amid rumors that she had become disillusioned and was secretly executed.

Although the party pledged itself to total sexual equality, in its internal habits it followed traditional patterns. Several women Communists holding high party posts were linked romantically to male party officials. One of Charles Ruthenberg's female companions became head of the party's research office, and a second became head of a major party front. William Foster's woman friend also received an important party office. Women were not well represented on the central committee in the C.P.'s early years. Of the six central committees from 1921 to 1929, three had no women members at all, and the highest percentage on the remaining three was 8 percent.

Statistics of uncertain reliability suggest that two-thirds of the Communist party's members were proletarians. The working-class character of the party, however, depended heavily on its immigrant base. As the party recruited more native-born Americans, it also became less proletarian. In the C.P.'s early years between 30 and 40 percent of the party's members belonged to trade unions. Bolshevization also aimed at increasing union membership, and in this it succeeded in part. Union membership rose to close to 50 percent. Party members were geographically concentrated in New York (about a quarter of the total membership in 1923), Chicago, Boston, northeastern Minnesota, Cleveland, and Detroit. The party had a few members in the South and in the rural Midwest and only a small membership on the West Coast.

Rank-and-file Communists sustained the party by attending its weekly club meetings, demonstrating for its causes, selling its newspapers, and supporting its auxiliary organizations. The C.P.'s professional cadre, however, dominated the party. The number of Communists who earned a living from employment in a party office or in a party front, newspaper, or labor union where the party had influence was enormous compared to the C.P.'s small size. Very few party functionaries, even high Communist officials, earned a generous income. Salaries were low and paychecks were late or simply skipped if party funds were low. The work was often difficult and tedious and sometimes dangerous. There was no job security. The career of a full-time Communist functionary had few economically attractive features. Most cadres likely could have prospered much more outside the Communist movement.

Communist cadres received spiritual, not monetary, compensation for their work. They believed themselves to be building a movement that would liberate mankind from economic, intellectual, and social suppression. Idealism of a markedly messianic form characterized many Communists. Although American communism had its share of opportunists, there is no reason to doubt the sincerity of most Communists. In the 1990s communism has been in power in the Soviet Union for over 70 years and was in power in Central Europe for over 40 years. The results of communism's totalitarian oppression, cultural stultification, and economic failure are apparent and its history of mass murder is no longer deniable. In the 1920s and 1930s, however, it was still possible to dream of a Communist future of freedom and abundance.

What led these particular men and women to communism is not clear. It is not simply because they saw injustice and out of compassion or outrage turned to communism. Millions of Americans, no less sensitive, felt the injustices of society, but only a tiny fraction turned to communism. Nor were Communists more or less intelligent than others. Nor were people with neurotic personalities particularly attracted to communism. Communists had their share of people suffering from psychological disorders, but no more than their share. If it was any disorder that led to communism, it was a disorder of the soul, not of the mind in the ordinary sense. What stands out in the attitude of many Communists was their profound alienation from American culture and their certainty that they possessed the knowledge and the right to impose a new social order.

Chapter Three

The Heyday: The 1930s

Buoyed by the Great Depression and intoxicated by its faith that a new revolutionary upsurge was imminent, the Communist party began the 1930s far more optimistically than its objective situation warranted. The party itself was not in a healthy condition. The cost of expelling Lovestone's supporters and Cannon's Trotskyists had been high; not only was the party deprived of a small but important segment of its cadres, but the survivors were bewildered and confused about what was expected of them. For the next several years, even the party's most successful forays were frequently succeeded by the Comintern's scathing second-guessing.

Moreover, the demands placed on Communists around the world by the ultrarevolutionary doctrines of Stalin's "Third Period" were particularly out of place in the United States. The injunction to struggle most resolutely against Socialists and other partisans of the left as the major enemy of the working class made little sense in a country where no kind of anticapitalist ideology had made even marginal headway. Bristling pronouncements about the imminence of the class war in which only the Communists represented the interests of the working class were delusions in a society where moderate labor unions had never enrolled anywhere near a majority of the working class.

Nonetheless, the collapse of the American economic system set in motion by the stock market plunge of October 1929 seemed to confirm the apocalyptic predictions of the Third Period and provide real evidence of the need for a truly revolutionary posture on the part of Communists.

Within a few months unemployment increased more than tenfold. Whole industries, such as automobile and textile manufacturing, were devastated and, with them, entire communities. By October 1931 more than 9 million people were out of work. The banking system came to the edge of collapse in 1932. Agricultural prices, hardly robust in the 1920s, plummeted further, threatening farmers with ruin.

Millions of Americans had become casualties of the capitalist system. Some were convinced that only a fundamental alteration in the American economic system could repair the damage. Others were prepared to listen to new ideas. And the first postcrash protests the Communists managed to stage fostered the illusion that even the tiny, heretofore ineffectual Communist party might be able to lead masses of American workers in the near future.

In late 1929 for the first time the Communist party began to plan political demonstrations designed to lead to clashes with the police. Several violent confrontations took place in New York, during which party members and the authorities fought pitched battles with rocks, clubs, and mounted police, turning parts of Lower Manhattan into battle zones. On 6 March 1930, in response to Comintern instructions to hold an "International Unemployment Day," the party sponsored mammoth demonstrations in cities around the country. More than 1 million people were reported to have appeared at rallies. The largest crowd and the most violent action took place in New York, where more than 100 were injured in a bloody melee.

Although initially the party exulted that the huge turnout marked a turning point in its fortunes and signaled "the birth of the mass Communist Party in the United States," the euphoria quickly faded.[1] Subsequent demonstrations aimed at mobilizing the unemployment proved far less successful. Comintern critics complained that demonstrations were no substitute for determined, dogged efforts to build up the party organization. Party strategists concluded that the success of the March 6 demonstrations owed less to party influence over the American working class than to its being the first opportunity many people had to voice their concern over unemployment.

If Communists were to have a lasting influence, they had to build organizations. Thus, the party quickly created a series of Unemployed Councils to give some structure and stability to the movement to fight this scourge. At first, in reaction to a directive from the Comintern, the responsibility for setting up and leading the councils was placed in the hands of the Trade Union Unity League, the party's dual-union movement. The TUUL held a National Unemployment Conference in New York at the end of March and a convention in early July, neither of which was particularly successful or able to attract delegates beyond the narrow confines of the party itself. Part of the difficulty stemmed from the party's demands, summed up by the slogan "Work or Wages," for unemployment relief at the expense of profits and for a seven-hour workday. Even party members could not take these unrealistic demands seriously; the program of the New York conference cautioned workers that they should "have no illusions that the government will grant these measures of partial relief."[2]

In August the party finally unveiled a specific proposal for the unemployed. The Workers Unemployment Insurance Bill suggested payments equal to workers' prior wages, but no less than $25 a week plus $5 for each dependent. The program was to be financed by a tax on incomes and capital. While the bill often provided a useful propaganda tool to rally the unemployed, frustrated party leaders like Earl Browder complained that far too often, Communist speakers emphasized that before such a bill could become law, "we must overthrow capitalism and establish a Workers' Government."[3]

The party's scorn for political reform was just part of the Third Period mind-set. It was not the Communists' task to ameliorate the sufferings caused by capitalist society or put bandages on a system that was in its death throes. If the American Communists were unable to recognize that to attract workers they had to offer them concrete proposals and suggestions short of revolution, the Comintern was more insightful. In October 1930, in the course of rebuking the Americans for their prior failures, its Political Secretariat demanded that "the fight for full social insurance, especially unemployed insurance," be placed at the center of the program of immediate demands.[4]

Even when the Communist party took this suggestion to heart and began emphasizing unemployment insurance in its demonstrations, the demonstrations themselves continued to be confrontational. During the fall of 1930 the Unemployed Councils led protests before city councils, state legislatures, and unemployment agencies. In New York a bloody riot resulted after Communists tangled with Mayor Jimmy Walker at a Board of Estimate hearing (one party speaker denounced the Mayor as "a grafting Tammany politician and a crook"), but funds were quickly appropriated for unemployment relief. Communists led rent strikes, fought against evictions by returning furniture to homes, and organized hunger marches to dramatize the plight of the poor. In numerous cities, party members were at the forefront of efforts to assist the poor, often battling long odds, government hostility, and frequently, official violence.[5]

The party also took the lead in creating the National Campaign Committee for Unemployment Insurance, which gathered 1.4 million signatures on a petition demanding that Congress enact such legislation. Rebuffed at efforts to present the names to Congressional leaders in Washington in February 1931, the Communist demonstrators dispersed, but not before their spokesman, Alfred Wagenknecht, warned that next time they would arrive at the Capitol "with organized mass power."[6]

Despite the more practical bent of its work with the unemployed, the American Communist party was still unable to satisfy the Comintern. In March 1931 Moscow once again raked the Americans over the coals for their failure to build an organization capable of articulating coherent demands, enlisting large numbers of the unemployed, and leading them in struggle. The Comintern complained about abstract demands, poor direction by the TUUL unions, and lack of leadership. American party representatives added their two cents: the fight against evictions had saved thousands of homes of unemployed workers but left no organizational traces, and the Unemployed Councils functioned only by dint of the prodigious energy of a handful of party cadres. Measured in terms of what should have been possible and what it felt it should achieve, the party was failing badly.[7]

Not until late 1931 did the party find an effective leader of the unemployed movement. He was an unlikely functionary named Herbert Benjamin, a party member since 1921, who prepared for his new assignment in Moscow in September 1931. The Comintern had just freed the Unemployed Councils from the tutelage of the TUUL. The Americans came up with a new list of demands that included "full wages to all workers unemployed from any cause whatsoever." To push for it and other, less sweeping proposals, the C.P. called for a National Hunger March on the nation's capital.[8]

Units of marchers, largely composed of Communists, set off from various parts of the country toward Washington in November 1931. Early in December 1,600 men and women arrived in the jittery city, awash with rumors of an impending clash. A conciliatory police chief negotiated with Benjamin, arranged for housing, and allowed the marchers to parade to Capitol Hill and sing the "Internationale." After being refused audiences with leaders of Congress or the president, the protesters created a national organization—whose top officers were all Communists—and peacefully left town.

Not all the hunger marches organized by the party were as peaceful as the first one in Washington. In March 1932 between 3,000 and 5,000 people marched on the Ford Motor Company headquarters in Dearborn, Michigan, with demands for jobs and a halt to foreclosures on the houses of autoworkers. Stopped by police, the marchers were barraged by tear gas and water hoses; they retaliated with rocks. The police opened fire, killing four demonstrators. Despite efforts at official intimidation, a massive funeral procession paid homage to the dead, who included three Communists.[9]

Similar in style to the hunger marches, the Bonus March drew more public sympathy. Designed to pressure Congress to approve early payment of previously promised bonuses to World War I veterans, the March brought 20,000 demonstrators to Washington by June of 1932. Although Communists were prominent among the authors of the idea and the marchers, they did not control the event. They did, however, take the lead in occupying abandoned government buildings as shelters. Late in July, following defeat of the Bonus Bill, federal troops under the command of General Douglas MacArthur cleared the district of the veterans and burned their Anacostia campground. Government officials justified their actions on the grounds that they had nipped a revolutionary plot in the bud. MacArthur insisted that the country "was one week before a revolution."[10]

The new, hard line toward Communist-led protests continued at the Second National Hunger March in December 1932. One column of marchers engaged in a bloody skirmish with police in Wilmington, Delaware. Once the marchers reached Washington in early December, they were shunted into an isolated cul-de-sac and surrounded by a large contingent of police brandishing weapons. After tense negotiations, 2,500 marchers under Communist leadership were finally allowed to parade to Capitol Hill in the midst of a government display of force. After presenting petitions to Congressional leaders, the marchers quietly dispersed.[11]

However minimal the concrete results of such militant demonstrations, they did help to establish the Communist party as the boldest and most visible opponent of American capitalism. Even the exaggerated, oftentimes frenetic rhetoric and responses of the authorities gave the party more credibility. Some Americans, looking for ways to protest against the deepening misery, regarded the Communist party as the only or the most effective option.

Although the Communists gained considerable publicity from their leadership of these militant demonstrations of the unemployed, they did not have the field entirely to themselves. While the party's organization and discipline had enabled it to do better than many other groups anxious to help the unemployed, it soon faced challenges from those with other solutions to the plight of the jobless, including Socialists and the Blue Shirts, a quasi-military unit founded by a Catholic priest. Although the Communists agreed to attend a conference with one of the Socialist leaders of the unemployed, Karl Borders, they quickly seized control of the gathering and denounced him as a Social Fascist. Borders, nonplussed, went on to set up a Federation of Unemployed Workers Leagues of America that soon claimed to have more than doubled the Unemployed Councils' claimed membership of 40,000.

The Communists themselves understood their problems, which reflected both the transient character of the unemployed and the suffocating control over them exercised by party functionaries. Despite a facade of independence, the Unemployed Councils were run by party members, carrying out decisions reached in party caucuses. Non-Communists felt themselves excluded and quickly lost interest in an organization over which they had no influence. While critical of such practices, party leaders seemed unable to escape from them.

Dual Unionism

The same serious problem bedeviled the party's efforts to build up its dual unions, created on order from the Profintern. At the initial meeting of the Trade Union Unity League in August 1929, there were three full-fledged unions and a number of other provisional leagues claiming to represent 50,000 workers. In fact, the Communist unions were weak and small, the leagues merely shadow organizations; the TUUL never managed to go past the level of running a few spectacular strikes, despite the abundant weaknesses of the American Federation of Labor, which had been losing members and was largely limited to skilled workers in a few industries.

The TUUL was entirely controlled by the Communist party. Not only were its leaders drawn from the party's ranks, but its program, its strategy, and its rhetoric all were carbon copies of the party's own. In the overheated rhetoric of the Third Period, it saw its goal as destroying the "fascist" American Federation of Labor, building "united fronts from below," and supporting the "revolutionary political struggles" of the Communist party. And, like the party itself, the TUUL was despondent about the disjunction between its expectations and the results. "The objective conditions were never better for building militant revolutionary unions, but objective conditions do not create organizations," complained Jack Johnstone.[12]

While few party members worked in the basic industries that TUUL unions had targeted, even those who did often did not join the TUUL union. Employee repression and fear for their jobs led many Communist unionists to hide their affiliation. When the TUUL did get involved with a strike, its demands for a workers' government or unemployment insurance sometimes pushed immediate issues of wages and working conditions aside. By October 1930 the situation was serious enough for Comintern leaders to chastise the unions and warn that they had to avoid "abstract politicizing of strikes, and must raise political demands which correspond to the strike struggles."[13]

The National Textile Workers Union symbolized the party's opportunities and failures. The NTWU was founded in 1928, one of the earliest of the dual unions. In March 1929 it sent an organizer named Fred Beal to Gastonia, North Carolina. He built a union at the Loray Mill, where a strike broke out on 1 April. In the face of state pressure and vigilante violence, the NTWU sent in Communist reinforcements from the North. Following a pitched armed battle in which the chief of police was killed, 15 union leaders were tried for murder. The strike was crushed, and several of the convicted defendants jumped bail and fled to the Soviet Union.

Although the heroic Gastonia strike bolstered Communist confidence, demonstrating that the party could lead native-born, white workers, it ended with the rout of the strikers. In the aftermath, Albert Weisbord, the union leader, fell afoul of factional intrigue in the Communist party and was purged. Early in 1931, under the leadership of Edith Berkman, the NTWU managed to spark a strike in the American Woolen Company mills in Lawrence, Massachusetts. Ten thousand workers returned to their jobs after a week, during which the union leadership was arrested, but claimed a partial victory. In October, however, when another strike broke out in Lawrence after a wage cut, the NTWU faced competition from AFL and independent unions. After weeks of disunity, the strikers were routed. NTWU leaders were deported or jailed and the union was sharply criticized by the Soviets for having "isolated themselves" from the workers. By January 1932 the NTWU was down to 2,000 workers.[14]

The National Miners Union (NMU), set up to challenge John L. Lewis's United Mine Workers, did not fare much better. During 1931 mine worker militancy sparked a series of strikes led by non-Communist insurgents in West Virginia and eastern Pennsylvania. In western Pennsylvania, however, the Communist-led NMU directed a strike of 40,000 coal miners. Twenty-five thousand miners temporarily joined the NMU, and a substantial number briefly joined the Communist party. Intoxicated by its achievements, the NMU leadership and William Foster, sent in to direct events, resisted efforts to end the strike, which nevertheless collapsed after a prolonged, three-month struggle. The Comintern blasted the American Communists for a host of failures, most notably their inability to recognize that "the revolutionization of the striking workers" required deploying "all their energy in the struggle against the employers so as to win the strike."[15]

Meanwhile, however, NMU organizers were trickling into Harlan County, Kentucky, where a bloody United Mine Workers strike had been broken in May 1931. By the fall 3,000 miners in one of the most repressive and poorest areas in America were members of the Communist-led National Miners Union. A strike began on New Year's Day in 1932, but since most NMU members were already blacklisted, it did not succeed to any great extent. Just to be sure, however, the mine owners and their hired thugs terrorized the country. An NMU organizer was gunned down in broad daylight, and dissidents were arrested. Delegations of prominent sympathizers recruited by such party fronts as the National Committee for the Defense of Political Prisoners arrived in Harlan County. On one such venture the well-known writer Theodore Dreiser was arrested for adultery. Congress investigated and national newspapers and magazines focused attention on events in this feudal stronghold. The publicity, however, could not save the Harlan County strikers or the NMU. Later in 1932 its president admitted that it now played "an insignificant role in these life and death struggles of the miners." By the end of 1933 it was, for all practical purposes, defunct.[16]

The only TUUL union that achieved a modicum of success in the first few years of the 1930s was the Needle Trades Workers Industrial Union, based on the largely Jewish needleworkers in New York. But it too never enlisted more than a small fraction of the membership of competing mainline unions. While the Communists' efforts at dual unionism floundered, the party's revolutionary rhetoric did not fare well in the electoral arena either.

Political Struggles

The Communist party mounted a major effort in the 1932 election, determined to spread its message that capitalism was doomed and only the party's revolutionary program offered any hope of salvation. Its central demand, unemployment insurance, was buttressed by calls for no wage cuts, relief for farmers, equal rights and self-determination for blacks, an end to repression, and support for the Soviet Union. A nationwide speaking tour for the party's ticket of William Foster and James Ford only added to the attention received by Ford, the first black to be nominated for national office by any political party in this century.

Foster set the campaign's tone in a book he published that year entitled *Toward Soviet America.* In shrill terms he looked forward to a civil war to destroy American capitalism, suppress competing political parties, destroy religion, nationalize industry, and collectivize agriculture along Soviet lines. "The working class cannot itself come into power without civil war," he warned, before going on to predict that an "American Soviet Government will be organized along the broad lines of the Russian Soviets" with "the Communist Party functioning alone as the Party of the toiling masses."[17]

The Communist vote did double, going from over 48,000 in 1928 to over 102,000. Moreover, as Communists were quick to note, many of their supporters were not citizens and thus unable to cast ballots. Also, many Communist votes were probably not counted. Nonetheless, the Socialist party's candidate for president, Norman Thomas, drew more than eight times as many votes as Foster, approximately 884,000. (Franklin Roosevelt, the Democrat, won with 22.8 million votes, with Republican Hoover trailing with 15.7 million.)

One of the few bright spots in the campaign was the support the party ticket received from intellectuals. The League of Professional Groups for Foster and Ford issued a manifesto endorsing the Communists as the only way out of the crisis of capitalism; "as responsible intellectual workers we have aligned ourselves with the frankly revolutionary Communist Party." It was signed by such luminaries as John Dos Passos, Sidney Hook, Matthew Josephson, Granville Hicks, Edmund Wilson, Malcolm Cowley, Sherwood Anderson, Theodore Dreiser, Lincoln Steffens, and Langston Hughes.[18] The league was only one of several party-led organizations for intellectuals that exhibited surprising vitality during the Third Period. The John Reed Clubs, founded in 1929, had as their goal bringing proletarian culture to the workers. Their numerous art exhibits and small magazines, like *Partisan Review,* gave struggling young artists and writers opportunities to find audiences for their work. Talented writers such as Richard Wright were drawn into the party's orbit through their auspices.

Intellectuals, however, were hardly the stuff of revolutionary dreams.

It was to the working class that the party looked to swell its ranks, but workers were not flocking in. Through the 1932 elections the party's membership figures gave little cause for optimism. At the beginning of the decade only 7,500 people were enlisted in the Communist party. Well into 1932 membership remained stuck around 9,000. It jumped to 18,000 right after the election, the first substantial growth in the Communist party since the early 1920s, prompting optimistic predictions that at long last the party was about to start moving, but in the first half of 1933 membership once again began to decline, falling to 15,000.

In the midst of this disheartening situation, having accomplished so little with so many opportunities, the party underwent a shift in leadership. For several years, ever since the ouster of Lovestone, a group of longtime party figures had been jockeying for power. The disputes were more personal than ideological. All the contestants pledged their loyalty to the Comintern. Max Bedacht, Robert Minor, William Weinstone, and a handful of others had been shunted aside to other jobs. The most formidable candidate for leadership, Foster, was handicapped by ill health. During the 1932 campaign Earl Browder, heretofore an important but obscure party professional, began to emerge as a public figure. Eschewing revolutionary bombast, the former accountant brought an emphasis on organization, financial accountability, and party building to the troubled organization. Browder was soon the undisputed leader of the party and the subject of a minor cult of personality.

He was an unlikely leader of a revolutionary party. Born in Kansas in 1891 to a family of old American stock, Browder dropped out of school to help support his family. He tried his hand at a variety of occupations, including a small business, before settling on accounting. Influenced by his father, Browder had joined the Socialist party as a young man. Working in Kansas City before World War I, he sampled several small radical sects, most notably one run by his future comrade William Foster. Browder spent time in prison during the war for refusing to register for the draft; he moved to New York and joined the Communist party upon his release in 1920.

The following year, still working as an accountant, he was asked to put together a delegation to attend the inaugural meeting of the Red International of Labor Unions, or Profintern, in Moscow. He played a role in convincing Foster, then a prominent union organizer outside the Communist party orbit, to attend the Profintern congress. After Foster secretly joined the Communist party during the trip, Browder became one of his chief lieutenants in the Trade Union Educational League. For the rest of the decade he labored in Foster's shadow, before being sent to Moscow in 1926. For much of 1927 and 1928 he was in China, working for the Pan-Pacific Trade Union Secretariat, a Communist organization.

When the Communist party sought to solve its leadership crisis in 1930, Browder was hardly the most obvious choice. A colorless functionary, he was not well known in the party. Nevertheless, his very anonymity proved an advantage. Because of his absence from the country, he had been removed from some of the factional intrigue. His very blandness mitigated the hostility some felt to Foster. His administrative competence and methodical style were attractive qualities in an organization needing both. In 1934 he became general secretary and for the next decade was hailed in the party press as the undisputed leader of the movement.

Fragile Alliances with Socialists and Labor Unions

All of the Communist party's difficulties were compounded by the formidable challenge posed by the new president, Franklin Delano Roosevelt. Before the election, the Communist party had dismissed FDR as a carbon copy of the Republican Herbert Hoover. His bold New Deal proposals of the first 100 days were attacked as an American version of fascism. By the middle of 1933, however, Communist leaders admitted that they had underestimated his appeal and that Roosevelt had succeeded in duping even some rank-and-file Communists into the belief that he was doing something about the depression. In response, at an Extraordinary National Conference in July 1933, which ratified Browder's accession to leadership, the C.P. sternly denounced the fascist tendencies of the New Deal and insisted that the party had to redouble efforts to establish itself within the working class.

Despite its being dead in American waters, the Communist party of the United States would not have changed course, even ever so slightly, had not the Comintern been concerned by the need to cooperate with Socialists after Adolf Hitler's rise to power in January 1933. In an "Open Letter" the Comintern, while harshly critical of the Socialists, suggested a united front, the better to drive a wedge between Socialist leaders and their followers. Dutifully, the C.P. and its front groups offered to cooperate with such bodies as the AFL, the Socialist party's Young People's Socialists League, and the International Ladies' Garment Workers' Union as a means, as party organizer Clarence Hathaway put it, "of exposing these treacherous mis-leaders as the opponents of united action, as the enemies of the workers." The united front was a "road which takes the masses over the political corpses of these leaders."[19]

The Communist move deeply divided the Socialist party, itself in the midst of a debilitating factional struggle between the old guard, largely based in the New York needle trades, and younger, more militant forces grouped around Norman Thomas. Communists and some individual Socialists such as J. B. Matthews, Reinhold Niebuhr, Heywood Broun, and independent radicals like A. J. Muste cooperated on united May Day committees, a National Committee to Aid Victims of German Fascism, and committees to free imprisoned labor leader Tom Mooney and the "Scottsboro boys," nine black youths convicted of rape in a notoriously unfair trial. These, however, were small, ephemeral groups, stymied by the refusal of the Socialist party to participate as an organization and largely limited to Communist party members. Still, they represented an effort by the party to break out of its Third Period isolation.

The first of the Communists' large front groups was the American League against War and Fascism, founded in September 1933, the vagaries of whose existence are testimony to the shifting line of the Comintern on the question of Germany. In August 1932 Willi Munzenburg, the Comintern's master propagandist, organized a World Congress against Imperialist War in Amsterdam. Although not originally directed against fascism, it soon merged with a Communist-inspired antifascist organization. An American delegation took up the challenge of creating an American branch; under the direction of J. B. Matthews, Socialist and other non-Communist support was obtained in mid-1933. When Socialists belatedly discovered that Communist control of the gathering had been assured by the inclusion of a large number of paper organizations controlled by the Communists and that the Communist party had no intention of observing a truce on attacks on them, they withdrew, leaving the handful of non-Communist "fellow travelers" too isolated to resist party control even if they had wanted to.[20]

Socialist tolerance for Communist tactics was further eroded in February 1934 when several thousand Communists invaded a Socialist party rally at New York's Madison Square Garden in support of beleaguered Austrian Socialists being brutally murdered by their own right-wing government. Fist fights broke out and chaos resulted after Communist leaders tried to seize the podium. Enraged Socialists denounced the Communists as "moral lepers," and many prominent intellectuals who had been associated with the League of Professional Groups for Foster and Ford broke with the party over the issue. The American League against

War and Fascism lost several of its remaining Socialists, dismayed by the "insurmountable" obstacles to building a united front.[21]

The party's revolutionary posturing enabled it to attract individuals totally alienated from the political and economic system, but limited its ability to cooperate with other radical, much less reformist groups. By the time of the "Open Letter," the TUUL unions were woefully weak. Often merely duplicates of the Communist party itself, they were anathema to many independent unionists unhappy with the AFL. Even when such TUUL unions as the Auto Workers Union succeeded in leading a series of strikes in 1933, their success was short-lived; within a year the AWU was moribund once again, and one party official confessed that it "is today organizationally very weak."[22]

The major exception to the TUUL's stagnation was in the fertile fields of California, where the Cannery and Agricultural Workers Industrial Union battled long odds and fierce repression to organize farm workers. The CAWIU had led several small, unsuccessful strikes in the Imperial Valley in 1930, notable chiefly for the prominent role played by Eugene Dennis, a future party leader. After several years of stagnation, CAWIU sparked a second series of strikes in 1933 among workers harvesting more than a half dozen different crops, including peas, lettuce, raspberries, cherries, melons, grapes, and cotton. While most of the strikes were lost through a combination of fierce employee resistance and mistakes by inexperienced organizers, as many as 10,000 impoverished migrant laborers joined the CAWIU and fought for higher wages and better working conditions in strikes later immortalized by John Steinbeck in his novels *The Grapes of Wrath* and *In Dubious Battle.*

The passage of the National Industrial Recovery Act in 1933 was a death knell for the TUUL. Section 7A of the act gave employees the right to collective bargaining. Although the Communist party bitterly denounced the provision as a ploy, it sparked an upsurge in union membership that left the Communist-created unions far behind. Even though the TUUL unions claimed to have enlisted an additional 100,000 members by early 1934, bringing their total to 125,000, it is likely that the numbers were vastly exaggerated, since Communist spokesmen and the unions themselves reported continued stagnation. Moreover, independent unions sprang up and quickly surpassed their TUUL counterparts in size, while the once-moribund AFL enjoyed a resurgence as well.

A series of dramatic strikes during 1934 drove the final nails in the TUUL's coffin. Several violent mass strikes took place in which TUUL unions played only minor roles. Even more galling was that other radical sects played influential roles. The first big conflict, the Auto-Lite strike in Toledo, Ohio, was led by an AFL union with support from A. J. Muste's radical splinter group. Originally named the Conference for Progressive Labor Action, it had become the American Workers party early in 1934. An ordained minister turned militant radical, Muste was, to the Communists, both dangerous and threatening. In Minneapolis truck drivers launched a major strike that soon shut down the entire city. While the TUUL was nowhere to be seen, the Teamster Union local directing the strike was dominated by Trotskyists. Bitter enemies of the Communists, the Trotskyists had, ever since their expulsion from the CPUSA in 1928, tried without much success to establish a mass base. Their creative leadership of the Minneapolis Teamsters briefly gave them hope that their revolutionary moment had come.

Another major strike of 1934 found the Communists on the sidelines. The party's National Textile Workers Union had led several strikes among New Jersey silk dye workers in late 1933, but was nowhere to be found when 500,000 workers left their looms in August 1934 at the behest of the AFL's United Textile Workers. The industry-wide strike was brutally quashed, but Communist leaders assailed their union organizers in the TUUL for having underestimated the AFL. The maritime strike in San Francisco did have a substantial Communist presence, and its leader, an Australian-born ex-sailor named Harry Bridges was either a close ally of the party or a secret Communist himself. Focused largely on demands for a union-controlled hiring hall, the strike shut down the docks and, after National Guard troops killed two men trying to reopen them, led to a brief general strike of 100,000 workers. While the party's Central Committee hailed the strike as "truly the greatest revolutionary event in American labor history," it was disappointed that the key role had been played by the AFL's International Longshoremen's Association; the Marine Workers Industrial Union of the TUUL provided aid and moral support, but was too small and discredited to have an impact. Bridges, however, had been far more concerned with winning a strike than standing by abstract formulas. His leading role in the strike assured the Communists a strong role in the West Coast's maritime unions.[23]

While several TUUL unions were already defunct, the Communist party still hoped to keep the remaining unions alive and negotiate their entry into the AFL as a body. In December 1934, however, Comintern leaders suggested disbanding the TUUL and returning its members to the AFL. The party quickly ordered the dissolution of the remaining, supposedly independent unions. With the exception of a group of metalworkers who entered the Machinists Union intact, and the Fur Workers, led by Ben Gold, who were actually larger than their AFL counterpart, the other TUUL unions simply collapsed, and the dual-union federation was closed up in March 1935.

Changing Demographics of Party Membership

Following the "Open Letter" of 1933 and Browder's consolidation of power in the C.P., party membership once again began to rise in the latter half of 1933, reaching 18,000 at the end of the year, the same number as at the end of 1932. By the end of 1934 it had grown to 26,000, the largest one-year increase in party history. Actually, nearly 50,000 people had become Communists in the first four years of the decade, but considerably more than half of them had dropped out. Membership fluctuation was always a problem. Although one cause was the shifting party line, that was clearly not a major factor in the early 1930s, when party policy was relatively stable.

A major source of dissatisfaction was the tedium of party life. Unit meetings were supposed to be the most significant point of contact between party members and the party. But they were frequently long, tedious, and dull. Many clubs were composed of old-timers suspicious of newcomers and speaking an indecipherable jargon. New members, when they were not ignored, sometimes were buried with assignments and work calculated to test their revolutionary ardor. One party conference complained that "there is a tendency to confine Party meetings to routine and organizational details, divorced from the living problems of the class struggle."[24]

The party put much of the blame on a lack of trained and experienced leaders. Few of the unit leaders were paid functionaries. Many of them were foreigners and leftovers from the days of fierce factional in-fighting of the 1920s. Even if they were energetic and enthusiastic, the strictures of the Third Period often precluded cooperating with other groups, and the party itself was so small that its initiatives were often futile. While some local clubs participated energetically in a variety of activities, more of them were turned inward, engaged in seemingly endless efforts to raise money for the *Daily Worker* or some party auxiliary.

The typical American Communist of the early 1930s was a white, foreign-born male, between the ages of 30 and 40, and unemployed. In 1931, two-thirds of all party members had been born abroad, and only about one-half of them were as yet American citizens. By 1935 the proportion of American-born Communists had climbed to 40 percent. Since the party saw its natural constituency as workers in basic industry, and many of them were foreign-born, its immigrant membership was less of a concern than the ethnic composition of those immigrants.[25]

The two largest ethnic components of the party were Finns and Jews, neither of whom were prominent in heavy industry in America. Finns were concentrated in the upper Midwest, Jews in New York, San Francisco, Cleveland, Philadelphia, and a number of other big cities. The most serious absence was that of Catholics from the Irish, Italian, and Polish communities, although there were small centers of party strength in Eastern European immigrant communities in the Pittsburgh area. To add to the party's woes, many of its foreign-born members—7,000 in 1934—remained active in insular foreign-language groups, which monopolized much of their time and often paid little attention to events in America. While the proportion of foreign-born was gradually shrinking in the first half of the 1930s, the proportion of the unemployed was rising. In 1932 fully 40 percent of the members were out of work, and by mid-1935, 52 percent were unemployed. Only a minority of Communists were trade unionists, despite the party's focus on unions. In 1935, after years of effort and cajoling, one-third of the membership belonged to a union, a smaller portion even than in the late 1920s. Less than a quarter of party members were women in 1935, and from the party's perspective, far too many of them—around half—were housewives, not workers.

During this era the C.P.'s membership was concentrated in only a few cities. One-third of the entire party was located in New York, with other large concentrations in Chicago, Cleveland, Detroit and San Francisco. Well over 75 percent of the party's entire membership could be found in those cities. The South, with the exception of Birmingham and a few pockets in North Carolina, Georgia, and Tennessee, was a vast wasteland. Between the Mississippi River and the West Coast—apart from the Finns in the Upper Midwest—there were only a few hundred Communists. There were less than 1,000 Communists in all of California as late as 1932, although party membership there began to rise dramatically in the next few years.

The party was not happy with the small number of young people in its ranks. The Young Communist League grew steadily during the Third Period, reaching 8,000 by mid-1935, but fell far short of the numbers party elders hoped for. Moreover, Gil Green, its leader, complained that its membership composition was "extremely poor," with far too many students and unemployed and not enough young workers.[26] Despite its small size, the Communist youth movement not only was an important source of future party leaders but also proved to be one of the more active and successful sectors of party activity in the Third Period.

For much of the 1930s the center of Communist strength among students was the New York City college system. City College of New York and Brooklyn College saw frequent confrontations between young Communists and the school administrations over issues ranging from compulsory military training (Reserve Officer Training Corps) to war and peace. Communist students were admonished, denounced, disciplined, and suspended. In 1931 they formed the National Student League, which also established an active chapter at Columbia University. The NSL managed to create, with Socialist students in the Student League for Industrial Democracy, one of the earliest and most successful united fronts in this era to combat American militarism. Their activities in 1933 and 1934 included student strikes against war, during which thousands of college students took the "Oxford Pledge," a commitment originating at Great Britain's Oxford University to refuse to fight for their country. Under the auspices of the NSL and organizations in which it had substantial influence, 25,000 students participated in antiwar activities in April 1934 and 175,000 a year later.[27] The National Student League was never larger than 1,000 members. Aside from New York schools, it established chapters at a few state universities in the Midwest and West Coast and several expensive and elite private universities. Its articulate and active members, however, included a number of future Communist party leaders and journalists including Joseph Starobin, Joseph Clark, and Robert Hall.

Perhaps the most disappointing area of recruiting was among American blacks. The Comintern had stunned the C.P. in 1928 by issuing a resolution defining blacks in America as a subject nation and calling for self-determination for Negroes in the Black Belt, that portion of the old Confederacy with a black majority. Not even the black leadership of the party had supported such a resolution; it seems to have been Stalin's inspiration. For more than a year, American Communists admitted they were very reluctant about "approaching our Negro work from such an angle." In August 1930 the Comintern issued another resolution demanding that self-determination become the central slogan for party work in the South.[28]

Self-determination never helped the Communist party in its efforts to recruit blacks. It was so incendiary a proposal to whites in the South that it merely increased the party's already heavy burdens in the region. The

Comintern's focus on the black question had originally been prompted by complaints from black Communists that the party did not pay sufficient attention to their community and even harbored racists within its own ranks. In the early 1930s the party launched a campaign against "white chauvinism" in an effort to demonstrate that it would not tolerate racism. A prime target was the foreign-language clubs. In one celebrated "trial," August Yokinen, a Finnish Communist in New York, was expelled for barring blacks from a party dance.

The Yokinen trial was a landmark in party history, the first in a long line of efforts to demonstrate that, unlike other institutions in the United States, the Communist party would punish members who discriminated against blacks. Yokinen, who barely spoke English, was tried publicly before a "people's court" in March 1931. He was prosecuted by a white Communist who charged him with serving the capitalists and endangering the Communist party. He was defended by a black Communist who blamed his client's guilt on "this vile, corrupt, oppressive system." Expelled from the C.P. for his behavior, Yokinen accepted the verdict and pledged to fight against white chauvinism in the future. His trial, however, had brought him to the attention of the Immigration Department, and he was deported to Finland the following year.[29]

The antichauvinism campaign undoubtedly emphasized the party's commitment to working on behalf of American blacks. But its immediate effects were not uniformly positive. A series of antichauvinism trials suggested that the party was rife with racists. As in later years, it provided an opportunity for settling scores or embarrassing other comrades. Nevertheless, the 1930s marked the party's first substantial successes among American blacks. In 1930 there were fewer than 1,000 blacks in the party. The League of Struggle for Negro Rights, created to push for self-determination, never achieved a mass base in the black community. With a few exceptions such as Chicago, the Unemployed Councils did not make inroads among blacks, nor did many join TUUL unions. Two dramatic southern trials and the controversies that followed them, however, gave the party visibility and credibility in black America—the Herndon case and the Scottsboro trial.

Angelo Herndon was a black Communist organizer arrested in Atlanta in 1931 and convicted of inciting to insurrection for attempting to organize an unemployed demonstration. Sentenced to 20 years in prison, he quickly became a focal point for national protests; his conviction was eventually overturned. Not the least of the benefits the party gained from the event was that Herndon's lawyer, Benjamin Davis, Jr., scion of one of the most distinguished black families in Atlanta, became a Communist. Davis eventually became one of the party's leading black figures.

The same year of Herndon's trial, nine black youngsters in Alabama were convicted of raping two white women on a freight train. The age of the defendants, the lynch mob atmosphere of the trial, and the considerable evidence that no rape had occurred turned the Scottsboro case into one of the major historic symbols of Southern racism. The Communist party won the intricate battle with the National Association for the Advancement of Colored People (NAACP) for control of the legal defense of the boys. For years, the International Labor Defense, the party's legal arm, fought in the courts to save them, while the party orchestrated a loud and vigorous propaganda campaign to save their lives. The effort won the party credibility in the black community and entrée to black churches, social groups, and civic organizations. For many black Americans the party was the only predominantly white organization willing to confront Southern racism head-on.

Communist militancy bore some fruit in the South. In 1931 party organizers from Birmingham had helped black Alabama sharecroppers build an embryonic union. Organizing efforts were horrendously difficult and dangerous, with several murders of leaders by local police. In one shoot-out in Reeltown, Alabama, seven people were killed. Nevertheless, several thousand people joined the Sharecroppers Union.

None of the party's efforts, however, seemed to produce results commensurate with expectations. Few Southern blacks joined the C.P. As late as March 1934 there were less than 250 Communists in Harlem, and the party there was torn by accusations that some of its black cadres were too nationalistic, leading to the appointment of James Ford to oversee party activities in the area. By 1935 the party's activities on behalf of Ethiopia, its united fronts with other segments of the black community, and its ability to recruit whites to support black causes had improved its standing. Still, while blacks were more sympathetic to the C.P. than whites, this did not translate into any substantial membership. Between 1934 and 1936, blacks made up just over 9 percent of total party membership.

From Third Period Communism to the Popular Front

The transition from the Third Period to the Popular Front that followed was not a dramatic one. As we have seen, beginning in 1933, the Comintern and the obedient American Communist party began to back away from the more rigid formulations of the revolutionary line. A major factor was Hitler's consolidation of power in Germany and his destruction of the powerful German Communist party. As early hopes of his speedy overthrow faded, the Soviet Union became more and more concerned about the danger that fascism posed to its security. The growing strength of fascism in other European nations, particularly France, raised fears that without coalitions with other political forces, Communists elsewhere would suffer the same grim fate as they had in Germany.

By early 1935 Communist-controlled groups active among students, the unemployed, and minorities were involved in several coalitions with non-Communists, although usually the Communists insisted on leading the coalition. No clear strategy had evolved, in large part because of divisions within the Soviet Union and the Comintern. The Seventh Comintern Congress, repeatedly postponed while new policies were being hammered out in Moscow, finally met in August 1935. Its dominant figure was Georgi Dimitroff, the Bulgarian Communist identified with opposition to fascism ever since his dramatic trial and vindication on charges of having conspired to burn the German Reichstag. The resolutions adopted at the congress called for a Popular Front against fascism that could include even middle-class elements.

In the United States the Communists did not anticipate the new line. Relations with such independent radicals as Muste had deteriorated in 1934 after he unified his American Workers party with the Trotskyists. Communists also denounced another Socialist, the writer Upton Sinclair, after he won the Democratic nomination for governor of California in 1934. Despite pleas by Sam Darcy, the C.P.'s California leader, to make a deal with Sinclair's EPIC (End Poverty in California) movement, the party suggested that Sinclair was doing the work of fascists and lambasted him for differing from the Roosevelt administration "only in that he plunges ahead towards its fascist goal with greater speed."[30]

Sinclair's victory in the California Democratic primary with his radical EPIC platform was not the only sign that a significant segment of voters were turning to left-of-center politics. In 1934 the populist Huey Long of Louisiana, the La Follette brothers of Wisconsin's Progressive party, and the Farmer-Labor party of Minnesota Governor Floyd Olson ran successful state-level campaigns on platforms more radical than the New Deal. Sensing that political forces well to President Roosevelt's left were gaining strength, Browder received Comintern approval in late 1934 to pursue a plan for a broad-based Labor party that would challenge the Democrats. This proposal was more rhetoric than reality since Browder explicitly rejected cooperation with people like Olson and demanded that this new Labor party be controlled by Communists and their allies. The C.P.'s leaders proclaimed, "Communists enter the movement for a Labor party only with the purpose of helping the masses to break away from the bourgeois and social-reformist parties and to find the path to the revolutionary class struggle." The party's attacks on FDR remained strident; just a month before the Seventh Congress, party leaders were still identifying the New Deal and Roosevelt with American fascism.[31]

The Seventh Comintern Congress, in addition to its general about-face in calling for a worldwide Popular Front, specifically ordered a shift in the American Communist party's posture. Dimitroff pointedly castigated those Americans who persisted in failing to understand that it was FDR's right-wing critics who represented the fascist danger; "one must be very partial to hackneyed schemes," he explained, not to see that it was Roosevelt's enemies against whom the party should be struggling. The stunned Americans made no reply, but immediately after returning home, the C.P. inaugurated a shift in its view of the president.[32]

The Congress marked another milestone in the Communist party's history. From 1919 until 1935 Comintern meetings featured open discussion of American policy. Comintern representatives were dispatched to America to oversee the party, and American delegates were in permanent residence in Moscow. No apologies were made for the Comintern's mission of being the directing center of the world Communist movement with the task of overthrowing capitalism around the globe. After 1935, in line with its new policy of cooperating with bourgeois governments to combat fascism, the Soviet Union played down the activities of the Comintern. Party leaders like Browder and Foster traveled to Moscow for private consultations and conferences to iron out disagreements or problems. As the official history of the Comintern notes revealingly: "The day-to-day management of the parties passed directly into the hands of the parties themselves."[33]

The Popular Front in America did not spring into being full-blown. It took the party two years to embrace Roosevelt fully, but its stops and starts about him did not prevent it from establishing a series of close and useful alliances with other forces in American political and social life. From late 1935 to 1939 the C.P. enjoyed the greatest successes in its history, never to be matched again. Not coincidentally, during this era the basic directions of American and Soviet foreign policy were in congruity and the party was most moderate in its views of domestic politics. Even though the party was doing what the Comintern wanted and what many of its members found congenial, it still took the organization a lengthy period of time to adapt to its new role.

The first major hurdle the party had to leap was how to deal with Roosevelt's bid for reelection in 1936. After returning from the Seventh Congress, Browder continued to insist that it was necessary to build a Farmer-Labor party in rivalry to FDR. The party's preferred allies, the various independent progressive and labor parties and the new industrial union movement, however, were enthusiastic about Roosevelt and unwilling to do anything to jeopardize his reelection. Comintern leaders, meanwhile, were nervous that an isolationist Republican might replace FDR and further complicate the USSR's policy of collective security against Hitler.

Browder and Foster were summoned to Moscow in March 1936. They returned home with Comintern approval for a new policy. Having argued with Comintern leaders that Communist support for FDR would cost him votes, Browder suggested that he himself run for president on the Communist ticket but focus his campaign on the theme that the Republicans had to be defeated at all costs. His suggestion was accepted. The Communist election campaign of 1936 reached more Americans than ever before. Browder was invited to such prestigious forums as the National Press Club to air his views. The mainstream press covered the party's activities far more thoroughly than ever before. And, brushing aside Socialist charges that the Communist party had softened its indictment of the capitalist Roosevelt, Browder focused his attacks on Republican Alf Landon.

The election results were quite pleasing to the party. Roosevelt, of course, won in a landslide of 27 million votes, with Landon a poor second at 16 million. Coming in a far distant third with 892,000 votes was William Lemke of the Union party, a bizarre coalition of angry populist farmers, assorted demagogues, and various hatemongers. The vote for Socialist Norman Thomas plummeted to 18,000, only a fifth of Thomas's 1932 level, and reflecting both the attraction of Roosevelt's New Deal and the disarray of the Socialist party. While the Communist vote declined from 1932, to 80,000, local party candidates ran ahead of the national ticket, indicating that voters who took their cues from the party had understood Browder's suggestion that they vote Democratic for president. In New York, local C.P. candidates out-polled Socialist party nominees for the first time.

It took another year before the C.P. fully embraced President Roosevelt, however. Ever so cautiously, the party shifted its viewpoint to draw closer to the New Deal. In a series of steps, most coming after consultations in Moscow between Browder and Comintern officials, the party gradually invited itself into the Democratic party, abandoning hope that it could draw Farmer-Labor supporters, Progressives, and other leftists out of the Roosevelt orbit and into the Communist camp. In October 1937 President Roosevelt made a historic speech in Chicago urging the United States to join with other "peace-loving" nations to quarantine aggressors, and the context left no doubt that Nazi Germany and Fascist Italy were the aggressors FDR had in mind. Although public reaction to the speech was less than enthusiastic, to American Communists it was the signal they had been waiting for. This presidential endorsement of collective security, the Soviet Union's highest priority, marked the party's full embrace of FDR. He was hailed as the American leader of the Popular Front, and Browder demanded that "everyone must line up on one side or the other. Whoever is opposed to collective action for peace is an enemy of peace, an agent of the international bandits."[34]

Communists and the CIO

Having jettisoned the strident language and militant tactics of the Third Period, the Communist party found numerous opportunities to expand its influence. None was as important as the labor movement, where a revolutionary upheaval gave the C.P. a golden opportunity to break out of its prior isolation. The abandonment of the TUUL came just at the moment when John L. Lewis, long the bête noir of the Communists in the labor movement, resigned as vice president of the AFL and, along with a handful of other leaders of industrial unions, set out to create the Committee for (later Congress of) Industrial Organizations (CIO). Despite its reservations about Lewis and nervousness about splitting the labor movement just months after its own attempt at a split had given up the ghost, the C.P. found itself in an enviable position. The CIO began an ambitious campaign to create thriving unions in such industries as automobiles, steel, electronics, shipping, and transport and among white-collar workers. Lewis and his chief aide, John Brophy, were desperate for experienced organizers; hundreds of veteran TUUL organizers were available. The CIO leaders cut a deal with the Communist party and welcomed their organizers. Dedicated, knowledgeable about the industries, committed to unionization, and willing to work for low pay, they were godsends to the CIO. Communists were not the only radicals recruited by the CIO, but they were among the most numerous.

Party organizers were particularly prominent contributors to the Steel Workers Organizing Committee (SWOC). The C.P. had a base in the ethnic communities of western Pennsylvania and Ohio. In addition to union organizers, the party threw the resources of the C.P.-led International Workers Order, a fraternal organization with ties to the immigrant worker communities of the steel towns, into the campaign to unionize steelworkers. At one point more than one-quarter of all SWOC organizers were party members. Despite their yeoman work in building the SWOC, Communists always took a back seat within the union hierarchy. The SWOC was firmly in the hands of Lewis's old friends from the UMW like Philip Murray, although one secret Communist, Lee Pressman, served as counsel for the SWOC and, eventually, the CIO itself. Lewis himself believed that he was using the Communists, reportedly noting once, "Who gets the bird, the hunter or the dog?"[35]

Party strength was not uniform throughout the CIO. In some unions, such as the Amalgamated Clothing Workers and the Textile Workers, the party's presence was minimal or nonexistent, particularly at the upper levels. In several smaller CIO unions the Communist presence was limited to the top echelon of union leaders. Several other unions had some Communists in the leadership and in modest numbers among the rank and file. Only among the Fur Workers was there a significant Communist presence in the membership. (Ben Gold, leader of the Fur Workers, was an open member of the party's central committee.) Far more frequently, Communists, in on the ground level of the union, held positions in the top or secondary leadership of unions whose membership was overwhelmingly non-Communist.

Two of the largest CIO unions did have a significant party presence. A number of the leaders of the dramatic sit-down strike in Flint, Michigan, that put the United Auto Workers on the map were Communists. Within the union's leadership, Wyndham Mortimer was a secret member of the Communist party, and lawyer Maurice Sugar was, at the very least, a close ally. Most of the union's leaders, however, were not Communists. For many years Communists and their allies fought a pitched battle with their adversaries for control, culminating with Walter Reuther's defeat of the Communist-aligned faction in the 1940s. The director of organization of the United Electrical, Radio, and Machine Workers Union (U.E.), James Matles, was also a secret Communist, as was its secretary treasurer, Julius Emspak. Many second-tier leaders of the union were more open about their party affiliation. After another bitter struggle for control, the pro-Communist forces succeeded in gaining the upper hand and isolating the U.E.'s anti-Communists.

Other CIO unions were led by men either in the party or very close to it. The Transport Workers Union, largely Irish, was dominated by a Communist caucus and led by Michael ("Red Mike") Quill, a flamboyant Irishman who proclaimed that "I would rather be called a Red by the rats than a rat by the Reds." Communists played a key role in building the TWU. The president of the United Cannery, Agricultural, and Packing and Allied Workers Union was Donald Henderson, another party functionary. The tiny Federation of Architects, Engineers, Chemists, and Technicians was dominated by a party caucus, as were the State, County, and Municipal Workers and the United Office and Professional Workers. Several of the maritime unions, including the National Maritime Union, the International Longshoremen's and Warehousemen's Union (ILWU), and the Marine Cooks and Stewards were led by men with close ties to the party.

All in all, about 40 percent of the CIO's unions had significant Communist connections by the end of the 1930s. This did not automatically translate into benefits for the party, however. As noted, party membership among the union rank and file was minimal. Many of its unionists were secret members, too afraid or too cautious to proclaim their political affiliations openly. Some Communists who had spent many years in the labor wilderness with the TUUL had no desire to endanger their new union careers. Other Communist unionists saw no conflict between union and party objectives during the Popular Front era. So long as the party's policies focused on support for the New Deal, their political views did not lead to conflict with the vast majority of their fellow union members. Moreover, the Communist party, in deference to its trade union "influentials," relaxed its discipline over them. Many of the party's best cadres had been thrown into work for the CIO; for some of them it became the primary focus of their effort and loyalty. By the mid 1940s party caucuses in unions had been disbanded, Communist union leaders negotiated issues directly with party leaders, and, for the sake of labor unity and amity, Communists even acquiesced with resolutions denouncing communism introduced at union conventions.

Not all party members or leaders were enthusiastic about the party's new moderation and caution. Unhappy about the whole-hearted embrace of both Franklin Roosevelt and John L. Lewis, William Foster complained to the Comintern late in 1937 that "the party was following at the tail of Roosevelt and Lewis." Uncomfortable that the party was ceding the leading role in the political and labor arenas to other forces, he demanded that it carry out its activities more openly and that its union members cease hiding their loyalties. In Detroit, Foster was supported by William

Weinstone, a longtime party functionary who did not care if Communist activities in the United Auto Workers threatened the alliance with John Lewis. Weinstone had encouraged a series of wildcat strikes that embarrassed Lewis and other CIO leaders. Browder pointedly reminded his colleagues in 1939 that "our greatest problem today is breaking down all suspicions in the minds of people who have no other obstacles to collaboration with us except their suspicions." As a result of its desire to cement the alliance with non-Communist unionists, the party's Politburo removed Weinstone from his position as district organizer and rebuked Foster.[36]

The New Deal, Antifascism, and the Democratic Front

The essence of the Democratic Front policy, a variant of the Popular Front line officially adopted early in 1938, was that the Communist party had agreed to accept a junior and hidden role in the New Deal and labor movements. Recognizing that "our Party, as a Party, will not be admitted into this progressive force . . . we should support the progressive movement, not demanding the admittance of our Party, not making this a condition for our support of the democratic forces, but showing by our activity in the campaign, by our energetic support for the progressive candidates, that our party is a constructive force entitled to entrance in the progressive movement, thereby paving the way for entrance at a future time."[37] Integral to the new line was acceptance of policies, methods, and rhetoric formerly scorned by the Communists. The party justified its retreat from revolution and socialism on the grounds that liberalism, bad as it was, was preferable to the reactionary conservatism that was the only alternative. Going even further than support for the "lesser evil," the C.P. lauded such American heroes as Thomas Jefferson and proclaimed that "Communism is Twentieth Century Americanism." Patriotic songs became staples of party rallies, and party ideologues proclaimed truces with such erstwhile enemies as Zionism and Catholicism.

Just how much the new line involved a Communist surrender of radical impulses was revealed in 1938, with the advent of the "Roosevelt recession," an economic downturn exacerbated by FDR's decision to cut back key New Deal programs, including reductions in work relief jobs of the Works Progress (later Work Projects) Administration (WPA). Rather than issuing a militant denunciation of the president, the party blamed the recession on a "sit-down strike" by capitalists aimed at FDR. At the same time, Communist spokesmen blamed everyone in the administration except President Roosevelt for the arms embargo that weakened the antifascist government of Spain.

The sine qua non of the Popular Front was antifascism. Opposition to Hitler's advances had driven the Comintern from the revolutionary dogmatism of the Third Period to collective security. By itself antifascism would not have accounted for the enormous growth in Communist popularity after 1935—the Comintern had been antifascist during the Third Period as well. But the policy of uniting with Socialists and liberals to fight Hitler had tremendous appeal, and nowhere was its appeal more evident than in Spain.

The Spanish Civil War, beginning in 1936, captured the attention of the world. The Spanish Republic's Loyalist government, a coalition of moderate and left-wing parties, faced a revolt of extreme nationalists led by Spanish army generals and supported by Nazi Germany and Mussolini's Italy. Partly in response to the widespread view that America's entry into World War I had been linked to the selling of weapons, in the 1930s the U.S. Congress enacted a series of neutrality laws, one of which provided for an embargo on arms sales to any nation involved in a war. Isolationist sentiment in America was so strong that after the Spanish Civil War began, Congress invoked an arms embargo. In the U.S. House of Representatives only John T. Bernard, a Minnesota Farmer-Labor congressman with extremely close links to the Communist party, voted against the embargo. The Loyalists received aid from the Soviet Union and were bolstered by a ragtag international army drawn primarily from the Popular Front left. Three thousand Americans, most of them Communists, made their way to Spain to fight in the Abraham Lincoln and George Washington Battalions of the International Brigades. They took enormous casualties—more than half died. At home the Communist party raised large sums of money for humanitarian and technical assistance to Spanish Loyalists. While the Roosevelt administration remained faithful to neutrality legislation prohibiting aid to either party in the conflict, the Communist party's prestige soared among liberals and radicals.

The new line did wonders for party membership. Just before the Seventh Congress there were 30,000 Communists. Membership jumped to 41,000 in the spring of 1936, where it stagnated for a year. Then, following the party's enthusiastic embrace of Roosevelt in the fall of 1937, membership began to spurt. At the end of 1937 it stood at 62,000, and a year later it was 82,000. In just over three years membership had almost tripled, with the largest increases coming when the party was most closely tied to FDR. The new members flooding into the party were only a portion of those whom the Communists now influenced. Party front groups like the International Labor Defense and the American League against War and Fascism boomed. Earl Browder boasted that many non-Communists looked to the party for political guidance: "Millions of people consider and are influenced by our decision."[38]

Many of those people were white-collar workers and professionals. Office workers, teachers, lawyers, and doctors joined the party in substantial numbers. During the last half of the 1930s about 40 percent of the party belonged to a union; a substantial proportion of these were members of one or another of the CIO's white-collar unions. Nothing better symbolized the changing nature of the party than the growth of a native-born majority. In the summer of 1936 the proportion of foreign-born members finally fell below 50 percent; it continued to decline for the rest of the decade. While the proportion of all Communists who lived in New York continued to climb, reaching 40 percent in 1938, party organizations prospered throughout the country. In mid-1937, 12 of the party's 35 state organizations had more than 1,000 members; only three had fewer than 100.

The party's greatest success came among American Jews. Many of the native-born, white-collar or professional New Yorkers it recruited were Jewish, attracted to the C.P. because of its fervent opposition to fascism. After the Seventh Congress the party also toned down the assimilationism and hostility to Jewish culture that had marked the Third Period. Nor were Jews the only ethnic group to benefit from the new tolerance. In 1938 Israel Amter reminded party members that "it is necessary that our comrades be not only good Communists, but good Germans, good Jews, good Irishmen."[39] The International Workers Order, a party-controlled fraternal organization structured to provide low-cost life insurance and organized by ethnic units (Hungarian, Jewish, Slovak, Serbo-Croat, Italian, and so on), boomed during the Popular Front, reaching 150,000 dues payers by 1939 and spreading Communist influence throughout foreign-born communities.

The new line also facilitated Communist involvement in electoral politics. From their self-imposed isolation during the Third Period Communists moved to active and, in a few cases, remarkably successful work in mainstream American politics. Although the party's greatest success came in those states where party membership was large, the local configuration of political forces also had a significant effect on whether Communists were able to overcome the suspicion and hostility with which they were regarded by many Americans.

New York City's system of proportional representation and state law allowing several political parties to run the same candidates for office enabled Communists to gain considerable influence in the politics of the Empire State. The American Labor party, originally formed by the fiercely anti-Communist needle trade unions, quickly became a center of party strength and a crucial factor in New York politics. Allied with such popular left-wing politicians as Vito Marcantonio, Mike Quill and Adam Clayton Powell, willing to support Mayor Fiorello La Guardia, and drawing on the 30,000 Communists living in New York and the numerous organizations and unions over which they exercised control, the party even managed to elect two open Communists, Benjamin Davis and Peter Cacchione, to the City Council in the 1940s.

At the other end of the country, Communists in the state of Washington gained control of the Washington Commonwealth Federation, with the help of its leader, Howard Costigan, a secret party member. The WCF was itself a major faction within the state Democratic party; riding its coattails, more than a dozen secret party members were elected to the state legislature. In California several high-ranking state officials had close relations with the Communist party. The Minnesota Communists reached an understanding with Farmer-Labor Governor Floyd Olson in 1935 and bars to their membership in the Farmer-Labor party were lowered. During the administration of Governor Elmer Benson party members and their allies held high positions in the executive branch.[40]

While Communists never made substantial headway in the South, during the Popular Front period they were able to build alliances with Southern liberals. Party members set up the Southern Negro Youth Congress, which attracted a number of talented college students to its activities. The Southern Conference for Human Welfare, created to push New Deal programs, from its beginnings had a small Communist contingent influential beyond its size because its members held key positions.

While they created a niche for themselves in the political and labor worlds, the Communists also built future troubles as well. The essence of the Democratic Front was that party members were not obliged to proclaim their Communist loyalties openly. Everyone maintained the charade that they were "progressives." In many cases, however, the labor leaders and politicians with whom they dealt knew very well that they were Communists. So, too, did their enemies. During the Third Period, Communists had not deigned to hide their affiliations. In the Popular Front years they did, leading some to conclude that they had something shameful to conceal and others to assume that many, or most of those with whom they were associated, were simply progressives and not party members. It was a potentially explosive situation, one that occasionally caused both the party and its allies some embarrassment in the late 1930s but was to have far more serious consequences after the Nazi-Soviet Pact and again after World War II. In 1938 a special committee of the House of Representatives, set up to investigate "un-American" propaganda, known as the Dies Committee, attacked both the CIO and the New Deal for their alliances with Communists. In Minnesota, Communist ties contributed to Governor Benson's 1938 electoral rout as well as to Congressman Bernard's defeat. (Not always discreet, Bernard had underlined his links to the C.P. by inserting articles from the *Daily Worker* into the *Congressional Record.*)

As in other areas, the Popular Front enabled the party's work with students to thrive. In December 1935 the party-led National Student League merged with the Socialist-dominated Student League for Industrial Democracy to form the American Student Union. Although the ASU never got much larger than 20,000 members, it attracted many of the most engaged and articulate student activists of the decade. It was also the scene of bruising battles between the Communists and New Dealers on one side and the Trotskyists and Socialists on the other over the issue of collective security. The Communists likewise dominated the American Youth Congress, formed in 1934, with delegates from numerous youth organizations. Few of the organizations represented in the AYC were Communist-dominated, but secret Communists and the party's allies constructed a coalition that consistently endorsed party positions, a task made easier by the party's moderation. By 1939 the AYC claimed to represent nearly 5 million young Americans.

The same situation obtained among blacks. Party efforts to organize demonstrations on behalf of Ethiopia won it support in Harlem. Following the Seventh Comintern Congress, the party quietly but steadily began to downplay its self-determination doctrine in the interests of forming alliances with other black organizations. The League of Struggle for Negro Rights was disbanded and party energies directed to the National Negro Congress, a broad-based delegate organization committed to mobilizing American blacks to fight for full economic and political equality. Open Communists were soon prominent within the NNC, which included more than 550 groups. For several years the Communists cooperated with its president, A. Philip Randolph, a leading Socialist and trade union leader. The party also played an active role in black cultural life. Communists and their allies dominated a variety of Harlem cultural institutions. Several prominent black entertainers cooperated with the party, most notably Paul Robeson.

Communist organizing among unemployed workers also benefited from the new policies. For several years in the mid-1930s the party's major effort had been to gain passage of the Lundeen Bill, a plan for unemployment insurance far more radical than the Wagner-Lewis Bill that eventually became law. In April 1936 the Communist-dominated Unemployment Councils united with the Socialist party's Workers Alliance. Although the new organization kept the Socialist name and Socialist David Lasser remained president, Herbert Benjamin, the Communist organizer of the hunger marches, became executive director. Several followers of A. J. Muste's unemployed group, notably Arnold Johnson and Louis Budenz, joined the Communist party, and it soon had effective control of the Workers Alliance. The new body soon shifted its attention to organizing WPA workers rather than the unemployed; by 1939 more than three-quarters of its members were on the government payroll.

Because the interests of its members were so heavily dependent on decisions by the executive and legislative branches, the Workers Alliance devoted much of its time to lobbying for relief. It developed close ties to a dozen congressmen and such New Dealers as Aubrey Williams, deputy director of the WPA. Since both the WPA and the alliance had an interest in raising appropriations for relief, the government agency encouraged demonstrations to pressure Congress to allocate more money. Moreover, such New Dealers as Williams, while clearly not Communists themselves, were willing to cooperate with the party during the Popular Front years.[41]

A similar situation prevailed in the field of culture. In the last half of the 1930s the C.P. was able to enlist the support of many of America's most distinguished artists, writers, and intellectuals. The small, revolutionary John Reed Clubs were ordered disbanded late in 1934, to be replaced by a more broadly based League of American Writers (LAW). The transition was not entirely smooth; some of the John Reed Clubs, notably the one in New York, resisted, continuing to publish its lively journal, *Partisan Review.* The LAW was inaugurated at an American Writers Congress held in 1935, shortly before the Seventh Comintern Congress proclaimed the Popular Front. As a result, the Communist domination of the Congress was still quite overt. By 1937, when the second gathering took place, the theme was combating fascism, most of the prominent Communists had disappeared from the program, and such luminaries of American culture as John Steinbeck, Ernest Hemingway,

James Farrell, Lewis Mumford, Van Wyck Brooks, William Carlos Williams, and Theodore Dreiser graced the league's activities.

The American Artists Congress meanwhile had enlisted comparable prominent artists into a Communist-influenced body. It was in Hollywood, however, that the Popular Front struck pay dirt. Actors, actresses, and screenwriters flocked into the Hollywood Anti-Nazi League and offered the Communist party both glamour and contributions. Communists quickly became a strong force in several Hollywood unions, particularly the Screen Writers Guild. Meanwhile, Communist troubadours like Pete Seeger and Woody Guthrie played a major role in developing and popularizing modern folk music.[42]

While the Popular Front enabled the Communist party to end its isolation, it did not end attacks on the party. In fact, it created a new set of enemies on the party's left. A number of radical intellectuals, who had been attracted by the party's revolutionary commitment and fervor, as well as its staunch hostility to bourgeois society during the Third Period, were made unhappy by its bows to respectability and moderation later in the decade. Disillusioned by the party's subordination of art to politics, they began to cast about for alternatives.

The most obvious was Leon Trotsky. Not only was his combination of radical cultural criticism and revolutionary politics attractive, but the growing Stalinist attack on Trotsky culminating in the Moscow Trials energized some Americans into coming to his defense. Although Trotskyism as a political movement remained both small and, outside of one dramatic series of strikes in Minneapolis, largely ineffective, it gained some support among intellectuals. *Partisan Review*'s editors, Philip Rahv and William Phillips, joined with James Farrell, Mary McCarthy, and Dwight Macdonald to form the core of an opposition to the Communist party that aligned itself with Trotskyism. Other intellectuals associated themselves with John Dewey's inquiry into Stalin's charges that Trotsky had been betraying Bolshevism from 1917 onward in league with various counterrevolutionaries and foreign intelligence services—an investigation that concluded he was innocent. (Later, while in exile in Mexico, Trotsky would be murdered by an NKVD assassin.)[43]

The intellectual war of words grew quite heated as the decade drew to an end. Supporters of the party and the Soviet Union demanded total endorsement of Stalin's actions; dissenters, even those expressing the mildest of doubts about Trotsky's guilt or the purge trials, were harshly read out of the Popular Front. The trials themselves were grotesque spectacles in which veteran Bolsheviks such as Zinovyev, Kamenev, and Bukharin (all later executed) confessed to fantastic treasonous plots with, variously, Trotsky, White counterrevolutionaries, and the intelligence services of Japan, Great Britain, and Germany. Their confessions appear to have been won by a combination of threats to execute their families and appeals to their Bolshevik mentality that they could serve the historic destiny of the party by self-sacrifice. Even more barbaric than the public show trials was the semisecret mass terror of the mid- and late 1930s in which the NKVD executed more than 1 million persons and sent more than 10 million to Gulag labor camps, where the majority died of malnutrition and overwork. The two leading journals of American liberalism, the *Nation* and *The New Republic,* either endorsed Stalin's murderous acts or suggested that it was best to remain silent about them for fear of endangering the antifascist coalition. In response to a manifesto issued by the Committee for Cultural Freedom condemning totalitarianism in all its guises, signed by 140 prominent intellectuals, including John Dewey and Sidney Hook, the Communists and their allies produced an indignant denunciation of the charge that Nazi Germany and the Soviet Union were similar. With consummate bad timing, it was issued just days before the Nazi-Soviet Pact brought an end to the the Popular Front.

The anti-Stalinist Communist movement did not make much headway in the 1930s. Trotskyists succeeded in building a strong base among Minneapolis Teamsters in the early 1930s and led a successful strike among New York hotel workers in 1934. That same year Trotskyists began an intricate set of mergers with other radical groups in an effort to compete more successfully with the Communists. Their Communist League of America merged with A. J. Muste's American Workers party, following Trotsky's orders to his supporters around the world to seek coalitions with non-Communist leftists.

The newly christened Workers party remained a tiny sect with no more than 2,000 members, so in 1936 Trotskyist leaders Jim Cannon and Max Shachtman engineered another merger, this time with the much larger Socialist party, itself in the process of lurching to the left. This maneuver alienated Muste, who, prompted by a religious experience, abandoned political radicalism. Ensconced within the Socialist party, the Trotskyists busily worked to convert its militants to their brand of bolshevism. By 1937 the Socialist party expelled the Trotskyists when, under orders from Trotsky, the latter denounced their Socialist comrades for betrayal of the class struggle. The expelled Trotskyists took with them a substantial number of former Socialists, including most of the S.P.'s youth division. Early in 1938 they formed the Socialist Workers party and joined the newly created Trotskyist Fourth International.

Next to the Trotskyists, the most significant of these small groups was the followers of Jay Lovestone, the C.P. leader whom Stalin himself had deposed in 1929. Although it never recruited more than a small cadre of members, Lovestone's "Communist Party (Majority Group)," later renamed "Communist Party (Opposition)" and then the "Independent Labor League of America," did include several talented organizers and intellectuals, including Will Herberg and Bertram Wolfe. Lovestone and several of his aides played an important role in the factional wars within the United Auto Workers in the late 1930s, allied with the anti-Communist caucus headed by union president Homer Martin. A Lovestoneite leader, Charles Zimmerman, for many years was a powerful figure in the International Ladies' Garment Workers Union.

The Communist party's adoption of the Popular Front fueled the anger and the energy of the Trotskyists and the other tiny Marxist-Leninist sects that popped up during the decade. They regarded the party's willingness to mute its revolutionary goals and make alliances with bourgeois forces as a betrayal of the revolution; likewise, they bitterly condemned Stalin for abandoning the cause of proletarian internationalism. As the Communist party became more moderate, they found it more distasteful. None of these groups enjoyed much success. While they often provided trenchant criticisms of Stalinism or the Communist party's opportunism, their strident calls for even more militant actions fell on deaf ears.

While the Communists could point to the Soviet Union as their model, independent Marxist-Leninists had to make the more complicated argument that Stalin and the world Communist movement had betrayed true Marxism-Leninism. To Americans discontented with capitalism or American society, their ideological carping often seemed merely an ineffective and futile course, compared with the thriving social and political movement offered by the Communists.

The Nazi-Soviet Pact of 1939

The Communist party's position in American life, however, was always a hostage to Soviet foreign policy. While the tremendous advances the party made during the Popular Front had given it a solid foothold in institutions throughout American society, its willingness to jeopardize everything it had achieved to serve Soviet interests became apparent immediately after Stalin and Hitler reached an agreement in 1939 on a nonaggression pact that paved the way for World War II.

When the pact was signed on 23 August 1939 the way was cleared for the German invasion of Poland, the Soviet seizure of the Baltic states and eastern Poland, and Foreign Minister Vyacheslav Molotov's infamous remark that fascism was just "a matter of taste." American Communists were dumbfounded. After a few weeks of indecision and confusion about the meaning of this momentous event, Earl Browder began to receive shortwave radio messages from Moscow with instructions on how to interpret the war between Nazi Germany and the Western Allies.[44]

In mid-September a tumultuous meeting of the American Communist Politburo reached agreement that the conflict between Nazi Germany and the western democracies was an imperialist conflict and issued a demand that America remain neutral. A C.P. paper explained, "The previous alignment into democratic and fascist camps loses its former meaning. The democratic camp today consists, first of all, of those who fight against the imperialist war."[45] At the end of the month the Comintern sent another secret message to the American Communists demanding that they break with the New Deal; at the end of October, after Browder had been indicted on old charges of using a false passport and President Roosevelt had denounced the Soviet invasion of Finland, the C.P. returned to the rhetoric of the Third Period, castigating the Roosevelt administration as protofascist and "Hitlerian," calling for united fronts from below, and denigrating the value of "bourgeois democracy."

This abrupt about-face had serious consequences for the party's hard-won status within American society. Most of the front groups that had achieved prominence were destroyed or severely weakened by defections of liberals unable to stomach the new policies. The League of American Writers lost so many of its luminaries that its letterhead had to be abandoned. The National Lawyers Guild lost virtually all of its liberal members. The American League for Peace and Democracy (formerly the American League against War and Fascism) dissolved. David Lasser resigned from the Workers Alliance and created a competing organization that soon surpassed its Communist rival in membership. Joseph Lash, the Socialist leader of the American Student Union, was expelled from the organization for opposing the pact. A. Philip Randolph angrily quit the National Negro Congress after it denounced FDR and praised Soviet foreign policy.

The party's political relationships also tattered. In the state of Washington defections wracked the Washington Commonwealth Federation.

The California Popular Front splintered. Prominent leaders of New York's American Labor party launched an all-out battle against Communist influence in their organization, leading to the formation of the rival anti-Communist Liberal party in 1943. Only in Minnesota, where traditionally strong isolationist sentiment provided an ideological rationale for the party's new position, did the Communist alliance with non-Communist leftists hold up. The party even flirted with right-wing isolationists it had previously accused of fascism.

The Communists were more fortunate within the union movement. John L. Lewis, the CIO's leading figure, shared their antiwar attitude. As a result, Communists in the CIO had fewer problems in switching from endorsement of collective security to a neutrality that regarded Great Britain and France as no better than Nazi Germany. Communists supported strikes in war industry plants on the grounds that national security could not be used to muzzle labor militancy.

Party membership was also severely affected. Although few party functionaries resigned, many ordinary Communists, particularly Jews, either quit or drifted away. Party officials estimated the loss to be 15 percent in one year, but it was probably much higher; in April 1942 party membership stood at only 50,000, half what it had been just before the pact.

The Communists launched a major campaign to keep America out of the "imperialist war," replacing the American League for Peace and Democracy with the American Peace Mobilization. Warning that "The Yanks Aren't Coming," the *Daily Worker* denounced Great Britain as a totalitarian and imperialist power as evil as Germany. The *People's World,* the leading West Coast C.P. paper, called Great Britain "the greatest danger to Europe and all mankind" and said the British were "intent [on] spreading the war." One party publication for Jews advanced the contorted view that "what is happening to the Jews of Palestine today, under British rule, does not differ essentially from what is happening to the Jews under Nazi rule."[46]

Perhaps more important than the loss of members and sympathizers, however, was the loss of trust and goodwill that had been so carefully built up in the last half of the 1930s. The Communist party had demonstrated that none of its principles was as precious as loyalty to the foreign policy of the Soviet Union. Anyone privy to its prior history would have known that lesson already, but no incident in the past had the emotional pull or prominence given this demonstration of fealty in 1939.

The full significance of this lesson did not immediately sink in, because this new era would prove to be of relatively brief duration, lasting only one and a half years, until the Nazi invasion of the Soviet Union would turn the C.P. from isolationists to fervent supporters of the Allied cause. With a great deal of relief, the Communist party would resume its hostility to fascism and support for Roosevelt's administration.

Chapter Four

The Failed Gamble, 1941–1959

After the Nazi invasion of the Soviet Union in June 1941 the Communist party hastily shifted from uncompromising opposition to U.S. involvement in World War II to fire-eating support for American intervention in the war. The American Peace Mobilization, the C.P.'s chief antiwar front group, hurriedly renamed itself the American People's Mobilization, but saving its initials did not prevent death from embarrassment over its blatant flip-flop. The loss of the APM, however, was trivial compared with the party's opportunity to recreate the antifascist Popular Front. By June 1941 the C.P. stood in danger of losing many of the gains of the late 1930s as its anti-Roosevelt and antiwar stance isolated it from New Deal liberals who supported Roosevelt's program of aid to the anti-Nazi belligerents and mobilization of American military forces. Even in the CIO, the C.P.'s anti-Roosevelt stance was placing the Communist-aligned unionists on the defensive and emboldening the CIO's anti-Communist faction. With the Nazi invasion, however, Communists could once more make common cause with liberals and support a policy that was parallel to that of the U.S. government.

Once America entered the war in December 1941 and the United States became a military ally of the Soviet Union, the Communist party unreservedly threw its support behind the American war effort and behind Roosevelt's war policies. The enthusiasm of Communists for the war effort allowed repair of much of the damage done to relations with liberals. Indeed, not only was the Popular Front alliance renewed, but Earl Browder believed that the extraordinary conditions of World War II required a fundamental transformation of the American Communist movement.

In late November 1943 Roosevelt, Churchill, and Stalin met in Teheran, Iran, to plan the defeat of Nazi Germany and the shape of postwar Europe. To Browder, Teheran signaled "the greatest, most important turning point in all history." The United States and Great Britain through their alliances with the Soviet Union had, Browder believed, put aside efforts to destroy communism's motherland and accepted the Soviet Union as a partner in a new postwar world. For its part, the Soviet Union had dissolved the Comintern in 1943 and no longer urged its allies in the West to foment revolution. Browder saw no realistic prospect for revolution in America after the war and expected "Europe west of the Soviet Union probably will be reconstructed on a bourgeois-democratic, nonfascist capitalist basis, not upon a Soviet basis."[1] It was the duty of Communists, Browder said, to prevent American reactionaries from using the fear of revolution to sabotage U.S.-Soviet goodwill. Browder, acknowledging that he was departing from orthodoxy, pledged not to "raise the issue of socialism in such a form and manner as to endanger or weaken national unity" and said Communists were "ready to cooperate in making this capitalism work effectively."[2]

Even before Teheran, Browder signaled the direction he was taking in the dissolution of the Young Communist League. In October 1943 the YCL reorganized as the American Youth for Democracy (AYD). The AYD's program made no mention of socialism or ties to the Communist party. Instead, the AYD emphasized U.S.-Soviet cooperation and a vague "progressive" program that was compatible with the reformism of Roosevelt's New Deal. Above all, the AYD backed any program that promoted the war effort, claimed that Washington, Jefferson, and Lincoln had all supported "universal conscription for youth . . . as a permanent feature of American life," and warned that "in the dark corners of America where treason lurks voices are being raised against the establishment of postwar universal compulsory military training."[3] In line with Browder's thinking, Communists supported Roosevelt's 1944 proposal for harsh punishment of striking workers and called for continuing the labor movement's no-strike pledge into the postwar period.

Browder's most dramatic symbol of the new direction of the Communist movement was the transformation of the Communist party into an advocacy group. Traditional Communist theory had seen the Republican and Democratic parties as bourgeois class parties, the Tweedledum and Tweedledee of American capitalism. Even during the Popular Front of the late 1930s, when the C.P. had worked within the New Deal coalition, it had continued to maintain its formal political independence. In 1944 Browder redefined America's two major parties as coalitions through which "diverse tendencies of political thought" and "local and regional interests" expressed their aspirations. He concluded that Communists should work within the two-party system and expand their wartime alliance with mainstream liberals and the labor movement behind Roosevelt's policies. This, Browder, concluded, would promote a foreign policy conducive to a postwar U.S.-Soviet entente and the maintenance of New Deal reforms.

Browder implemented his restructuring in 1944 by renaming the Communist Party USA the Communist Political Association (CPA). The 1944 CPA convention bore little resemblance to the founding conventions of the Communist Labor party and Communist party in 1919. Beneath pictures of Marx, Trotsky, and Lenin, the 1919 conventions had shouted violent slogans, pledged themselves to the overthrow of the American government, and hailed those who had resisted military service in World War I. The 1944 convention took place beneath portraits of two non-Communists, Franklin Roosevelt and Winston Churchill, and one Communist, Joseph Stalin, and displayed banners hailing more than 9,000 Communists serving in the American armed forces in World War II. In 1919 the Communist party's manifesto declared, "Communism does not propose to 'capture' the bourgeoisie parliamentary state, but to conquer and destroy it." The CPA provided for the expulsion of any Communist who "conspires or acts to subvert, undermine, weaken or overthrow any or all institutions of American democracy."

In every arena where Communists had strength Browder threw their support behind FDR and the Democratic party. The CIO had grown significantly in power during the war, and frustration with government-imposed wartime restrictions on the use of union economic leverage renewed the call of union militants that the CIO explore the creation of a national Labor party. Communists weighed in against a Labor party and backed the strategy of Sidney Hillman. Hillman, a leading CIO figure and head of the Amalgamated Clothing Workers, was a close friend of President Roosevelt. In 1943–44 Hillman made the CIO's Political Action Committee into a powerful electoral machine that worked with the Democratic party. Hillman welcomed Communist activists into CIO-PAC, and they staffed a number of its offices. Although Republicans tried to make the CIO-PAC (and the Communist role in it) into an issue in the 1944 election, the organization proved to be one of Roosevelt's major campaign assets. It raised about a fifth of all the funds in the Roosevelt campaign and distributed millions of pieces of literature, and its massive voter registration and turnout efforts reversed a current of voter apathy that threatened FDR's reelection.

In New York, Communists had long been a minority in the American Labor party, whose leadership had been dominated by anti-Communist Socialists and liberals led by David Dubinsky of the International Ladies' Garment Workers Union. In 1943 Communists formed an alliance with Hillman and his Amalgamated Clothing Workers and took control of the ALP. (Dubinsky and his allies left the ALP to form the anti-Communist Liberal party). The Hillman–Popular Front alliance made the ALP the New York affiliate of the CIO-PAC and shifted its role from that of a balance of power between the two major parties to that of a left-wing adjunct to the Democratic party. In 1943 Communist Benjamin Davis had won a seat on New York's City Council running under the C.P. label. Early in 1945 Davis reregistered as a Democrat and made plans to run for reelection under the Democratic party label with the support of the very embodiment of politics-as-usual, Tammany Hall. In Harlem, Communists formed a loose alliance with Adam Clayton Powell, a rising star among black Democrats. In East Harlem, a Puerto Rican area, Communists had a much firmer alliance with Congressman Vito Marcantonio. Marcantonio in 1944 ran and won the election with the simultaneous nominations of the ALP, the Democratic party, and the Republican party. In New Jersey, Communists used their influence in liberal and labor circles to block those who wanted to create a state third party modeled on New York's ALP. Communists gave their support to the corrupt Jersey City political machine of Frank Hague in a Democratic primary, asserting that attacks on Hague by the state's Democratic governor, a liberal reformer, risked disruption of the Democratic organization and Roosevelt's loss of the state in 1944.

In California, Communists first gained a role in Democratic party politics in the late 1930s through their role in the Democratic Federation for Political Unity and the election of Culbert Olson as governor in 1938. Communists were particularly close to Lieutenant Governor Ellis Patterson and were among his staunchest supporters in his successful election to Congress in 1944 as a Democrat. California Communists also developed an alliance with Robert W. Kenny, the state's attorney general and a likely Democratic gubernatorial prospect. In Minnesota, Communists were part of the dominant Popular Front wing of the Farmer-Labor party, a radical third party that in the 1930s had dominated the state's politics. In 1944 Communists convinced the Farmer-Labor party to give up its independent existence and merge with the smaller and very non-radical Democratic party. Several concealed Communists and close allies, such as the former U.S. senator and governor Elmer Benson, served on the state executive committee of the merged Democratic-Farmer-Labor party (DFL). In Washington State, Communists had dominated the Washington Commonwealth Federation, the state's leading liberal political body, since its founding in 1935. In 1944 Hugh De Lacy, the WCF's leading figure and a close friend of the Communist party, won election to Congress as a Democrat. In March 1945 the WCF dissolved itself, announcing that it was no longer needed because "progressives" of its type had been integrated into the Democratic party.

American Communism's Postwar Strength

In the spring of 1945 American communism was once more in flood tide. Membership in the CPA was about 63,000 with nearly 10,000 additional Communists on leave due to military service. Over half of the party's members were trade unionists, well over half were native-born, and, the payoff of many years of effort, the Communist Political Association had finally developed a following among blacks, who made up over 10 percent of its membership. International Publishers and New Century Publishers, both party-aligned, put out more than 2 million books and pamphlets a year. The Sunday edition of the C.P.'s *Daily Worker* had a circulation that usually topped 65,000; weekday issues ran between 20,000 and 25,000. On the West Coast the C.P.'s *People's World* had a strong readership, and the party still retained more than a dozen foreign language newspapers that circulated in the tens of thousands in various immigrant communities. The Yiddish-language *Freiheit* retained a circulation above 20,000 as late as 1947. Also maintaining C.P. ties to immigrant communities was the International Workers Order (IWO), headed by the veteran Communist Max Bedacht. The IWO, which reached a membership of nearly 185,000 in 1947, linked together Communist-run ethnic fraternal societies that proved themselves successful purveyors of insurance at competitive rates. The IWO provided Communists with financial support and contact through its immigrant-ethnic societies with sectors of the CIO and the Democratic party. Through the Abraham Lincoln School in Chicago, the San Francisco Labor School, the Walt Whitman School of Social Science in Newark, the Thomas Paine School in New Rochelle, the Samuel Adams School of Boston, and the Jefferson School of Social

Science in New York, Communists enrolled ten of thousands in part-time courses in politics, labor organizing, vocational training, art, philosophy, and Marxism-Leninism.

Communists led or were dominant partners in th leadership of one large CIO union; the United Electrical, Radio, and Machine Workers; and 17 smaller CIO affiliates. In all, CIO unions with Communist-aligned leaders represented about 1,370,000 unionists, a quarter of the CIO's total. In addition, Communists were partners, although not dominant ones, in the ruling coalition of the million-member United Auto Workers, the CIO's largest affiliate. Communist unionists also controlled the leadership of many state and local CIO councils, particularly those in New York City, California, Minnesota, Wisconsin, and Washington. The CIO's anti-Communist wing was nearly equal in size and increasingly aggressive. Even so, the Communist-led wing was firmly allied to the largest group in the CIO, a centrist group led by CIO president Philip Murray. After using them in the union's initial organization, Murray eliminated most Communist activists from his own United Steel Workers, but was willing to work with Communists in other unions and included several Communists in CIO central headquarters posts. The CIO's general counsel and the editor of its newspaper were both concealed Communists. Murray did not want a factional struggle to disrupt CIO unity, and without Murray's support CIO anti-Communists could only complain and do little. (Although Communists maintained a strong role in the CIO, they held only a toehold in the larger, and largely anti-Communist, AFL.)

Mistrust of communism was deep, however, and CIO Communists found it easier to hide their communism than to acknowledge it and overcome suspicions. The network of secret Communist militants also functioned as a source of support for Communist union leaders as they sought increased influence in the labor movement. Such secrecy, however, had its price. Unionists not allied with the Communist circle often were manipulated by the shadowy Communist network and deeply resented the duplicity used to maintain its secrecy. Whatever their intent, Communists' habits of secrecy and exploitation of their concealed network gave a conspiratorial cast to their union activities.

At the end of World War II popular hostility toward communism was also lower than it had been at any time since the Bolshevik Revolution. Public support for harsh anti-Communist laws dropped toward 40 percent in public opinion polls, still showing deep enmity but significantly lower than the 70 percent support measured for such laws in the late 1930s. That decline was due to the C.P.'s support for the war, its taking on the symbols of patriotism, and its endorsement of mainstream political positions such as reelecting President Roosevelt. Chiefly, however, the decline in popular distrust of communism reflected a decline in hostility toward the Soviet Union.

Most Americans appreciated the tremendous sacrifices in blood the Soviet Union was making to defeat Nazi Germany. The success of the wartime alliance encouraged many Americans to see the Soviet Union in a new light. In a prime example, during the war Joseph E. Davies, American ambassador to the USSR in the late 1930s, wrote *Mission to Moscow*, a popular book that was made into a movie. Davies described the Soviet Union as a progressive society evolving in the same direction as the United States and insisted that those condemned in Stalin's hideous purge trials were guilty of the crimes with which they were charged. Ambassador Davies described Stalin, one of this century's most infamous mass murderers, with the words "his brown eye is exceedingly kindly and gentle. A child would like to sit on his lap and a dog would sidle up to him."[4] The fervor of American anticommunism was not inspired by a critical philosophical examination of Marxism-Leninism or by fear of the popular support commanded by Earl Browder, William Foster, or the Communist party itself. Rather, most Americans feared what they saw in the Soviet Union. They loathed American communism not for itself but for the Soviet communism that they believed—quite accurately—that American Communists wished to bring to this nation. Consequently, the spread of a benign view of the Soviet Union during World War II drastically reduced hostility toward American communism.

The Duclos Article

Earl Browder's springtime came to an end with an article by Jacques Duclos, a leading French Communist, in the April 1945 issue of a French Communist journal. Duclos denounced Browder's Teheran doctrine for "erroneous conclusions in no wise flowing from a Marxist analysis" and for "a notorious revision of Marxism" that had led to the "liquidation of the independent political party of the working class." He denied that the Teheran agreement could be interpreted to call for "a political platform of class peace in the postwar era."[5] American Communists judged that Duclos's essay was a Moscow message; Duclos had no reason to concern himself with the American movement unless at Moscow's direction. Further, Duclos quoted from unpublished minutes of meetings of American

C.P. leaders and from William Foster's private criticism of Browder's doctrine, material available to Moscow but not to Duclos.

The Duclos article became public in the United States in May, and there ensued a brief period of turmoil in the Communist Political Association as members absorbed the Soviet message. In June the CPA's national committee transferred executive power from Browder to a secretariat headed by Foster. In July an emergency national convention with only minor debate dissolved the CPA and reconstituted the Communist Party USA with Foster as chairman. The new secretariat denounced Browder as "an unreconstructed revisionist . . . a social-imperialist . . . an enemy of the working class . . . a renegade . . . an apologist for American imperialism."[6] Browder's close confidants repudiated his doctrines and supported Foster's elevation. Before the Duclos article Foster had been nearly alone in questioning Browder's policies, and even he had acquiesced when early in 1944 he received a message from Georgi Dimitroff, former head of the Comintern, that Moscow approved of Browder's strategy. Lacking any pool of anti-Browder cadres to draw upon, Foster accepted the conversion of Browder's former lieutenants and allowed most to retain their offices.

The Communist party officially expelled Browder in February 1946; he made no attempt to organize an opposition group either in or outside the party. Browder went to Moscow and appealed his ouster; Stalin's foreign minister heard Browder out but refused to reinstate him. The Soviets did, however, give him a post as the American distributor of Soviet nonfiction books. (The book venture failed; Browder lost most of his life's savings and gave it up in 1949.) Browder unsuccessfully asked to rejoin the party in 1948 and continued to regard himself as a Communist until the late 1950s.

The Communist Party Reconstituted

Foster's health prevented him from taking on the Communist party's organizational responsibilities. In 1946 Eugene Dennis took Browder's old title of general secretary. Although Dennis had been closely associated with Browder, he was a Comintern-trained Moscow loyalist who abandoned Browder at the right moment and assisted Foster in returning the party to orthodoxy. Foster retained the title of chairman and kept overall control of the ideological direction of the party, while Dennis became its organizational leader.

Eugene Dennis was born Francis X. Waldron in 1905 in Seattle, Washington. His father was the son of Irish immigrants and his mother the daughter of Norwegian immigrants. After brief attendance at college Dennis first joined the IWW and then, in 1926, the Communist party. He became a TUUL organizer in California and fled to the Soviet Union in 1930 to avoid arrest on state criminal syndicalism charges. For several years he worked as a Comintern representative under the name Tim Ryan in the Philippines, South Africa, and China. In 1935, using the name Eugene Dennis, he returned to the United States and took up the post of secretary of the Wisconsin C.P. In Wisconsin Dennis used the party's newly adopted Popular Front stance to solidify an influential Communist role in the Wisconsin CIO. He became American representative to the Comintern in 1937 and in 1938 became part of the American C.P.'s national leadership. Neither an orator or an ideologist, Dennis was an exemplary Communist bureaucrat.

Foster, resurrecting Lenin's theory that imperialism was the final stage of capitalism, asserted of the United States that "no other nation in history, not even Nazi Germany or militarist Japan, ever set for itself such all-inclusive imperialist goals" and held that only the Soviet Union blocked America's imperialist path.[7] As for the role of American Communists in this contest, Foster explained that "in no country have the workers and other democratic forces so great a responsibility in the present world crisis as here in the United States," because here "the axe must be applied to the root of the evil" and "the power of finance capital, the breeder of economic chaos, fascism and war, must be systematically weakened and eventually broken."[8] Foster, however, disavowed immediate revolution as left sectarian and said, "First, the workers should enter into organized co-operation with the poorer farmers, the Negro people, with the progressive professionals and middle classes, with the bulk of the veterans, for joint political action against their common enemy, monopoly capital, and in such forms as to culminate eventually in a broad third party movement. Secondly, this great political combination must be led by the workers, by the trade unions."[9]

After Browder's fall, American Communists' praise for Stalin, always sycophantic, became even more so. Alexander Bittleman announced, "Stalin's greatness and genius stand out so clearly and beautifully that progressive humanity has no difficulty in recognizing them. . . . To live with Stalin in one age, to fight with him in one cause, to work under the inspiring guidance of his teachings is something to be deeply proud of and thankful for, to cherish." The party's best known female organizer, Elizabeth Gurley Flynn, called Stalin "the best loved man on earth of our time."[10]

The end of Browderism did not bring a return to the militant sectarianism of Third Period communism. The Popular Front strategy of working in mainstream politics continued, but the nature of that participation changed. From 1936 to the 1939 Nazi-Soviet Pact and from the 1941 Nazi invasion of the Soviet Union into 1945, Communists had supported established liberal leaders, generally cooperating with all who did not actively oppose the C.P. or the Soviet Union's foreign goals. After Browder's ouster, Communists increased the price for their assistance and demanded that their non-Communist allies take a more strident line in defense of the Soviet Union. In Minnesota, for example, leaders of the Popular Front faction of the Democratic-Farmer-Labor party lauded the Finnish government's censorship of criticism of the Soviet Union (a requirement imposed on Finland after its defeat by the Soviet Union in World War II) and stated that such criticism ought to be similarly punished by American courts. In the fall of 1946 the CIO and several major liberal advocacy groups sponsored the General Conference of Progressives to map out a common labor-liberal political stance. The CIO's Philip Murray marred the Popular Front tone of the gathering with an extemporaneous attack on communism; former Minnesota governor Elmer Benson, one of the presiding officers and an ally of the C.P., promptly stalked off the platform to protest Murray's remarks.

Communists and their allies also shifted the ethical basis of their foreign-policy pronouncements. During the war Communists emphasized common ground with liberals by invoking the democratic values expressed in the Roosevelt-Churchill Atlantic Charter and President Roosevelt's Four Freedoms speech. After 1945 such concepts were awkward in a defense of Soviet policies in Eastern Europe. Instead, the Communist party and its allies shifted attention to what they called America's "swaggering militarism" and "Truman imperialism," maintaining that growing cold-war tensions resulted from American aggression. The party, which under Browder had supported continued conscription in peacetime, shifted after Browder to abolition of the draft and a quick military demobilization and withdrawal from Europe and Asia. (The latter themes were popular with Americans tired of wartime sacrifices and anxious for peace and plenty.)

Communists believed that the postwar domestic situation offered fertile ground for their post-Browder militancy. With the surrender of Nazi Germany and Japan in 1945, wartime controls no longer restrained

American workers, and pent-up demands produced the largest strike wave since 1919. This time the American left, having prospered during World War II, was not reeling from official prosecution as it had been in 1919. Returning veterans in World War I had tended toward hostility to unions and often volunteered to break strikes; World War II veterans generally supported the labor movement. The labor movement also appeared ready to break its alliance with the Democratic party. The Truman administration's failure to support the unions in the strike wave offended labor leaders, and Truman's seizure of the railroads in 1946 in order to stop a railroad strike infuriated the powerful rail brotherhoods. A. F. Whitney, the leader of the rail unions, called for labor to defeat Truman if he attempted reelection in 1948, and in numerous CIO union conventions delegates irritated with Truman's policies passed resolutions calling for a labor-controlled political party. Communists also believed that the United States faced an economic "catastrophe, within the next three to five years, the likes of which we have never seen before . . . and will assume a depth and proportion which will dwarf the economic catastrophe of 1929–1933."[11]

Other trends were adverse to Communists prospects, however. Public suspicion of the Soviet Union began to grow once more as Stalin disregarded wartime declarations that Europe would be reconstructed on the basis of democracy and national independence. The Soviet Union kept its territorial conquests of the Nazi-Soviet Pact (eastern Poland, eastern Romania, Latvia, Estonia, and Lithuania) and sliced off part of Finland. In Poland, Bulgaria, Hungary, Czechoslovakia, and eastern Germany, Soviet occupation troops installed Communist-dominated governments and began a brutal assault on non-Communist political forces. By 1948 all had been reduced to Communist police states modeled on Stalinist totalitarianism and firmly under Moscow's imperial control. Moscow's frustration of democracy in postwar Eastern Europe dismayed many liberals who had made common cause with Communists in the late 1930s and during the war when they faced the common enemy of Nazism. Dismay turned to alarm when Communists outside the area of Soviet occupation adopted an aggressive stance. The French and Italian Communist parties, already significant political forces by right of winning more than a quarter of the popular vote, attempted to use their control of the major part of the labor movement to destabilize the economy and bring themselves to power. In Greece a Communist guerrilla army fought for power first against British troops and then the Greek army. In China, the world's most populous nation, Communist armies under Mao Zedong defeated the government of Chiang Kai-shek and forced his retreat to Taiwan.

The spread of Communist rule into Eastern Europe and Asia sufficed to renew popular hostility toward communism. Revelations of Soviet espionage—usually factual but sometimes given exaggerated importance—further exacerbated public fears. In the spring of 1945 federal authorities discovered that *Amerasia,* a journal on Pacific affairs whose editors were close to the Communist party, possessed thousands of pages of security classified government documents. Authorities failed to get search warrants for much of the evidence in the case, evidence thus rendered inadmissible in court. Consequently, the government convicted only two of those involved, and those under plea bargains. The evidence, although inadmissible in court, was incontrovertible, and when the affair became public in the summer of 1945, it revived the aura of espionage that had long clung to American communism. Elizabeth Bentley, a longtime Soviet spy who had been recruited from C.P. ranks, quietly turned herself in to the FBI in 1945. Her testimony, usually but not always reliable, about her work for her deceased lover, a leading Soviet agent, uncovered a sizable although low-level Soviet espionage network in Washington, D.C., during World War II. Bentley's 1948 testimony to the House Un-American Activities Committee (HUAC) was followed by the testimony of Whittaker Chambers, who was a senior editor for *Time* magazine, a former American Communist, and a former Soviet spy. Chambers's testimony provided evidence of a Soviet network in the State Department in the 1930s and led to the imprisonment of Alger Hiss, a former high-ranking American diplomat.

American cryptographers also partially decoded Soviet messages and turned up information that led in 1950 to the arrest in Great Britain of Klaus Fuchs, a scientist who had worked on the atomic bomb project in the United States. Fuchs's confession led the FBI on a trail that resulted in the arrest and execution in the United States of Julius and Ethel Rosenberg for stealing U.S. nuclear secrets. Collectively, these cases and others convinced many Americans that Communists were not merely radical dissidents but traitors who threatened the nation's security.

The defection of Louis Budenz, editor of the Communist party's *Daily Worker,* further strengthened the public's belief in the link between American communism and Soviet espionage. In the fall of 1945 Budenz told HUAC that the American Communist party was a direct arm of the Soviet government and every American Communist a potential spy. Budenz's description gave a distorted picture of the American C.P. The party did what it thought Moscow wanted because it identified the Soviet Union with the future of communism, not because it was in any administrative sense a Soviet agency. Ideologically, American Communists owed their first loyalty to the motherland of communism rather than to the United States, but in practice few American Communists were spies. The Soviet Union recruited spies from the Communist movement, but espionage was not a regular activity of the American C.P. The party promoted communism and the interests of the Soviet Union through political means; espionage was the business of the Soviet Union's intelligence services. To see the American Communist party chiefly as an instrument of espionage or a sort of fifth column misjudges its main purpose.

Communist leaders interpreted Budenz's defection as a sign of ideological laxity and in 1946 purged several hundred members suspected of deviating from the post-Browder orthodoxy either to the right (toward Browderism) or the left (toward open espousal of revolution). Some of these expelled for left deviation formed short-lived splinter organizations such as the Maritime Committee for a Communist Party and the Workers Freedom League. These expulsions, along with the confusion inside the party caused by Browder's fall in mid-1945, put an end to the surge of membership growth. From its 1945 high of 63,000 the C.P. dropped to 50,000 in 1946. One of the party's disappointments of this period was its regaining only a portion of the 10,000 party members who had entered military service. For many young Communists, military service had been a major discontinuity that had removed them from the "progressive" environment in which they had grown up. In America's mass armed forces of World War II these young Communists met the full variety of American life and discovered the yawning gap between the beliefs of ordinary young Americans and the assumptions of the Communist movement. After the war, despite a major effort by the party, most Communist veterans failed to reestablish links with the C.P. and joined other veterans in the pursuit of domesticity and a share of the burgeoning consumer culture.

Even so, Communist growth resumed in 1946 and reached about 70,000 in 1947–48. Rapid turnover continued, however, and most new members left the movement within a year. The party remained geographically concentrated, with about one-third of its membership in New York, but its reach had spread to new areas, including 2,000 members in the South, once a desert of Communist support. The C.P. claimed some 1,700 neighborhood clubs (its most active units), 3,000 industrial (job-related) clubs, 200 clubs for professionals, and several hundred clubs for its student and youth adherents. In all, the party claimed affiliates in 600 American cities and towns. Although the C.P. did not match its 1939 membership high of 100,000, in terms of its institutional power through the labor movement, numbers of full-time party functionaires, financial resources, and influence and prestige in liberal and labor circles, Communist strength was never higher than in the immediate postwar period.

The Progressive Party and Disaster: 1946–1948

In repudiating Browderism, Communists also repudiated Browder's acceptance of the American two-party tradition. In November 1945 Eugene Dennis told Communists "to create the conditions and base for organizing a major third party nationally." Meeting Foster's criterion for a third party (a broad coalition of workers, farmers, blacks, and middle-class progressives led by the union movement) was a formidable task, however, and Communists did not move immediately to creating a third party. Dennis also cautioned that a "majority of the labor and progressive movement still has to be convinced and won over for a third party" and specified only that the "American people must have an alternative to the two-party strait-jacket; they must be in a position to have a choice in 1948 other than between a Truman and a Dewey."[12]

The 1946 California primary defeats of two C.P. allies (Congressman Ellis Patterson for the Democratic Senate nomination and Attorney General Robert Kenny for the Democratic gubernatorial nomination) demonstrated the risks of the new policy. The smooth relationship between the California CIO, the left wing of the California Democratic party, and the Communist party had been disrupted. Dennis commented, "The adverse results in many of the primaries were due . . . to the sectarian and one-sided positions which sections of the progressive labor movement, including certain [Communist] Party forces, developed toward all Democrats, including progressives like Kenny and Patterson in California, and toward other and more conservative, middle-of-the-road or wavering pro-labor Democrats." (Kenny shared that assessment, blaming his defeat on "a Frenchman named Duclos.") Dennis explained that Communists, "while pursuing an independent workingclass policy and expanding its independent political organizations and activity [laying the basis for a national third party in 1948]," should also "help influence a progressive regrouping within the Democratic party [i.e., possibly challenge Truman within the Democratic party]." Communists pursued this two-track policy through the presidential candidacy of Henry Wallace.[13]

Wallace, secretary of agriculture for FDR's first two terms, had headed programs that pulled farmers back from disaster in the early 1930s and were among the New Deal's proudest achievements. In 1940 Roosevelt rewarded Wallace with the vice presidential nomination. As vice president, Wallace had been extremely popular among advanced New Dealers, and his People's Century speeches advocating a vague worldwide New Deal embodied the idealistic vision of the wartime Popular Front. Wallace's militant liberalism and eccentric personality, however, did not endear him to Democratic professionals. In 1944 Roosevelt dropped Wallace from his ticket and replaced him with the more moderate Truman. As a consolation prize FDR appointed Wallace secretary of commerce, and Wallace remained a leading spokesman of the New Deal wing of the Democratic party after FDR's death. As the cold war developed, Wallace grew increasingly uneasy about Truman's policies toward the Soviet Union. He did not regard the Soviets as aggressive and felt that Stalin's desires could be accommodated. In a September 1946 speech Wallace advocated American recognition of Soviet supremacy in Eastern Europe and deplored the developing anti-Soviet alliance of the United States and Western Europe. The president fired him a few days later.

Wallace's public recognition and liberal reputation made him a natural rallying point for those unhappy with the president, and in the fall of 1946 those were many. Truman had replaced veteran New Dealers with men more comfortable with the politics of special interests, and many of the former saw in Wallace a return to New Deal idealism. Labor leaders distrusted Truman, public opinion polls put his popularity at abysmal levels, and Democratic activists feared he would drag down the entire party to defeat.

Wallace developed a forum for his views by becoming the editor of *The New Republic* and by setting out on a nationwide speaking tour that attracted enthusiastic crowds. The National Citizens Political Action Committee (NCPAC) and the Independent Citizens Committee of the Arts, Sciences, and Professions (ICCASP) also rallied to Wallace's cause. The NCPAC began as a 1944 subsidiary of CIO-PAC for organizing nonunion liberals; Elmer Benson of Minnesota, an old Communist party ally, chaired the committee. The ICCASP spoke for advanced liberals among the scientific, artistic, and cultural elite. Although Roosevelt had won reelection in 1944, the war years had seen a major decline in liberal strength, and in 1946 Republicans won control of Congress. The NCPAC and the ICCASP represented those liberals who believed that liberal fortunes could be restored through stronger organization: through liberal solidarity with each other and with the labor movement. Communists and their allies were regarded as integral, although unacknowledged, partners in this coalition. Progressive solidarity, then, required that no one object to or acknowledge the role of Communists in the liberal alliance. Further, in view of Communist attitudes, liberal unity could be achieved only if non-Communists refrained from divisive questions about Stalin's policies in Eastern Europe. In December 1946 the NCPAC and the ICCASP merged to form the Progressive Citizens of America (PCA). Communists saw the PCA as an embodiment of the union-led progressive coalition of workers, farmers, blacks, and middle-class progressives. Wallace was also the perfect candidate for such a coalition.

The PCA gave Wallace the skeleton of a national political organization. How Wallace would use the PCA, however, was unclear. Should he challenge Truman for the Democratic nomination? This put the least strain on existing political arrangements and, if successful, put Wallace in an excellent position to win the presidency. On the other hand, denying an incumbent president his party's nomination was a difficult task. A third-party candidacy would be risky, but it would allow progressives to break the restraints placed on them in the Democratic party by its Southern conservatives and patronage-oriented big-city political organizations. Wallace, like the Communist party, kept his options open.

The small anti-Communist Union for Democratic Action (UDA) challenged the PCA's claim to speak for organized liberalism. In May 1946 *The New Republic* carried a long letter to the editor from James Loeb, head of the UDA, that in retrospect was the first shot in a nationwide liberal civil war. Loeb wrote that liberalism's problem was ideological rather than organizational. He argued that liberal revival depended on severing the link developing in the public's mind between liberalism and Soviet tyranny, a link forged by liberals who defended or ignored Stalin's conduct. Further, Loeb argued, the unacknowledged alliance between liberals and Communists betrayed democratic values. In view of the Communist party's totalitarian ideology, liberals could not associate with it without compromising their integrity. In January 1947 the UDA reorganized itself into the Americans for Democratic Action (ADA). The ADA attracted the support of some veteran New Dealers (Eleanor Roosevelt most prominently), young liberal activists (Hubert Humphrey, for example), the leaders of the anti-Communist wing of the CIO such as Walter Reuther of the UAW, and AFL figures such as David Dubinsky of the ILGWU. The ADA declared its intention to drive Communists from their concealed role in liberal and labor politics.

In the CIO Philip Murray sensed fratricide, and he took steps to discourage the fight. At his instigation the 1946 national CIO convention adopted a resolution stating, "We resent and reject efforts of the Communist party or other political parties and their adherents to interfere in the affairs of the C.I.O. This convention serves notice that we will not tolerate such interference."[14] Murray, nonetheless, maintained the de facto alliance between CIO Communists and his centrist group. He continued to hold the CIO anti-Communists in check and did not eliminate Communists from their positions in the CIO. The resolution warned Communists that Murray would do so, however, if they endangered the CIO. CIO Communists not only did not contest the resolution, they supported it. Michael Quill, the concealed Communist head of the Transport Workers Union, chaired the subcommittee that drafted the resolution. Later, in March 1947, the CIO executive board, again at Murray's instigation, urged CIO officials to abstain from participation in both the PCA and ADA. This, Murray hoped, would either warn both organizations that the CIO wanted liberal peace or at least isolate the CIO from the fight.

The domestic reverberations of international events, nevertheless, pushed the two sides toward a showdown. Early in 1947 a worsening financial crisis forced Great Britain to withdraw support for Greece's right-wing regime, then fighting Communist insurgents. In March 1947 President Truman asked the Congress to approve aid for the Greek government and announced the Truman Doctrine of military and economic aid for any nation resisting Communist takeover. In June 1947 Secretary of State George Marshall announced a plan to deal with Europe's deepening economic crisis, a crisis that had brought economic recovery from the war to a halt and threatened to bring Communist parties to power in France and Italy. The Marshall Plan provided for massive American economic aid for a coordinated European recovery program that would include Eastern Europe and the Soviet Union. If Eastern European nations participated, the plan would tie their economies to the West and destroy Stalin's plans for a Soviet sphere of influence.

Stalin responded by urging European nations to reject American assistance unless the United States channeled aid to separate recovery programs for each nation. When Western European countries accepted an Anglo-French plan for a single European recovery program, the Soviets walked out of the Marshall Plan negotiations. Stalin also forced Eastern

European nations under Red Army occupation to withdraw from the negotiations. American liberals split over these events along the lines of the PCA-ADA fissure. Wallace and the PCA denounced the Truman Doctrine as "Truman Imperialism"; the ADA supported Truman. The ADA endorsed the Marshall Plan; Wallace and the PCA greeted the Marshall Plan skeptically and denounced it altogether after the Soviets left the negotiations. The cold war, at home and abroad, began in earnest.

Toward a Third Party

Throughout most of 1947 American Communists continued to follow their two-track strategy. Events in California highlighted this policy. Hugh Bryson, head of the CIO's Marine Cooks and Stewards Union and a concealed Communist, and Robert Kenny, the former attorney general and political ally of the Communist party, were both prominent figures in California liberal-labor politics. Kenny argued that Wallace should remain a Democrat and the liberal left throw its resources into key Democratic presidential primaries, particularly those in the western states. Wallace victories in prominent primaries, he felt, would stampede nervous Democrats toward nominating Wallace as the only alternative to losing with Truman. In July 1947 Kenny formed the Democrats for Wallace to campaign for Wallace delegates in the western states. At the same time Bryson called a founding convention for the Independent Progressive party of California (IPP). Kenny regarded Bryson's third party as quixotic as well as competitive to his effort. He met with William Foster to urge Communists to restrain Bryson and wound up in a shouting match with a Los Angeles C.P. leader who had come to make a case for the IPP. Foster refused to choose. Both initiatives proceeded.

With the exception of Bryson, most CIO Communists inclined against a third-party venture. The leading Communist-aligned union in California, Harry Bridges's ILWU, backed Kenny's initiative and blocked Bryson's effort to get CIO support for the IPP. Also in September Communists and their allies at the New York CIO convention, where they were the predominant influence, made no move to support a third party. In October, at the national CIO convention, the Communist-led wing did not raise the third-party issue and agreed to a foreign policy resolution that in all but name endorsed the Marshall Plan. Eugene Dennis commented, "We Communists are not adventurers and irresponsible sectarians. We are not going to isolate ourselves. We never did and do not now favor the launching of premature and unrepresentative third parties or independent tickets."[15] All of this suggested that although the C.P. was maintaining its options, it would not pursue a third-party venture. Its own criteria made significant union support a fundamental requirement, and such support did not exist.

In early October the Soviet Union announced the formation of the Communist Information Bureau (Cominform). Cominform linked nine European Communist parties in an anti–Marshall Plan political program and pledged an aggressive attack on what it termed American imperialism. In a sign of its confrontational stance, Cominform's founding conference criticized French and Italian Communists for not having attempted an insurrectional seizure of power in 1944 in the chaos that followed liberation from Nazi occupation. No American Communists attended the founding of Cominform, and the American party never joined. Cominform remained throughout its existence chiefly a vehicle for Soviet coordination of European Communist activity. The days of Comintern agents coming west to tell the American party what to do or of American Communists journeying to Moscow to present their policies to a Comintern committee were past. Still, American Communists lived, as one historian (and former leading Communist) put it, in a "mental Comintern" and followed Moscow's guidance by indirect means. American Communists discerned Soviet wishes in much the same way the U.S. government and academic "kremlinologists" analyzed Soviet policy: by reading between the lines of Soviet press reports, noting who was standing nearest to Stalin at public events, and assessing the tone of speeches of Soviet leaders.[16]

It took a few weeks for the texts of speeches at the Cominform conference to reach the West and for American Communists to interpret them. By mid-October 1947 the Communist party's leadership decided that Moscow had launched an all-out political attack on the West. American Communists hastened to join the assault. The two-track policy ended; Communists shifted to exclusive support for a third party. Communist political leaders informed their supporters in the labor movement that they were to support a third party even if the cost was a break with Murray and other centrist CIO leaders.

Henry Wallace knew his constituency included Communists, but he never dealt with the Communist party directly. The relationship existed through members of Wallace's inner circle who were close to the party and through liberal and labor leaders who worked with Communists in various liberal-left political arenas. The unhealthy nature of this relationship manifested itself in Wallace's third-party decision. As soon as Communists learned of their leaders' decision for a third party, they and their allies began advocating that option in the arenas in which they operated. Wallace and his close advisers began to receive delegations, letters, telegrams, and phone calls from a variety of political clubs, civic groups, ethnic associations, and labor unions urging him to lead a new third party. The publisher of *The New Republic* remembered that Wallace's office became "Grand Central Station" and "there were steady deputations led in to see Henry [Wallace]. Phil Murray would criticize the third party—on the following day a 'rank and file' delegation from some painters or auto workers local in New York or New Jersey would troop in to tell Henry that Murray did not speak for the membership."[17]

Wallace and his close supporters had been unsure about what to do, but the flurry of activity in November and December made it appear that a broad segment of labor and liberal-left activists had swung to enthusiastic support for the third-party path. In fact, the swing of opinion was not among thousands of activists but an end to the indecision of Foster, Dennis, and a few other Communist leaders. The indirect relationship between Wallace and the C.P. and the concealed role of Communist activists in the labor movement and in local liberal organizations led Wallace to misjudge support for a new party. In late December 1947 Wallace and the PCA announced that they would form a new Progressive party that would run Wallace for the presidency and field candidates for congressional, state, and local offices as well.

CIO Communists on the Defensive

Even as Communists embarked on the risky path of the third party, the tide of events turned against them. Since the 1930s Communists had been partners (although not controlling ones) in the ruling coalition in the United Auto Workers, the CIO's largest and most dynamic union. Walter Reuther, an anti-Communist, had won the UAW's presidency in 1946, but the coalition of which the Communists were a part retained control of the UAW's executive board and limited the effect of Reuther's victory. At the November 1947 UAW convention, however, Reuther's caucus routed its opponents. Reuther fired scores of Communists from the UAW's staff and set about eliminating Communists from offices in UAW locals. Another major labor ally of the Communist party, Joseph Curran, president of the CIO's National Maritime Union (East and Gulf Coast sailors), also broke with the C.P. In 1947 Curran won total control of the NMU and drove the once-dominant Communist faction out of the union.

Curran's and Reuther's victories exacerbated the damage Communists sustained in the passage of the Taft-Hartley Act in 1947. Taft-Hartley, one of the achievements of Republican control of Congress in 1947, limited the protections accorded unions in the National Labor Relations Act (Wagner Act) of 1935. One Taft-Hartley provision restricted legal protection given unions to those whose leaders signed non-Communist oaths. This struck directly at the power of concealed Communists. Communist union officials faced grim choices. If they did not sign, their unions would lose legal protection. While some unions were strong enough to bargain with employers without the protections of the National Labor Relations Board (NLRB), most were not. Union Communists could resign from the C.P., sign the oath, and keep their offices. Their break with the party needed to be thorough, however, or they faced federal prosecution for falsely signing the oath. Hugh Bryson, for example, signed the non-Communist oath but was convicted of perjury when he failed to convince a court that he had actually left the Communist movement.

Taft-Hartley's political fallout, moreover, damaged Communists as much as the oaths. Leaders of the AFL and the CIO hated the law's reduction of union power and were grateful to President Truman when he vetoed the act. Congress overrode Truman's veto, but labor's gratitude remained and the breach between Truman and labor began to heal. Further, Taft-Hartley's passage brought home to union leaders the importance of the 1948 election. If the Congress stayed Republican and the presidency went Republican as well, labor faced the passage of even harsher antilabor legislation. The institutional viability of the modern labor movement, created in the 1930s under the legal protection of the NLRB, was at stake. Union survival required Republican defeat. To most labor leaders, and to Philip Murray in particular, defeating the Republican presidential candidate and unseating the Republican majorities in Congress looked difficult enough without adding the burden of dividing the anti-Republican vote. Most union leaders decided that a viable third party would guarantee Republican victory. They set out to make sure it didn't happen.

Within weeks of Wallace's third-party decision Murray severed the center-left alliance in the CIO and set about breaking the back of the Communist position in labor. In January 1948 the CIO executive board voted 33 to 13 to oppose the third-party movement. Although the resolution did not bind individual CIO unions, it bound the CIO's national staff, and Murray eliminated third-party supporters (largely Communists) from

CIO offices. The policy also bound state and local CIO central bodies. John Brophy, who had bitter memories of his alliance with Communists in the UMW in the late 1920s, carried out Murray's directive to eliminate Communists from CIO central bodies. CIO officials also ousted Communists from their once-strong role in the CIO's Political Action Committee. When the American Labor party became the New York affiliate of Wallace's party, the CIO-PAC severed its relationship to the ALP. The Amalgamated Clothing Workers, the ALP's chief union support, also withdrew its participation.

For many years CIO anti-Communists had lectured CIO centrists that Communist unionists could not be trusted, saying that although most unionists regarded politics as secondary, Communists treated it as primary. If Communist politics and union needs clashed, anti-Communists preached, CIO Communists would put the party before the CIO. For most of the CIO's existence, however, Communist politics and CIO interests had not clashed. Before the cold war was underway in earnest, most CIO centrists did not regard the passage of occasional pro-Soviet resolutions at union conventions as worth getting upset about. The third-party venture, however, was different. The third party endangered the CIO by disrupting the CIO's plan to defeat the Republicans in 1948. Communists had done what CIO anti-Communists had said they would do: put the C.P.'s political goals ahead of the CIO's union goals. Further, Murray regarded the Communist decision to require its labor cadre to support the third party a violation of the 1946 CIO convention resolution warning against C.P. interference in the CIO. The distinction between the CIO's anti-Communist wing and its Murray-led centrist majority became a mere matter of degree. For all practical purposes, the CIO split between an anti-Communist majority, which encompassed unions with three-quarters of its membership, and a shrinking Communist-aligned minority.

Communist unionists found themselves pressured by the C.P. for a forthright stand for Wallace, pressured by CIO leaders to disavow the third party, pressured by the government to sign Taft-Hartley non-Communist oaths, and often pressured by increasingly aggressive anti-Communist factions within their own unions. There was no unanimity of response as Communist unionists sorted out their attachment to Communist ideology, their loyalty to the institutional labor movement, and personal concerns for careers and family. Some chose communism, sometimes surviving but often being forced out of union staff jobs or losing union elections. As the CIO's legal counsel, Lee Pressman held a position of considerable prestige and importance, but he was also a concealed Communist. Murray would have kept Pressman if he had given up his Communist loyalties. Pressman, however, resigned as the CIO's legal counsel in February 1948 and devoted himself to the Progressive party. Only five CIO affiliates endorsed Wallace: the medium-size Mine, Mill, and Smelter Workers and four smaller C.P.-aligned unions.

Other CIO Communists chose the labor movement. "Red Mike" Quill, head of the Transport Workers Union, regarded a third party as political lunacy but initially acquiesced to the C.P.'s decision. He endorsed Wallace and as a member of the CIO's executive board voted against the anti-third party resolution. By April 1948, however, Quill had had enough. The third-party decision, along with the New York Communist party's opposition to a subway fare increase that would finance a wage increase for TWU members, forced him to choose. (The bulk of the TWU's members were New York subway and bus employees.) Quill abandoned the Wallace campaign, privately quit the C.P., and forced Communists out of the TWU. Many CIO Communists and their allies tried to finesse the issue by supporting the Progressive party as individuals but not committing their union. Albert Fitzgerald, president of the U.E., by far the largest of the C.P.-aligned unions, chaired the National Labor Committee for Wallace, but he refrained from asking the U.E. itself to endorse Wallace. Harry Bridges and his ILWU followed a similar course.

The third-party decision revealed the shallow roots of Communist influence among liberal-left political activists as well. The third-party decision alienated thousands of liberals, including many officeholders and would-be officeholders, active in local Democratic organizations; they had invested too much in the Democratic party to give it up for a new party. In particular, the third-party venture weakened Wallace forces in those states where they were strong in the Democratic organization. In Minnesota, for example, a Popular Front alliance had taken control of the Democratic-Farmer-Labor party state convention in 1946. A Popular Front majority that included several concealed Communists controlled the DFL state executive committee. Elmer Benson, later national chairman of the Progressive party, led the Popular Front majority on the DFL executive board.

The Wallace forces, then, already controlled the Minnesota DFL and were in a good position to send pro-Wallace delegates to the national Democratic convention. Wallace's third-party decision, however, forced them to adopt the difficult strategy of disaffiliating the DFL from the Democratic party and affiliating to the new Progressive party. An anti-Communist faction, led by Minneapolis mayor Hubert Humphrey, used the third-party decision to separate the hard core of the Popular Front alliance (the Communists and their close friends) from their more numerous but softer allies who liked Wallace but recoiled at abandoning the Democratic party. Further, the Popular Front faction of the DFL relied heavily on the manpower and money of the Communist-led Minnesota CIO. After the third-party decision the national CIO withdrew its support from incumbent pro-Wallace Minnesota CIO leaders and shifted it to an angry anti-Communist faction led by Humphrey's labor allies. In the spring of 1948 the Minnesota CIO executive board and the CIO-PAC board expelled third-party supporters from their ranks and forced the resignation of the CIO-PAC's Minnesota director, a concealed Communist.

In the DFL's party caucuses, Humphrey's anti-Communist faction won a solid majority of delegates and prepared to take control of the DFL at its state convention. Wallace's supporters, nonetheless, had won uncontested control of DFL state convention delegates from nine countries and half of the delegation of a tenth. Further, Wallace progressives, although a minority, had been accepted as delegates at dozens of country and congressional district DFL conventions and picked up scattered DFL county offices. If Wallace progressives wanted to stay in the mainstream of liberalism in Minnesota, they needed only to attend the DFL state convention and accept their minority status. Nor did remaining within the DFL mean abandoning Wallace's presidential candidacy; under Minnesota law Wallace's supporters could place his name on the ballot without actual organization of a new party.

Carl Ross, head of the Minnesota Communist party, supported the view of local leaders that progressives should remain within the DFL. However, when Ross visited Communist headquarters in New York in the period between the county conventions and the state DFL convention, he was told in inarguable terms that Communists and their friends must leave the Democratic party. The C.P. would not tolerate its Minnesota allies remaining in a DFL party that failed to join Wallace's Progressive party. After Ross's return, the Minnesota Wallace campaign announced that its supporters would boycott the state DFL convention and hold a separate convention. If the new party failed to be electorally viable, the once-powerful Popular Front alliance was finished as a force in Minnesota liberalism. Although Humphrey's faction could not eliminate all of the Wallace progressives from the DFL party, once they walked out, keeping them out was easy.[18]

Foreign Pressures and Electoral Defeat

Other events, international and domestic, combined to further weaken the Wallace campaign and to render the C.P.'s position vulnerable. Elections held shortly after Czechoslovakia's liberation from Nazi rule had produced a substantial Communist vote, but not a majority. Czechoslovakia's non-Communist political leaders, led by Eduard Benes and Jan Masaryk, knew that maintenance of their democracy depended on Stalin's goodwill; after all, the Soviet army occupied the nation. Consequently, Communists were major partners in the new government's ruling coalition, and Czechoslovakia deferred to the Soviets on foreign-policy issues. Czechoslovakia's democratically elected coalition government was seen as proof that Stalin would allow internal democracy in Eastern Europe as long as Soviet foreign interests were protected and local Communists received a share in power. In February 1948, however, a Communist coup d'état overthrew the coalition government and installed a harsh Communist tyranny. Masaryk died, having jumped or been thrown from his office window. Wallace defended the coup and advanced the argument, a preposterous one, that the Communist coup had merely preempted a reactionary coup organized by the American ambassador. The Czechoslovak coup did enormous damage to efforts of Popular Front liberals to defend Soviet conduct in Eastern Europe.

Nor was this the end of it. In June Stalin blocked land access to West Berlin, and the United States responded with a massive airlift to keep the Western-controlled enclave in East Germany free of Soviet control. Most Americans deeply resented Stalin's coercion, but Wallace defended the Soviet position. On the heels of the Berlin airlift came the break between Stalin and Josip Tito. Yugoslavia had been freed of Nazi occupation largely through the efforts of a Communist partisan army led by Tito rather than by the Soviet army. Tito installed a Communist regime and worked as one of Stalin's close allies. When Stalin replaced the Eastern European governments established immediately after the war with thoroughly Stalinized regimes, however, Tito insisted that Yugoslav communism retain its independence from Moscow. Stalin in 1948 launched a fierce political attack on "Titoism." Communist parties throughout the world purged those suspected of supporting "national" communism; in

Eastern Europe Stalin's lieutenants imprisoned or executed thousands for Titoism. In the United States the Stalin-Tito split further disconcerted liberals who had taken a benign view of Stalin's policies.

By the time of the Progressive party's July national convention, a portion of the soft liberal support for Wallace had fallen away. A disproportionate number of the delegates were hard-core Popular Front supporters—the Communists and their friends. The result was a convention majority oblivious to the disturbing impression it made on the press and the public. The fate of the Vermont resolution aptly demonstrated this insensitivity. Convention speeches and the platform text overwhelmingly conveyed the message that the United States, not the Soviet Union, had started the cold war and that only a change in U.S. behavior could end it. The Vermont delegation sought to dilute the lopsided nature of the platform by the addition of a sentence stating: "Although we are critical of the present foreign policy of the United States, it is not our intention to give blanket endorsement to the foreign policy of any other nation." On its face the amendment was innocuous, but to the reflexively pro-Soviet convention it hinted that Stalin's policies might be open to criticism. Without any awareness of the damage to their own cause, Progressive party leaders denounced the amendment and it went down to overwhelming defeat. Most Americans concluded that a party that could not pass the Vermont resolution could not end the cold war on terms acceptable to the United States.

Paralleling Wallace's fading star was the brightening of Truman's hopes. President Truman's popularity had continued at dismal levels through the first half of 1948, and Republicans looked forward to an easy victory. The Democratic national convention, however, was a turning point. In an unexpected floor battle liberal and labor forces led by Hubert Humphrey and the ADA inserted a strong civil-rights plank into the platform. The fight galvanized the otherwise listless convention, and Humphrey's impassioned advocacy of the equal-rights plank provided an emotional and moral highlight for the convention and a national radio audience. (The convention's action sparked a walkout by southern delegates and the formation of the racist States Rights party behind the presidential candidacy of Governor Strom Thurmond of South Carolina.) Truman accepted the plank and thereby extinguished the Wallace campaign's hopes of making inroads among black voters. Truman followed up with a rousing "give 'em hell" acceptance speech that foreshadowed his remarkable recovery of voter support in the fall.

In the wake of the party conventions, the leakage of non-Communists from the Wallace campaign accelerated. Publicly, only a few score quit the Progressive party, complaining of the defeat of the Vermont resolution or making veiled reference to Communists' role in the Wallace campaign. Privately, thousands ceased active participation. Among the latter were Robert Kenny, once Wallace's most articulate supporter on the West Coast. He later commented, in a reference to the Communist role in the third-party decision, "We needed a third party here [California] like a hole in the head. We had control of a second party and might have remained in control had it not been for this alien doctrine which came in from the East and dictated that the Left Wing sever itself from the Democratic party and go into seclusion as a separate Independent Progressive Party."[19]

As non-Communist progressives withdrew, Communists, without intending to do so, came to play a larger role in the Progressive party. As the Communist role increased, the outflow of non-Communist progressives further accelerated. As the general election approached, the Progressive party was not the broad coalition of unions, farmers, blacks, and middle-class progressives that William Foster had envisioned. Instead, the Progressive party became a narrow coalition of Communists, a handful of Communist-led unions, and several thousand liberal-left activists, independent radicals, and chronic political mavericks, along with a scattering of left-inclined figures from Hollywood and artistic circles who provided a dash of glamour.

The general election shattered Communist hopes. Truman won with 24 million votes, Republican Thomas Dewey was second with 21.9 million votes, and Thurmond of the States Rights party was third with 1,169,000 votes. Wallace came in fourth with 1,138,000 votes, 2.3 percent of the total. Since the 1930s American Communists had built up a formidable array of institutions and achieved a significant measure of influence in the labor movement and in liberal-left political circles. In 1948 Communists gambled these assets on the Progressive party and lost the gamble. The 1948 election broke the back of communism in America. In the years that followed American Communists suffered other defeats and setbacks. The Progressive party venture, however, was the movement's decisive defeat. What followed was a long dying.

The Long Dying

Something might have been recovered from the Progressive party debacle if the Republicans had triumphed. Perhaps the defeated Progressives could have made common cause with the defeated Democrats and placed part of the blame for Republican victory on anti-Communist liberals for having disrupted liberal unity. Yet not only had Wallace and the Progressive party failed, but Truman had retained the presidency and Democrats won control of Congress. The cold-war Democrats of the Truman administration and the anti-Communist liberals of the ADA were in the ascendancy.

The assaults on Communist enclaves in the labor movement, begun in 1948, continued in 1949 and 1950. Murray and other CIO leaders judged that Communist unionists had subordinated the survival of the labor movement to Communist political goals by backing the third party and dividing the anti-Republican vote. They also were mindful that in the face of the cold war and growing popular anticommunism the Communist presence in the CIO risked tainting the organization with disloyalty. CIO leaders concluded that Communists were an inherent threat to the institutional viability of the union movement and set about eliminating them. The 1949 national CIO convention ordered the small Communist-aligned Farm Equipment Workers Union (F.E.) to merge with the huge, and anti-Communist, United Auto Workers. The F.E. resisted, but UAW raids took most of its membership and it ceased to function. The CIO also lifted the charter of the influential Communist-led New York CIO Council, thus allowing the creation of a new central body, free of Communist control, in New York. Privately, Murray warned leaders of the Communist-aligned unions that even worse was in store unless they changed their ways. They did not: the U.E., largest of the Communist-aligned unions, responded with a preemptive attack on its large anti-Communist faction by expelling its leaders. The November 1949 national CIO convention reacted by denouncing the U.E. as Communist controlled. The U.E. was refusing to participate in the CIO by this point, and it is a matter of definition as to whether the U.E. was expelled or withdrew from the CIO.

The CIO brought formal charges against its Communist-aligned unions and, after hearings, expelled seven of them by late 1950. The CIO authorized its affiliates to raid the expelled unions or charted new anti-Communist bodies to take over their jurisdictions. AFL unions also raided the expelled unions. Harry Bridges's ILWU withstood anti-Communist assaults almost without loss. The ILWU, easily the best led of the Communist-aligned unions, provided its members with efficient collective-bargaining services. Further, Bridges and many of his lieutenants were heroic figures to many West Coast dockworkers for their role in the 1934 maritime strike that gave birth to the union. The ILWU, however, was the exception. The U.E., largest of the expelled unions, survived but lost more than half of its members to the newly charted CIO International Union of Electrical Workers or to other unions. Most of the smaller expelled unions were picked apart by AFL and CIO raids and disintegrated despite desperate efforts to save themselves by merging with one another. By the mid-1950s membership in the surviving Communist-aligned unions numbered about 200,000, a fraction of their once-impressive strength.

Neither the disaster of the Progressive party venture nor the destruction of its position in the labor movement caused the C.P. to reexamine its strategy. Instead, Communists turned inward and blamed their failures on internal enemies. Party leaders began a new hunt for members guilty of Browderism, conflating it with the Titoist deviation. In the purge trial of Hungarian Communist leader Laszlo Rajk (later executed), Stalin's agents fabricated evidence linking Rajk to American intelligence agencies through John Lautner, a 20-year veteran of the American Communist party and a leader of its work among Hungarian Americans. Testimony in the Rajk trial linked Rajk's (imaginary) crimes to Browder by claiming that the American Office of Strategic Services had smuggled Browder's Teheran speeches into Hungary to mislead Hungarian Communists. (Lautner had served with the OSS, the World War II predecessor to the Central Intelligence Agency.) In an anemic emulation of Stalin's bloody anti-Titoist purge, American C.P. leaders interrogated Lautner at gunpoint and expelled him from the party as an "enemy of the working class." His wife, a loyal Communist, divorced him. The evidence against Lautner was entirely false.

The American Communist party's most devastating internal purge was the white chauvinism campaign. Communists had for many years with modest returns invested a significant share of their manpower, energy, and resources in black recruitment and work for black causes. Communists were one of the first white political organizations that championed black rights. A number of Communists were beaten and a few murdered while working among southern blacks. The C.P., regarding itself as a band of revolutionary brothers free of the bigotry of the class-ridden and racist society in which it operated, sought to integrate black Communists fully into the internal social life of the party. By the postwar period Communists had developed a meaningful, albeit still small, following among black Americans, and the party's black membership had risen above 10 percent. There were, however, strains within the party due to the tension between its internal policy of racial integration and its external commitment to a quasi–black nationalist view of the place of blacks in American society. In 1949, in the wake of the Wallace catastrophe and the destruction of the CIO's Communist wing, some Communists began to suggest that blacks were emerging as the real revolutionary force in place of the (mostly white) working class as a whole. The rapid growth of anticolonial liberation movements in Africa and Asia reinforced that attitude. In the frustration of defeat, some Communists attributed the party's difficulties to its failure to recognize the revolutionary potential of black workers.

In October 1949 the chairman of the C.P.'s Negro Commission called for a party offensive against white racist attitudes in order to make the party worthy of the revolutionary potential of the black liberation movement. Other party leaders endorsed the call, and there ensued a massive internal hunt for "white chauvinists." Members, confused and angry at political defeat and steeped in an apocalyptic expectation of world war and fascism in America, took out their frustration on white chauvinism. Thousands of veteran Communists were accused of white chauvinism on the flimsiest of evidence. Use of the phrases "whitewash" or "black sheep" in casual conversation or the serving of watermelon at a social event sufficed to bring a party trial. Some party members recklessly charged others with white chauvinism to repay old scores or clear the ladder above them for promotion. The campaign lasted until 1953, when Foster denounced the campaign's excesses as left sectarian. In the meantime, thousands of Communists had been driven out of the movement. The historian and former Communist Joseph Starobin later wrote, "No single experience is remembered in retrospect with such dismay, even fifteen years later, by thousands of former Communists and their progressive sympathizers. Not a few have asked themselves: if they were capable of such cruelties to each other when they were a small handful of people bound by sacred ideals, what might they have done if they had been in power?"[20]

Government and Public Hostility

As cold-war tensions between the United States and the Soviet-led Communist bloc worsened after World War II, government pressure on the American Communist party, nearly absent since 1942, resumed. In March 1947 Lewis Schwellenbach, Truman's secretary of labor, suggested that the Communist party be outlawed. The president did not

endorse Schwellenbach's proposal, and it received an unsympathetic reaction from liberals, including such prominent anti-Communist liberals as
Eleanor Roosevelt. Indeed, in less than a month a C.P. appeal to members and liberal sympathizers for funds to fight Schwellenbach's plan
raised a quarter of a million dollars, a sizable sum in 1947.

Also in 1947 Truman issued an executive order setting up a loyalty
program for federal government employees. Although the program affected hundreds of thousands of government employees, it was not a
major blow to Communists, because federal employees were not a major
source of support for the party. The loyalty-security program caused
more trouble for former Communists than it did for members of the
party. In the late 1930s and 1940s several hundred thousand Americans
briefly had been Communists, and even more had joined various front
organizations. Most left the movement within a year or two. Some of
these former members later became government employees. These former Communists, by this time often holding moderate political attitudes,
were called to account for their onetime membership in an organization
that was at this point allied with the nation's chief foreign enemy. The
situation induced unease and even fear in many former Communists;
some were forced to go through humiliating loyalty hearings, and the
government fired several hundred as potential security risks. Some employees who had never associated with communism also faced investigations when acquaintances, out of ignorance or viciousness, confused
any type of unconventional behavior with Communist sympathies.

In 1948 the Congress considered strong anti-Communist legislation,
but the bill proposed by Senator Karl Mundt (Republican, South Dakota)
and Representative Richard Nixon (Republican, California) failed to pass.
Communists once more used the specter of anti-Communist legislation
as a fund-raising device, this time raising about a half million dollars as
well as considerable sympathy from a broad spectrum of liberals. In part
to head off passage of the Mundt-Nixon bill and Republican exploitation
of the issue in the 1948 election, the Truman administration in July 1948
indicted 12 Communist leaders under the Smith Act.

Congress had passed and President Roosevelt had signed the Smith
Act in 1940 during the period of the Nazi-Soviet Pact, when many feared
that fascist sympathizers among Italian Americans, Nazi sympathizers in
the German American Bund, and native anti-Semitic extremists such as
the quasi-fascist Silver Shirts might make common cause with Communists, Trotskyists, and other left revolutionaries. It was a time when
many Americans were frightened by the success, exaggerated by the

media, of subversive "fifth columns" and "Quislings" in paving the way for Nazi Germany's conquest of most of Europe. The Smith Act made it a crime to knowingly or willfully advocate the violent overthrow of the U.S. government. In 1941 the government indicted 29 and convicted 18 Trotskyists under the Smith Act, convictions upheld by the Supreme Court. By the time of the Trotskyist trial, Nazi Germany had invaded the Soviet Union, and the Communist position had changed from one of vicious hostility to the Roosevelt administration to all-out support, and the C.P. was no longer a target of the Smith Act. Consequently, far from opposing the use of the Smith Act against the Trotskyists, American Communists publicly applauded their prosecution. Earl Browder even provided advice (unsolicited) to government officials on how the Trotskyists could be convicted of violent revolutionary intent. Communists also applauded the government's Smith Act prosecution of 31 extremist anti-Semites and called for indicting isolationist congressmen who advocated limiting the American war effort to defense of the continental United States and prosecution of Norman Thomas, the Socialist leader who opposed the war on pacifist grounds.

The 1948 Smith Act indictments included the Communist party's chairman, William Foster; Eugene Dennis, its general secretary; and 10 other leaders. Party lawyers convinced the court to sever Foster's case from the rest on grounds of his poor health, and he was never tried. The trial of the remaining 11 did not begin until January 1949, and all those indicted remained free on bail. The government did not charge overt revolutionary acts, only that the defendants advocated the overthrow of the government. Communists rejected a defense centered on a claim that their advocacy was protected free speech under the First Amendment to the Constitution. Instead, the defendants presented a elaborate defense of party policy in which they claimed that since the mid-1930s Communist doctrine called for a constitutional path to socialism. The prosecution, however, hit hard at the inability of the defendants to explain how Browder's overthrow did not show a shift to a revolutionary stance and at the party's continued use of classic Marxist-Leninist texts that portrayed violent revolution as necessary to overthrow capitalism. The prosecution also brought in 13 former Communists, several of whom had been informants for the FBI while in the party, who testified that they had been taught that communism could only be achieved through the violent overthrow of the capitalist system.

The defendants and their lawyers adopted a confrontational stance throughout the trial; in repeated outbursts they orally abused Judge Harold Medina and sought to disrupt the trial. Judge Medina, who on occasion displayed personal distaste and hostility toward the defendants, found two of the defendants in contempt during the trial but waited until the end to act against the defense attorneys. He found all five attorneys in contempt and imprisoned them for a time. Medina ruled that the defendants' advocacy was not protected free speech because "there is a sufficient danger of a substantive evil [overthrow of the government]" to remove the advocacy from the realm of protected speech. The jury convicted the defendants. Medina sentenced 10 of the defendants to five years' imprisonment; he sentenced one, Robert Thompson, to three years in deference to his decoration for heroism in World War II.

Communists coordinated the disruptive tactics in the courtroom with a protest campaign portraying the trial as an inquisition. By the time of the trial, 1949, however, the C.P. had lost many of its allies. Further, the decision to fight the indictment by defending Communist doctrine rather than by taking a free-speech stance reduced sympathy from liberals. Many of the latter were prepared to defend the rights of Communists to advocate their beliefs but did not wish to place themselves in the position of defending those beliefs. In contrast to the party's success in 1946 and 1947 in using the Schwellenbach and Mundt-Nixon proposals as rallying points for fund-raising, attempts to use the Smith Act case to raise funds produced meager returns.

After the Supreme Court upheld the convictions in its *Dennis* decision in 1951, federal prosecutors indicted a series of lesser Communist leaders. The government successfully convicted just over 100 of the "second-string" leaders. Several of the second-string trials were replays of the *Dennis* case. After a time some Communist defendants rejected party advice, centered their defense on free-speech rights, and avoided courtroom confrontation. A number of federal judges also disliked the standard used in the *Dennis* decision to distinguish constitutionally protected speech from that which is not. In several cases trial judges directed acquittals or appeal courts set aside convictions on procedural grounds.

In 1957 the Supreme Court backed away from *Dennis* by voiding the Smith Act conviction of California Communist leaders in the *Yates* case. In the wake of *Yates*, courts dismissed many indictments of Communists or reversed convictions on appeal. By the late 1950s the Smith Act ceased to be an effective weapon against the Communist party. Of those convicted under the act, less than half went to jail, and those that did served relatively short sentences. A few states also prosecuted Communists under one or another state statute. These state prosecutions sent a few score Communists to prison, but states found their jurisdiction limited by the Supreme Court, and state prosecutions faded away by the latter half of the 1950s. Even so, state authorities seriously damaged the Communist party through their attack on the International Workers Order. The IWO provided the party with considerable institutional and financial support made possible by a substantial membership attracted to its low-cost insurance. State insurance regulators, spearheaded by those of New York, destroyed the IWO by forcing liquidation of its insurance programs.

In the Smith Act trials Communists were often startled to find party members turning up as prosecution witnesses. FBI Director J. Edgar Hoover began his career in federal law enforcement as a Justice Department agent investigating radicals in the post–World War I Palmer raids. After he became head of the FBI in 1924, he made surveillance of revolutionary organizations a regular activity of the FBI. Even so, it was not until World War II and, particularly, the development of the cold war, the evidence of significant Soviet espionage, and the emergence of anticommunism as a domestic political issue that Hoover received the expansion of FBI manpower and the backing he needed to make surveillance of Communists a major FBI activity. The FBI developed files on party clubs, party officials, and individual members as well as the activity of party fronts and of individuals allied closely to the party. FBI agents collected party literature, attended public meetings, and covertly trailed Communist organizers. On occasion FBI agents burgled party offices to copy documents and plant listening devices, and often the FBI read the mail of Communists or those close to the party. The FBI recruited hundreds of informants within the C.P. in the 1940s and continued to recruit more even as the party shrank in the 1950s. Most of the FBI's informants were ordinary party members with little responsibility who could do no more than report on the activities of their local party club. A few, however, held middle-level party positions.

Most of the FBI's activity was the passive one of gathering information. It provided evidence, and a number of its informants came forward as government witnesses in various prosecutions of Communists under the Smith Act or against concealed Communist union officials who signed the anti-Communist oaths required by the Taft-Hartley act. FBI information also often provided the basis for the elimination from government employment of individuals who were Communists or associated with the party and were security risks. (Several thousand federal employees lost jobs under the loyalty-security programs of the Truman and Eisenhower administrations. In most cases, however, those discharged as security risks were judged so on grounds having nothing to do with communism. Alcoholism, drug abuse, prior criminal activity, chronic gambling or other money problems, and deviant sexual activity were the most common reasons for security risk designation.)

The FBI also provided information from its files to state and local authorities that led to the discharge of state and local employees who had links to the Communist party. Hoover leaked FBI information to trusted journalists, without attribution, to identify concealed Communists. This usually resulted in newspaper stories that during this period of intense public anticommunism led to the disruption of whatever activity the concealed Communists were engaged in. More rarely, the FBI pursued the active disruption of Communist activity through planting false information that led Communists to take missteps. For example, in 1964 FBI agents planted false information that led party leaders to believe that William Albertson, head of the party's key New York organization, was an FBI informant. The party expelled Albertson, an entirely loyal Communist, based on the FBI's faked evidence.

Attacks on an Already Defeated Foe

The government's main blows against the Communist party fell after the 1948 election politically broke the back of American communism. Although few public officials or Communist leaders at the time realized it, the governmental attack on the Communist party was more in the nature of shooting the wounded than an assault on a dangerous foe. Judge Medina's finding in the *Dennis* case that "there is a sufficient danger of a substantive evil" was mistaken. From 1949 until the mid- and late 1950s the image of the American Communist movement to the public, to the government, and even to Communists themselves was based in large part on what the party had been and not on what it actually was at the time. From the mid-1930s until 1948 it had been a major force in the labor movement, it had been a significant participant in mainstream politics through its semiconcealed role in the liberal wing of the Democratic party in several key states and cities, and it had been an influential presence in prominent artistic and cultural circles. In those various arenas hundreds of thousands of Americans had contact with the Communist party either as allies, associates, or opponents. The latter also retained angry memories of the many times Communist strength, skill, or ruthlessness had defeated them. Nor should one forget that from the mid-1930s until 1948 several hundred thousand Americans briefly had been Communists. Until 1949 one could reasonably view the Communist party, by reason of its institutional strength, political influence, totalitarian goals, links to Soviet foreign policy, and habitual concealment as a threat to American democracy.

By 1949, however, all this was gone or fading fast, but the image of Communist strength lingered on. It took some years for the reality of the Communist movement's isolation and weakness to replace its aura of hidden strength. During its most influential period Communists had partially concealed their presence in order to avoid triggering an anti-Communist reaction. This habitual concealment, once a cover for strength, after 1948 covered weakness. Those hostile to the party often suspected that Communists once more concealed their strength when, in fact, it had melted away. Communists contributed to this misleading image by claiming strength, an act that reflected both a defiant, brave front and self-delusion. By the early 1960s the American Communist party was tiny, politically isolated, and possessed little influence. Government efforts against the party at this point were wildly disproportionate to the threat.

The image of strength also lingered because of the American Communists' link to the Soviet Union. American Communists saw themselves and were perceived as the American representatives of an international movement led by the Soviet Union. After World War II the Soviet Union emerged as a nuclear-armed superpower and the possessor of the world's most powerful land army. No longer isolated, the Soviet Union ruled an empire of satellite states in Eastern Europe and was allied with the victorious Communists of China, the world's most populous nation. Throughout Asia, Africa, and South America, Communist parties in their own right or as a part of anticolonial movements were on the march. American Communists drew tremendous psychological strength from the advance of communism in the postwar world. Americans who acknowledged and feared the growth of Communist strength abroad often attributed to the American party some of the strength of foreign communism.

America's basic stance in the cold war was defensive, that of "containment" of the Soviet expansion. Although in the long run containment succeeded, many Americans found a defensive stance frustrating. America had just emerged from a world war with Nazi Germany, Fascist Italy, and the Japanese Empire and from the economic privations of the Great Depression of the 1930s. Americans in the postwar period wanted to reap the benefits of peace and prosperity but found themselves without respite threatened by a nuclear-armed Soviet Union and communism expanding on every continent. Frustration with the restraint necessitated by America's defensive stance in the cold war, combined with anxiety about Soviet communism's threat to the enjoyment of peace and prosperity raised popular American anticommunism to new heights.

Anti-communist sentiment reached a fever pitch when a Communist army from North Korea invaded South Korea in June 1950. President Truman immediately committed American troops against the invaders. American troops first defeated Korean Communists in intense combat only to have their gains nearly erased by the intervention of Chinese Communist troops and a second round of combat even bloodier than the first. A mid-1951 ceasefire agreement halted major troop movements, but savage combat continued along the "ceasefire" line until the signing of an armistice in mid-1953. More than 54,000 Americans died in the Korea conflict, and another 100,000 were wounded. Nearly as many Americans died in the relatively short period of combat in the Korean War as died in the eight years (1965–73) of American military intervention in Vietnam. War coarsens a people. When Americans had brothers, fathers, or neighbors being shot at, blown up, killed, or wounded by Communist soldiers, many became impatient with the tedious legalisms of America's constitutional order and developed a preference for rough-and-ready justice toward domestic Communists. Angered by the deaths of Americans in Korea at the hands of Communists, many Americans felt that although it might be too difficult or too risky to destroy foreign communism, at least domestic communism could be smashed. That there was very little left to smash was not well understood and was, in any case, emotionally beside the point.

The intensity of popular anticommunism of the period produced an array of organizations and spokesmen, many responsible and sincere, along with a good number that were fanatical, hysterical, or opportunistic. Some of the anti-Communist exercises of the period seem comic in retrospect, although they were meant seriously at the time. In Mosinee, Wisconsin, local public authorities in cooperation with the American Legion staged a one-day mock takeover of the town by Communist troops, complete with the arrest of local political and religious figures, closing of local churches, and a Marxist-Leninist purge of the library. In Indiana local anti-Communist fanatics called for the removal of Robin Hood stories from local schools for fear that the stories of robbing the rich and giving to the poor prepared the way for Communist propaganda, and one popular magazine saw Red influence in the spread of rock and roll music. (Even at the time, most Americans regarded the Robin Hood threat as laughable, and the merry men of Sherwood Forest continued as heroes of children's literature. Nor did the charges of Communist influence noticeably reduce the popularity of rock and roll.) One unsophisticated American Army officer wrote a memo to guide security personnel entitled "Special Study: 'How to Spot a Communist'" that listed as danger signals of Communist allegiance such attributes as "heaviness of style and preference for long sentences" in writing and "such hobbies as 'folk dancing' and 'folk music.'" Embarrassed Army commanders withdrew the memo.[21]

McCarthyism

As with almost any issue of such salience with the public, politicians sought to exploit the issue or to prevent its use against them. By 1950 an anti-Communist consensus held sway in the Democratic party, among liberal advocacy groups such as the ADA, and in the AFL and the CIO. Nonetheless, the defeat of Popular Front liberalism in 1948 and Truman's leadership in the cold war did not prevent communism from becoming a partisan issue. Their long exclusion from national power frustrated many Republicans. Franklin Roosevelt had broken the tradition of a two-term presidency by winning a third term in 1940 and a fourth in 1944. Republicans thought themselves on the way back to power when they won control of Congress in 1946, only to have their expectation dashed in 1948 by Truman's come-from-behind victory. Many Republicans were ready to use any issue they could to pry the Democrats out of power.

Republicans and conservatives had complained of New Deal complacency regarding Communists since 1936, but the issue never gained public saliency until after World War II and the coming of the cold war. Liberal Democrats wanted to regard the issue as closed in view of the defeat of Popular Front liberalism in 1948. Republicans, however, were not inclined to let Democrats off with nothing more than a quiet "I told you so." Republicans called Democrats to account for the late 1930s and 1940s, when Popular Front liberals and Communists had been part of the New Deal coalition in some states. Moreover, the most partisan and irresponsible Republicans vehemently insisted that nothing had changed. Senator Joseph McCarthy (Republican, Wisconsin) was the most prominent of those who denounced officials of Roosevelt's and Truman's presidencies as front men or worse for a treasonous Communist conspiracy.

He assailed civil decency through his use of unsubstantiated testimony, anonymous informants, outright lies, and abusive assaults on witnesses. McCarthy also knew how weak American Communists were. Far from being fearful of communism, McCarthy's bullying tactics reflected mankind's unadmirable habit of kicking a man when he is down.

"McCarthyism" soon passed into popular political language as the name given to irresponsible accusations that someone was a Communist when, in fact, they were not. McCarthy began his attacks on the Democrats in 1950 with a speech charging that Truman's State Department knowingly kept secret Communists on its staff. Republicans found McCarthy's broad-brush assaults linking Democrats and the Truman administration to communism and treason useful in the partisan debate leading up to the 1952 election.

Joining the Republican assault on liberal Democrats were conservative Democrats from the South and West who had long resented domination of the national Democratic party by its liberal wing. Two congressional committees, the House Un-American Activities Committee and the Senate Internal Security Subcommittee (SISS) of the Judiciary Committee made the exposure of the Communist role in domestic institutions their principal concern. These committees, sometimes under responsible and sometimes under irresponsible leadership, launched investigations of the Communist role in Hollywood, in labor unions, in youth and students groups, in immigrant organizations, and so on. Congressional committees called hundreds of persons, including Communists, anti-Communists, and ex-Communists to testify about their experiences. Communists and friends of the party found themselves in a dilemma. Congressional committees had the authority to require witnesses to testify, and refusal could bring imprisonment for contempt of congress. A witness could refuse to testify only by invoking the Fifth Amendment to the Constitution, which forbids compulsory self-incriminating testimony. However, most Americans thought that when someone refused to answer a question because it might incriminate them, although it was one's right to do so, it indicated one had something to hide.

In 1947 HUAC attracted great public interest by investigating Communist influence in the Hollywood film industry. Ten film writers, most of whom were concealed Communists, refused to testify but declined to invoke their rights under the Fifth Amendment; Congress cited the "Hollywood Ten" for contempt, and they were imprisoned. In response to congressional investigations and the threat of a public boycott, major films, television, and radio companies instituted an informal blacklist of entertainers with Communist or radical links. The blacklist gradually died out in the late 1950s, but in the early and mid-1950s it retarded the careers of several hundred entertainers and drove some entirely out of the industry. After the imprisonment of the Hollywood Ten, most Communists chose to invoke the Fifth Amendment, thus legally frustrating HUAC and SISS but suffering a public relations and political defeat.

Much of the history of the Communist controversy in Washington in the 1950s was only indirectly connected to the history of the Communist party. Communism was the ostensible issue, the history of Communist activities was sometimes accurately and sometimes not so accurately exposed, and individual Communists from time to time found themselves dragged into a controversy or placed before a congressional committee. It was, for example, a HUAC investigation that led to the exposure of several State Department officials who had spied for the Soviet Union in the late 1930s. Even so, the thrusts and counterthrusts between Republicans and Democrats, between moderates, liberals, and conservatives of both parties, were as often aimed at each other as the Communists. Although HUAC hearings produced a great deal of information about Communist activities, the manner in which it conducted some of its investigations gave HUAC an often deserved reputation for partisanship, ignorance, and viciousness. During 1945–47, for example, Representative John Rankin (Democrat, Mississippi) dominated HUAC and was more interested painting Roosevelt's New Deal as a Jewish-Communist conspiracy than he was in exposing actual C.P. operations.

The sense of impending doom among American Communists increased in 1950 first with bloody combat between American and Communist troops in Korea and then with the passage, over President Truman's veto, of the McCarran Act. This act set up the Subversive Activities Control Board (SACB) and required organizations that SACB designated as subversive to register and provide information about their activities and membership. The act also authorized the government in a presidentially declared national security emergency to arrest individuals it considered potential saboteurs and spies. In 1953 the SACB ruled that the Communist party had to register, but nothing happened as the government and the party's lawyers fought a decade-long battle in the courts. In 1964 the Supreme Court emasculated the McCarran Act by letting stand a lower court decision that no party official could be required to register the party because such an act would be coerced self-incrimination that would place the official in jeopardy of the Smith Act. In the end, neither the Communist party nor any other organization registered with the SACB. The government prepared plans for detaining Communists in case of war with the Soviet Union and designated sites for detention camps. As the prospect of war declined after the end of the Korean conflict, the government sold or leased the sites for other uses. No detention camps were ever built, and no one was ever detained under the McCarran Act. Even so, in 1950, on paper at least, the act looked formidable, and the psychological state of Communists was such that they saw it as preparation for fascist rule.

In theory party members were hardened political soldiers in a revolutionary army. In practice many were summer soldiers of revolution. The party suffered a steady drain of members and a drastic drop-off in its friends and allies. The prosecution, harassment, and public hatred of the party also reinforced the apocalyptic expectations of party leaders and their sense of being a movement besieged. Communists, in the expression of Eugene Dennis, felt that it was "a few minutes before midnight." At midnight would come American fascism, a physical assault on the party resembling the systematic murder of party members in Nazi Germany and Imperial Japan, concentration camps, the extinguishing of political freedom, suppression of all labor unions, and world war.

Any questioning or even debate regarding party doctrine became a sign of weakness, and the party expelled those suspected of lacking confidence in the party's course. In 1952 the chairman of the Maryland C.P. wrote a pamphlet raising questions about the party's direction, and party leaders expelled him for "defeatism" after he had already been indicted and shortly before he would be convicted under the Smith Act. American Communists also clung tightly to even the most exotic Soviet doctrines. For example, Stalin crippled Soviet biology for decades by rejecting Mendelian genetics and holding to the pseudo-science of Trofim Lysenko, who claimed environmentally induced physical adaptations were genetically inheritable. American Communists in this period made adherence to Lysenkoism a criterion of Marxism-Leninism. Similarly, after having tolerated discussion of psychoanalysis for decades, the American party declared that Freudian theories were incompatible with communism.

Underground Foolishness

On 4 June 1951 the Supreme Court upheld the conviction of the eleven Communist leaders in the *Dennis* case. In the past year tens of thousands of Americans had died fighting Communist soldiers in Korea, and popular anticommunism burned at a white-hot level; American Communists were convinced that midnight was upon them.

Four of the eleven party leaders convicted in the *Dennis* case, free on bail since their indictment in 1948, evaded prison and disappeared. The four were Henry Winston, organizational secretary; Robert Thompson, leader of the New York C.P.; Gus Hall, acting general secretary while Eugene Dennis served a contempt of Congress conviction; and Gil Green, leader of the Illinois C.P. Sending Thompson underground illustrated the apocalyptic mood of Communists in 1951. Thompson had received a sentence of three years rather than the five years dealt out to the other defendants. With good behavior he would be out of prison in a year and a half. Communist leaders, however, feared the fascist crackdown would come within that period, and Thompson would return to a smashed party. Thompson, who had commanded a Communist battalion in the Spanish Civil War and served with heroic distinction with American forces in World War II, also argued that he was needed to lead guerrilla forces against the impending American dictatorship.

The party also helped its summer soldiers on their way out of the C.P. by ordering members to reregister. The party denied reregistration to members viewed as weak and dropped all who failed to reregister, nearly one-third of its membership. Party leaders felt that only a Communist movement reduced to its core of hardened Bolsheviks could withstand the long night of fascist oppression that lay ahead. This action elimination about 8,000 loyal but inactive Communists from party ranks. Under a plan in preparation since 1947, the party divided into several parts and layers. The open party organization under William Foster retained some 16,000 to 17,000 members. Communists expected that in a short time the open party would be made illegal and its members arrested or scattered.

Three layers of underground leaders and cadres backed up the open party. The "deep freeze" layer consisted of the four *Dennis* defendants who had evaded prison, some second-string Smith Act defendants who were evading trial, and several hundred other Communists regarded as vulnerable to prosecution. Deep-freeze cadres changed their names and took ordinary jobs, but continued to function covertly as party leaders. A second layer consisted of several hundred "operative but unavailable" party members who moved around the nation, often in disguise, as the liaison between the aboveground party and the deep-freeze leaders. A third layer, the "deep, deep freeze," consisted of several score Communists, mostly younger leaders, judged as possessing the qualities needed to rebuild the party if the other layers were destroyed. The party sent many of these reserve leaders outside the U.S. for safekeeping.[22]

The underground absorbed enormous amounts of energy and money.

Coordinating decisions between open party leaders and the deep-freeze leaders suffered from delays and often produced muddled policies. It was also complicated by imprisonment of several key party leaders. The party intended that Eugene Dennis, C.P. general secretary, go underground and function covertly. Fumbled planning, however, resulted in his being in prison for a short-term contempt of Congress conviction at the time of the *Dennis* decision; consequently he was unable to avoid imprisonment for his Smith Act conviction. Federal authorities also apprehended two *Dennis* case defendants sent underground: Gus Hall in October 1951, during a bungled attempt to escape to the Soviet Union through Mexico, and Robert Thompson in August 1953 in a California mountain hideout. Not only had Thompson not had occasion to organize a guerrilla force, his flight resulted in an additional prison term and the imprisonment of four other Communists, two of whom were important underground leaders, for harboring him in his fugitive status. While Thompson was in custody, an anti-Communist Yugoslav awaiting deportation beat him with a lead pipe and nearly killed him.

By the time the C.P. send its cadre underground, the FBI had established a large informant network in the party. Although a portion of those going underground dropped from its sight, the FBI retained surveillance on many. Hoover and the FBI saw the Communist party as a conspiracy involved in covert operations and were not surprised that hundreds of Communists suddenly went underground. The FBI was puzzled, however, when underground Communists failed to do much more than maladroitly continue their usual activity. The FBI knew that Communist leaders were telling their members that the underground was a defensive measure to thwart the coming fascist crackdown. The FBI also knew that there was no impending fascist crackdown, assumed (incorrectly) that Communists leaders knew that as well, and assumed that the purported reason hid a more sinister design. As time passed and the Communist underground continued business as usual, FBI perplexity grew. In some places underground Communists who thought they had avoided FBI surveillance were unnerved to find FBI agents at their door. The agents, however, came not to arrest them in the long-awaited roundup but to confront them in an attempt to provoke action that would lead the FBI to the purpose of the elaborate underground existence.

The underground experience imposed enormous psychological costs on its participants. The expectation of war and fascist dictatorship and the knowledge that the FBI had penetrated the underground led many Communists to live in fear. Cut off from accustomed neighborhoods, friends, and family (in some cases husbands and wives were separated for many months), many cadres experienced loneliness and periods of psychological depression, and a few suffered mental breakdowns. The underground also undermined ideologically the party's most valued members, particularly younger cadres designated as future party leaders. For party militants, communism was nearly a full-time existence. Many were employed by the party or one of its associated organizations during the day and attended party-related functions three or four nights a week. Further, most Communist activists socialized largely with other Communists. In New York, an area of Communist strength, Communists tended to live in the same neighborhoods (Sunnyside in Queens, for example)—many even in the same apartment building (one of the ILGWU's massive New York cooperative apartment complexes became a Communist favorite)—go to the same upstate summer resorts (Camp Unity in Wingdale), and send their children to the same progressive summer camps (Camp Kinderland in Hopewell Junction).

Most activists read almost exclusively from party-approved literature and attended C.P.-sponsored lecture series and study clubs. New York had eight Communist-aligned social/cultural clubs, such as the 1,000-member Prospect Workers' Club in the Bronx, which organized outings, dances, music concerts, and lectures where most in attendance were Communists, friends of the movement, and potential recruits. Communists even cultivated politically correct musical tastes. The folkishness of the Popular Front of the late 1930s and 1940s prompted Communist musicians, defining folk music as a "people's music" and folk artists as "people's artists," to pioneer a revival of traditional folk music styles through such groups as the Almanac Singers, People's Songs, and People's Artists. Attending a hootenanny where a talented Communist-aligned singer such as Pete Seeger mixed traditional folk material with topical leftist protest songs formed a standard part of Communist recreation. New York Communists with more chic tastes frequented Café Society Downtown or Café Society Uptown. At these nightclubs Communists artists, writers, and professionals and their friends listened to a format that mixed progressive politics, gutbucket jazz, and the musical talent of such artists as Hot Lips Page, Billie Holiday, and Josh White. (Black music along with folk music met party standards for political correctness.)

This Communist movement culture tended to ensure ideological uniformity and solidarity among activists and reinforce the bonds of shared experience and comradeship between members. Underground Communists were cut off from this environment; as part of their cover they socialized with non-Communists and avoided Communist-linked literature or activities. Many found the experiences of ordinary American life profoundly unsettling. For the first time many read extensively in non-Communist, Social Democratic, dissident Marxist, and Trotskyist literature. It took several years for the undermining process to mature, but when the party faced an ideological crisis in 1956–58, the vast majority of members sent underground in the early 1950s left it.

By the mid-1950s the peak in domestic anti-Communist fervor had passed. Much of the zeal of anticommunism was simply nationalism aroused by the cold war, inflamed by the hot war in Korea, and aimed at the domestic allies of the foreign enemy. American Communists espoused the cause of the Soviet Union, sided with Korean Communists in the Korea War, and even supported North Korean propaganda that American soldiers were war criminals waging bacteriological warfare. As one historian observed of one of the most irresponsible of the era's anti-Communists, "The Korean War put both a floor under McCarthy's influence and a ceiling above it."[23] The end of the Korean conflict in 1953 sharply reduced the stridency of popular anticommunism. McCarthy himself failed to temper his actions after Republicans gained the presidency and control of the Senate in 1953; by 1954, McCarthy's irresponsibility caught up with him. President Dwight D. Eisenhower quietly moved against him, and in December 1954 the Senate censured him and ended his power. The success of the Marshall Plan in restoring Western European prosperity and the creation of a military strong North Atlantic Treaty Organization reduced fears of Western Europe falling to Soviet domination. Stalin's death in 1953 and his replacement by less-aggressive Soviet leaders also lessened anxiety.

Slowly, events undermined Communist fears that it was a few minutes before midnight. In the 15 years from the end of World War II to 1960, the government imprisoned several hundred Communists under the Smith Act, for contempt of Congress, for signing false Taft-Hartley oaths, or other offenses. Most received sentences of five years or less, and most of those served less than three years, many much less. The government's prosecutions and the FBI's surveillance and harassment damaged the Communist movement, but these actions hardly constituted the fascist crackdown Communists expected. The long-feared mass roundup of Communists never occurred. Throughout the period the Communist party continued to function legally. Even during the peak of popular and official anticommunism in the early 1950s, the C.P. organized public protests, supported its beleaguered labor allies, recruited new members (although not many), ran candidates for public office (not many of these either), and circulated hundreds of thousands of copies of its newspapers, pamphlets, and books.

After Stalin's death, the new Soviet stance that "peaceful coexistence" with the West was possible undermined C.P. expectations of imminent war. In 1955 the new Soviet leader, Nikita Khrushchev, ended Stalin's cold war against Tito's national communism. American Communists had loyally implemented the anti-Tito purge, and its discrediting weakened the party's ideological stance. The strength of the American economy further disconcerted American Communists. Communist expectations of a massive depression to follow World War II, once confident, seemed increasingly shaky as rapid economic growth in the postwar years spread affluence to most regions of the nation, greatly expanded the middle class, and delivered a significant measure of prosperity to industrial workers. Middle-class and working-class values also tended to blend together in a mass consumer culture that increasingly characterized American life.

Reemergence, Reexamination, and Disintegration

In 1954 and 1955 the Communist party ordered its labor leaders to take their unions back into the mainstream labor movement on whatever terms they could gain. In 1954 a weakened Fur and Leather Workers Union dropped its long-time Communist leader, Ben Gold, and in 1955 merged with the much larger Amalgamated Meatcutters (AFL) on terms that destroyed what remained of Communist influence. Most of the small Communist-aligned unions followed a similar path into one or another mainstream union. On the other hand, the two strongest Communist-aligned unions, the United Electrical Workers (U.E.) and the West Coast longshoremen's union (ILWU) balked at the order. The U.E.'s national leaders, who still considered themselves radicals, held the Communist party responsible for reducing the U.E. to a fraction of its former strength. Having gone through so much, they refused to give up what was left, thus triggering a revolt by U.E. officials still loyal to Communist party guidance. In 1955 C.P.-led locals with at least 50,000 members (over a third of the U.E.'s remaining membership) seceded and affiliated with one or another mainstream union. Harry Bridges, secure in the loyalty of West Coast longshoremen and increasingly contemptuous of the party's leaders, also refused to enter the newly merged AFL-CIO. The ILWU remained independent and intact.

The Communist party also ordered those who had gone underground to surface in 1955 and 1956. For most this was an easy process, as their going underground had not broken any laws. They simply resumed their old names and returned to their old neighborhoods. Those who had evaded prison terms had a harder time. Henry Winston and Gil Green, convicted in the *Dennis* case, surfaced in 1956 and had to serve their original sentences plus additional time for evading jail. They remained in prison until 1961. (Winston developed eye difficulties in prison, and a combination of neglect and an unsuccessful operation by prison doctors led to blindness.)

The first public sign of rethinking of party policy came in January 1956 at an anniversary dinner for the *Daily Worker*. Eugene Dennis, the party's general secretary, and John Gates, *Daily Worker* editor, both only recently released from serving Smith Act convictions, called for a new direction for the party. That reexamination got underway in April at a meeting of the party's national committee. Dennis deplored the "few minutes before midnight" attitude, attributed the party's mistakes to a "deeply-ingrained left-sectarian approach," its doctrinaire use of Marxism, and excessive deference to "the experiences of other parties [the Soviets]." Looking back, he judged that the Progressive party might have been an error and that the break with Philip Murray and the CIO surely was.[24]

The process of reexamination that Dennis's speech triggered had its origins in the frustrations of American Communists with the failure of their policies since 1945. Yet foreign events immediately overtook this domestically initiated reexamination. In February 1956 Khrushchev gave a secret speech to a congress of the Communist party of the Soviet Union. Khrushchev told Soviet Communists that Stalin had committed enormous crimes, including the initiation of purges in the 1930s that had killed hundreds of thousands of innocent victims and created an atmosphere of terror that had poisoned Soviet society and stifled cultural and intellectual life, promoted a "cult of personality" that made him into a superhuman figure, and brutally suppressed any deviation from his wishes. In line with Khrushchev's announcement, leaders of the Soviet Union's satellite states revealed enormous Stalinist crimes in their own history. Satellite and Soviet sources also confirmed the anti-Semitic themes of several of Stalin's postwar purges.

Khrushchev disclosed only a portion of the mountains of corpses and rivers of blood that resulted from Stalinism, and most of what he announced was already known in the West. Regardless, American Communists and their sympathizers had not believed the tales of blood-soaked mass terror, rigged trials, and the lethal Gulag labor camps that had been reported by anti-Communists and carried by the mainstream American press. When Khrushchev's secret speech reached the West, Communists and their friends habitually referred to the "revelations" of Stalin's crimes. Dennis said that "the facts disclosed about the errors of Stalin . . . are, of course, new to us." Another party publication referred to the crimes of Stalin as "matters of which its [the American C.P.'s] members could not know." A leading party ideologist said, "The disclosure of the mistakes made under Stalin's leadership came as a stunning surprise." These statements in a literal sense were false. Too much evidence of the mass murder committed under Stalinism was public in the West for anyone to say they could not have known. In a psychological sense, however, the statements were truthful. American Communists did not know of the evils of Stalinism because they would not acknowledge anything not given Moscow's imprimatur. In the mental world of American Communists, Stalin's mass murders were visible only if Moscow could see them. Once Khrushchev gave Moscow's sanction to the charges against Stalinism, American Communists, in shock, suddenly saw bodies littering the landscape. [25]

In March American newspapers began to carry partial reports on Khrushchev's speech, and an authoritative summary from Communist channels reached American Communist party leaders in April prior to the meeting of the national committee. Initially Khrushchev's speech encouraged Dennis, Gates, and others to call for a rethinking of party policy. Gates quickly became the champion of radical reform. He repudiated achieving socialism through violent revolution and endorsed exclusive use of constitutional means. He came out for extending civil liberties to the enemies of communism and argued that in a Communist America the displaced capitalists should have the right to agitate for return of their property.

In early June the U.S. State Department distributed a translation of the full text of Khrushchev's speech, and American newspapers published portions of the text. Gates then published a full translation in the *Daily Worker,* thus insuring that all Communists had access to an authoritative (in Communist terms) exposition of the crimes of Stalinism. Peggy Dennis, wife of the party's general secretary, remembers that on reading the text "the last page crumpled in my fist, I lay in the half darkness and

I wept. . . . For Gene's years in prison. . . . For the years of silence in which we had buried doubts and questions. For a thirty-year life's commitment that lay shattered. I lay sobbing low, hiccoughing whimpers."[26]

Party newspapers and journals, publications that rarely printed internal debate, were for a time filled with angry, outraged, tormented, pain-filled letters, editorials, and resolutions revealing a membership in agony. Some letters blamed the party's situation on Foster, Dennis, or the Soviets. Others blamed the problems on the party's fundamental principles and demanded a radical renewal in the movement's philosophy. Most of the letters called for drastic change, but a minority would have none of this or very little. William Foster emerged as the champion of minimal change. He allowed that Stalin had made serious errors but indicated that these mistakes paled beside the achievements of the Stalin era in building socialism.

By late June 1956 Soviet leaders realized that some foreign Communists were drawing lessons from the criticism of Stalin that went beyond those Moscow wanted. Soviet publications carried essays that set out the limits of criticism and evinced a tone that resembled Foster's. Even so, by this point Gates and other American Communist reformers were no longer willing to defer to Moscow. In September 1956 the national committee adopted a platform for an "American road to socialism." It supported an expansion of the welfare state, endorsed civil liberties, and, although calling for eventual socialism, essentially adopted the position of militant New Deal liberals. The resolution had a tone of "national" communism in speaking of the need to base American communism on "Marxist-Leninist principles as interpreted by the Communist party of our country" and disavowing Leninist principles "which reflect exclusively certain unique features of the Russian revolution or of Soviet society."[27]

Although implicitly rejecting the policies of Foster that had prevailed since 1945, the resolution did not approach Gates's call for a thorough reform of American communism. Dennis, who had initially supported a reexamination of the party's position, recoiled at the Gates's radical reforms. Dennis wanted reform, but not too much. Moscow at this point intervened more directly by praising Foster in *Pravda*. Moscow's approval emboldened Foster, who had stood almost alone in April, and he found allies among older cadres and among black party members.

In Hungary the process of reform set in motion by Khrushchev's speech proceeded to the point that the Hungarian Communist party ousted the nation's Stalinist leaders and installed a reformist national Communist, Imre Nagy. Gates endorsed Hungarian national communism and called on the Soviets to respect the choice, a position endorsed by the national committee of the American Communist party. Foster opposed this position, and Dennis, uncomfortable with criticism of Moscow, abstained. The Nagy regime moved swiftly toward political democracy and withdrawing from the Soviet-led Warsaw Pact military alliance. This was too much for Khrushchev, and in November 1956 Soviet tanks entered Budapest and installed a Moscow loyalist in power. Soviet troops crushed a brave but poorly armed Hungarian resistance; thousands died, including Nagy. Gates and his reformers regretted the Soviet intervention, but Foster and his hard-line supporters endorsed it. Dennis ceased his fence-straddling and endorsed the Soviet action as "anti-fascist and pro-peace."[28]

In February 1957 a special C.P. convention met but failed to resolve the party's internal agony. Gates, Dennis, Foster, and their supporters avoided open debate of their differences. The convention papered over its deep splits with compromise language and balanced slates of offices. Its final resolution, although reformist in tone, was a strategic victory for Foster and his hard-liners.

Although after the Khrushchev "revelations" the great majority of party members rejected the party's traditional stance, they did not form a cohesive reform faction behind John Gates. Instead, members began to drop out of the party. The decisions were individual and usually private. Each member had a different breaking point when the news out of the Soviet Union or one of the Eastern European satellite states became too much to bear. Samuel Sillen, editor of the Communist-aligned *Masses & Mainstream* and one of the party's leading intellectuals, walked out of his office early in 1956 and never came back. Within a few months he was working as a commercial salesman. There were thousands of Sillens, and every week dozens left the movement. Every week the majority that might support drastic reform of American communism weakened as its supporters ceased to be Communists. Foster and his hard-liners stayed, and the party shrank around them.

Gates's inability to mobilize the majority stemmed from several factors. Some disillusioned Communists regarded Gates, a longtime party official, as too compromised to lead a renewed Communist movement. More importantly, however, was the impossibility of Gates's enterprise. Gates and the other reformers, by adopting political pluralism and putting aside the Soviet myth, eliminated from American communism the factors that constituted its identity. The link to the Soviet Union was crucial to American communism. The link to Soviet power gave American Communists psychological strength, both strength in their own minds and strength in the minds of their enemies. The belief that the Soviet Union had created a society where man no longer exploited man was fundamental to the worldview of American Communists. The Soviet vision proved to American Communists that it was possible to construct a socialist society and that they, because they consciously modeled themselves on Soviet Marxism-Leninism, knew how to construct a Marxist America. The Khrushchev "revelations" disturbed Western European Communists but were not for them the catastrophe they were for American Communists. The Communist parties of Italy, France, Spain, and Great Britain existed within radical subcultures that were a part of larger working-class cultures. In those more stratified societies something resembling classic Marxist class consciousness existed. Communism in those nations was one of the vehicles through which working-class aspirations and resentment found voice. The uniquely Communist attributes of linkage to the Soviet Union and the ideology of Marxism-Leninism shaped that articulation, but the worker-generated power that gave strength to Western European communism was independent of Moscow.

In America, however, the link to Moscow and the Soviet myth provided the power as well was the direction to communism. Western European Communist parties could, and the Italian party did, seriously explore what later became known as "Eurocommunism:" communism that was nationalized, democratized, and independent of Moscow. American communism, lacking a working-class subculture whose ambitions and grievances it could articulate, could not develop an "Americommunism." Take away Moscow and embrace democratic values, and American Communists would be just another group of radicals appealing to the egalitarian democratic beliefs that are deep in American culture and claimed as well by mainstream liberals and conservatives. Whatever it was that Gates was advocating, it was not longer communism, and most American Communists sensed this. Rather that support Gates in such a quixotic task, they left the party.

After the February 1957 party convention, Gates steadily lost strength as his supporters drifted out of the C.P., Foster's hard-line remnant grew proportionally stronger, and Dennis's center group shifted toward Foster. Dennis received an unmistakable message in March 1957 as to what direction Moscow wished him to take. The Soviet journal *International Affairs* carried an essay by "T. Timofeyev" on the American C.P. convention, interpreting its compromise resolution as defeat for the "revisionist and Right-opportunists" (Gates and his reform allies) and a victory for "the vital force of proletarian internationalism" (loyalty to Moscow). When Dennis and his wife had returned to the U.S. in 1935 they left a son in Moscow. The American-born son became a Soviet citizen and director of Moscow's Institute of the World Labor Movement under the name Timur Timofeyev. [29]

By the fall of 1957 Foster's hard-liners were strong enough to reduce party financial support for the *Daily Worker,* which Gates edited. Gates gave up, and in January 1958 he announced his resignation from the party. The *Daily Worker* folded with him; its last issue appeared on 13 January 1958. In February the party's national committee, led by Eugene Dennis and firmly in tune with Moscow, repudiated Gates's views as the "revisionist" product of "bourgeois ideology," concluding that "there is no place in the Party for a Gates or his ideology. The departure of such individuals will not injure but strengthen the Party."[30] The remaining reformers soon left or were pushed out of the party. What was left was the rump of a movement. In 1958, the party reregistered its members to get an accurate count of who had survived. The total was 3,000; the Communist party had lost over three-quarters of its members in two years.

Chapter Five

The Twilight Years, 1960–1990

Ironically, the collapse of the Old Left in the late 1950s took place just as the American political system became more receptive to radical ideas and proposals. The election of John F. Kennedy in 1960 seemed to symbolize a new era in American politics, as a younger generation began to move into positions of power and influence. The civil rights movement, which had been slowly gaining force throughout the 1950s, forever altered American political life in 1960 when the first sit-in demonstrations took place in the South. For the next few years black and white demonstrators and organizers mounted a fundamental challenge to Southern society within the limits of the Constitution.

Meanwhile, the American Communist movement was in complete disarray as the 1960s began. The Communist party, rocked by Soviet de-Stalinization and torn apart by internal strife, was on the verge of disintegration. Its membership had all but vanished, disillusioned with communism, exhausted by more than a decade of governmental assault, or convinced that American radicalism had no future. Some of its cadre remained loyal, but, like the surviving rank-and-file members, the Communist party was old, tired, and increasingly out of step with American life. Many party members were more concerned with keeping the organization alive as a comfortable old-age home than influencing American life; few had any hope of making an impact on American society.

While the collapse of the Communist Party USA raised the hopes of the various small Communist sects, which foresaw opportunities to recruit new members from among disillusioned party activists, these groups were so small they barely registered on any political seismograph. Radicalism of any sort seemed irrelevant in the middle-class and comfortable America of 1960.

McCarthyism Dies Out

While vestiges of McCarthyism remained, by 1960 the Supreme Court had effectively gutted the Smith Act, making further prosecutions impossible. It was also increasingly willing to find ways to limit the use of other anti-Communist legislation. The Kennedy administration did seek to compel individual Communists to register with the Subversive Activities Control Board and continued a long-standing government effort to have the party itself register, but such efforts were pale reflections of the more systematic and effective anti-Communist tactics of the previous decade.

One sign of the lessening effectiveness of the anti-Communist crusade was the new opposition to the House Committee on Un-American Activities, which had for decades been in the forefront of the effort to expose the activities of Communists and their sympathizers. In May 1960 HUAC came to San Francisco on one of its periodic forays to harass radicals. It was met by a large, well-organized demonstration, staffed by many students from the University of California. Police beat protesters and turned fire hoses on them. While the FBI and HUAC insisted the demonstration had been orchestrated by the Communist party, and could point to the presence of several well-known party figures, their efforts to discredit the protest by linking it to communism found fewer takers than in previous years. In campus communities like Berkeley, California, and Madison, Wisconsin, with a critical mass of old leftists and student bodies energized by the civil rights movement, government claims that outside agitators were to blame for protest fell on unsympathetic ears.[1]

Changes in the Communist world also vitiated warnings about the dangers of communism or the dire consequences of cooperating with Communists. Khrushchev's de-Stalinization campaign appeared to auger a less-threatening Soviet Union. In the late 1950s Communist China under Mao Zedong rejected Soviet leadership of the Communist bloc and adopted its own form of national Communism. This Sino-Soviet split destroyed the image of a monolithic Communist enemy. The Soviet Union, meanwhile, had lost much of its appeal to radicals, who dismissed it as a stodgy, status quo power. While a small group of disaffected Communists began to sing the praises of Mao Zedong and the Chinese revolution, many more were enthralled by Fidel Castro and the 1959 Cuban revolution.

Castro's appeal to American radicals was originally not related to the Marxism-Leninism he would soon openly avow. Rather, Castro's image as a flamboyant rebel seeking to establish his country's independence from the United States drew attention. Soon after he seized power in 1959 Castro began to defy the United States and transform his country's economy. The U.S. government harshly criticized Castro's violations of civil liberties and his wholesale expropriations of private businesses, including the property of American firms. In reaction, American admirers of the Castro revolution created the Fair Play for Cuba Committee (whose most notorious organizer was Lee Harvey Oswald, President Kennedy's assassin). The committee received support from such prominent intellectuals as James Baldwin, Jean-Paul Sartre and C. Wright Mills. The latter, a flamboyant radical sociologist, was a guru to the young students of the New Left. His influential "Letter to the New Left," written in 1961, urged them to be "realistic in our utopianism" and enthusiastically noted that "we are beginning to move again."[2]

American attacks on Castro and efforts to destabilize and overthrow his government on the grounds that it was Communist had the same effect on the New Left as Southern segregationist criticism of civil rights organizers on the grounds they were Communist agitators. They only confirmed for many New Leftists that anticommunism was a smokescreen behind which America bullied other nations and cooperated with their most reactionary elements to prevent genuine internal reforms to benefit the poor. The slow but gradual increase in U.S. involvement in Vietnam, beginning during the Kennedy administration and escalating under Lyndon Johnson, provided additional fodder for the growing conviction that opposition to Communist insurgencies lacked a moral basis.

A new refusal to embrace or even tolerate the domestic constraints of anticommunism went hand in hand with the increasing skepticism about the traditional anti-Communist foreign policies of the U.S. government. For many years, Communists had been pariahs in American political life. Regarded as agents for a foreign government, they were excluded from political coalitions and shunned not only by mainstream liberal politicians and groups but also by non-Communist radicals and reformers. Two of the larger peace groups during the Eisenhower years, Turn toward Peace and the Committee for a Sane Nuclear Policy (SANE), both excluded Communists. They did so partly out of principle, believing that Communist support for peace was based primarily on support for Soviet foreign policy. They also understood the long history of Communist efforts to infiltrate and take over groups. But their reluctance to cooperate with the Communists was also a matter of expedience, based on fear that the peace movement would lose whatever effectiveness it had if it was tainted by the presence of Communists. In May 1960 SANE planned to hold a big rally at Madison Square Garden. When Senator Thomas Dodd, Democrat of Connecticut, learned that the man in charge of organizing the rally, Henry Abrams, had a Communist background, he successfully pressured Norman Cousins, head of SANE, to fire him.[3]

Such "exclusionary" policies disturbed a growing number of people in the peace, civil rights, and student movements. In some cases they argued that the Communist party was weak and no threat to take over other organizations. In others they claimed that a civil libertarian position required openness to everyone. New radicals and some of their older mentors like A. J. Muste derided the anti-Communist "obsessions" of groups like SANE and protested that bowing to anti-Communist pressures was immoral. In 1963 Dagmar Wilson of Women Strike for Peace announced that her organization accepted anyone who shared its aims, including Communists: "I would like to say that unless everybody in the whole world joins us in this fight, then God help us."[4]

The Fair Play for Cuba Committee included not only Trotskyists, who soon came to dominate it, but also young Communists. Communists and other varieties of Marxists and Marxist-Leninists were among the organizers and leaders of the Free Speech Movement at the University of California at Berkeley in 1964. Martin Luther King, Jr., continued to work closely with New York attorney Stanley Levinson, despite warnings from President Kennedy and Attorney General Robert Kennedy that Levinson had Communist ties.[5]

The New Left and Communism

Students for a Democratic Society (SDS) provided the most dramatic example of the New Left's attitude toward Marxism-Leninism and Communists. The first organized embodiment of the New Left, it soon became the most prominent. Known as the Student League for Industrial Democracy until 1960, it was the youth wing of the League for Industrial Democracy (LID), a fiercely anti-Communist organization long identified with democratic socialism. From the beginning the parent group harbored suspicions that SDS was insufficiently anti-Communist. The presence in its small ranks of such red-diaper babies, as the children of

Communists were called, as Richard Flacks, Bob Ross, and Steve Max intensified the concern.

At its 1962 convention in Port Huron, Michigan, the SDS adopted a famous statement written largely by Tom Hayden proclaiming the birth of a new radical generation. LID, however, reacted angrily to language suggesting that the United States was the prime obstacle to a disarmament treaty with the Soviet Union and denouncing "an unreasoning anticommunism." Just as provocative was the SDS's initial decision to modify a constitutional provision excluding Communists from membership. It also sat a member of the Progressive Youth Organizing Committee, a C.P.-controlled group, as an observer at the convention.[6]

Spurred on by Michael Harrington, a young veteran of radical anti-Communist political wars, who had represented LID at Port Huron, the parent organization ordered a hearing, called SDS leaders on the carpet, and proceeded to fire the group's staff. While a compromise was eventually reached and the dismissed staffers rehired, the episode soured the SDS. Many of its leaders were now convinced that anticommunism was inevitably dishonest and manipulative and that Communists were less dangerous than their anti-Communist opponents. Jack Newfield, a journalist sympathetic to the New Left, complained that the "new radicals are still kids. . . . Their politics are not a finished product. . . . Even those emotionally sympatico with the Chinese or Cuban revolution are not moral monsters. . . . They should be exposed to the democratic atmosphere of SDS. . . . Why do Social Democrats always fear that political influence inevitably flows one way and that it is the democrats who must get subverted? Do bad ideas necessarily drive out good ideas?"[7]

In fact, young Communists did not pose a particular threat of infiltrating the SDS. Still reeling from its international and internal troubles, the C.P. was incapable of mounting a serious challenge even to such a young, organizationally chaotic group as the SDS. Nor were Trotskyists a major force. By 1959 the Socialist Workers party was down to fewer than 400 members. It founded the Young Socialist Alliance (YSA) in 1960, buttressed by the influx of a group of young Trotskyists unwilling to follow Max Shachtman and Michael Harrington of the Independent Socialist League into the Socialist party.

Shachtman had been one of the founders of American Trotskyism. By 1940 he and James Burnham, later an editor of the conservative *National Review*, had developed severe disagreements with Trotsky and James Cannon, leader of the Socialist Workers party. Shachtman argued that the Soviet Union was not a Socialist state but a bureaucratic collectivist state, where the means of production were owned by a new ruling class. His "third camp" position, opposed to both capitalism and Stalinism, attracted a small but intellectually distinguished group of adherents, including Irving Howe and Hal Draper. Shachtman's Trotskyist splinter group, the Workers party, formed in 1940, remained a tiny sect during the 1940s. At the end of the decade it changed its name to the Independent Socialist League. During the next decade it slowly abandoned its commitment to Marxism-Leninism, merging with the Socialist party in 1958. Not all of the Shachtmanites were willing to give up their Leninism for democratic socialist porridge, however.

Buoyed by their highly publicized support for the Cuban Revolution and black nationalist Malcolm X, the Socialist Workers party and the YSA enjoyed a modest growth in the early 1960s. Splits, however, had plagued the Trotskyist movement almost from its inception, and the 1960s were no exception. In 1959 Sam Marcy and Vincent Copeland led a group of dissidents concentrated in Buffalo, New York, out of the SWP and formed the Workers World Party (WWP). Although it never became very large and, in any case, soon abandoned Trotskyism for a brief flirtation with Maoism and then a more generic pro-Sovietism, the WWP did form a militant youth group in 1962 that stood well to the left of the SDS. The WWP's Youth against War and Fascism started with only 50 members but quickly earned a reputation as one of the most provocative organizations on the left, carrying flags from the Communist-led Vietnamese National Liberation Front at antiwar demonstrations and participating in a number of violent protests.

James Robertson, an ex-Shachtmanite, departed from the Socialist Workers party in 1964 and with about 200 members eventually formed the Spartacist League. Tim Wohlforth, another ex-Shachtmanite, was removed from the SWP leadership in 1963 and with a similar number of supporters went on to create the Workers League. Although other issues were also involved, both groups were unhappy with the SWP's close identification with Fidel Castro. Still another split from the SWP in 1964 by its Seattle branch led to the formation of the Freedom Socialist party, which eventually adopted a Socialist feminist perspective.

The Communist group that did eventually help to destroy the SDS was a relative newcomer to Marxist-Leninist ranks. The Progressive Labor Movement (P.L.M.), a colorful Chinese-oriented breakaway from the Communist party, was the most significant and notorious Communist organization in the early 1960s. Although several small groups of pro-Maoist dissidents had either split from or been expelled by the Communist party in the late 1950s, the core leadership of the P.L.M.—Milt Rosen, Mort Scheer, Fred Jerome, and Bill Epton—was expelled late in 1961. They had wanted the C.P. to become more politically aggressive, to proclaim its commitment to revolutionary Marxism, and to admit that there was no peaceful path to socialism. They were also adamantly opposed to the C.P.'s tacit support for liberal Democrats. In 1962 they formed the Progressive Labor Movement. By the time it became the Progressive Labor party in 1964, there were 600 members.

Progressive Labor first earned a reputation for militancy and violence as a result of its activities in New York's Harlem. Beginning in 1964 racial tensions began to boil over in city after city across America. In Harlem, America's most famous black neighborhood, the shooting of a teenager by an off-duty policeman in the summer of 1964 sparked a full-scale riot. Once the rioting began, Progressive Labor cadres worked hard to keep it going. Bill Epton, P.L.'s Harlem organizer, insisted in a speech that the state had to be smashed: "We're going to have to kill a lot of cops, a lot of these judges, and we'll have to go up against their army." P.L. also printed and distributed instructions for making Molotov cocktails. After the riot, a dozen P.L. members were jailed for contempt of court, and Epton himself was found guilty of criminal anarchy. During his trial one of his aides, who was actually an undercover policeman, played a tape recording of Epton's speech urging the murder of policemen and judges.[8]

By 1965 Progressive Labor had grown to 1,400 members and held its first convention in an atmosphere of exuberance. The organization seemed to offer a new brand of communism far more open, militant, and freewheeling than that peddled by the old-line C.P. Despite a commitment to democratic centralism, it was, at least in its early years, far more in tune with the new radicalism than the staid C.P. P.L., for example, sponsored trips to Cuba in defiance of the U.S. government's economic boycott. When called to testify before the HUAC regarding this and other matters, P.L.'s members mocked the committee and made no effort to hide their beliefs, unlike the Communists, who characteristically took the fifth amendment. One P.L. leader, Philip Abbot Luce, editor of the group's magazine and one of its more colorful and charismatic personalities, denounced the HUAC as "the scum of Congress." For the moment, though, P.L. had little interest in the SDS.[9]

Within a year, however, Progressive Labor underwent a reevaluation, sparked by Epton's conviction and the sudden apostasy of Philip Luce. In March 1965 P.L. expelled Luce on charges that he had become an FBI informer. Luce responded that his defection was due to disillusionment and disagreement with P.L. He also claimed that it was storing arms, training its members to conduct armed warfare, and secretly manipulating other organizations. Shaken by its troubles, P.L. tightened its discipline in 1966, denounced cultural radicalism, forbade its members from using narcotics, dissolved the "May 2nd Movement" (M2M), an anti–Vietnam War group it controlled, and decided to concentrate on recruiting members of the SDS into its ranks.

While not pleased by Progressive Labor's decision to send its members into the SDS, the latter group had long since abandoned its exclusionary rule banning Communists. SDS leaders themselves displayed little concern. In a 1965 speech, Carl Oglesby confidently noted that "those whose behavior runs athwart the deep SDS commitment to democracy just have no leverage over the democrats of SDS." The next two years were to provide a test of Jack Newfield's hope that exposure to the democratic ethos of SDS would convert Marxist-Leninists to the vision of participatory democracy.[10]

The civil rights movement provided much of the impetus for the SDS in its early days. Many members had gone south in the early 1960s to work with the Student Non-Violent Coordinating Committee (SNCC). Others had organized sympathy demonstrations on northern campuses. In pursuit of its vision of organizing the poor and powerless in urban areas, the SDS set up Economic Research and Action Projects (ERAP) in 1964. While frustration with the slow pace of change in the South and anger over the beatings and killings of civil rights demonstrators contributed to the radicalization of SDS and SNCC members, the war in Vietnam transformed American radicalism from a marginal force into a mass movement. Hostility to the war sprang from many sources, ranging from idealism to fear of being drafted to fight. More than any other issue, the war energized radicals, sparked the largest protests in American history, and provided opportunities for Marxist-Leninist parties to recruit members.

The first substantial antiwar demonstration took place on 2 May 1964 in New York City. Peter Camejo of the Young Socialist Alliance and Levi Laub of Progressive Labor were among the chief coordinators of the event. Soon afterward, the organizers set up the May 2nd Movement to fight the war and American imperialism. Under the control of Progressive Labor, the M2M began to sponsor demonstrations in cooperation with Youth against War and Fascism. The M2M also initiated a campaign for signatures on a pledge to refuse to fight in Vietnam. Its membership peaked at about 1,000 in 1965; it was dissolved in early 1966 when P.L. decided to send its cadres into the SDS.

The M2M's precedent of cooperation among radical groups set the tone for the antiwar movement. In April of 1965 the SDS called for a nonexclusionary march in Washington, D.C., to protest against the Vietnam War. Both the May 2nd Movement and the C.P.-controlled Du Bois Clubs endorsed the march, which drew 20,000 participants. While older peace groups denounced an "activity which is in fact more hostile to America than to war," and anti-Communist Socialists welcomed support only from those "not committed to any form of totalitarianism," SDS leaders shrugged off such complaints and charged those making them with trying to red-bait them. [11] Efforts to keep Communists out of the broader peace movement swiftly collapsed. Throughout the country many of the most dedicated, energetic, and effective forces in the antiwar movement were either linked to one or another Marxist-Leninist group or believed that excluding such people and groups was futile, counterproductive, or a surrender to McCarthyism.

In the summer of 1965 the National Coordinating Committee to End the War in Vietnam was set up with Frank Emspak as national coordinator. Emspak's father had been a union leader in the Communist orbit, and both Communists and Trotskyists strongly influenced the committee. Local antiwar committees, which bore the brunt of antiwar work, were united fronts, accepting as members all those opposed to the war and willing to work against it. The largest local antiwar group in the nation, New York's Fifth Avenue Vietnam Peace Parade Committee, was a broad united front including Fred Halstead of the Socialist Workers party, Robert Thompson of the Communist party, and Levi Laub of Progressive Labor, coordinated and held together by the venerable A. J. Muste.

Attracted by the large numbers of politically disaffected citizens in these antiwar groups, various Communist organizations saw them as attractive recruiting grounds and places to push their own programs. And as frustration and anger over the Vietnam War grew, increasing numbers of protesters found Marxist-Leninist analyses of American society and prescriptions for changing it cogent. Not that there was agreement among these groups. Opposition to the war sprang from many sources, and depending on their perspectives, opponents had a number of solutions for ending it. The Communist party, in concert with many liberal and moderate opponents of American involvement in Vietnam, called for negotiations between the United States and North Vietnam. The Socialist Workers party and many New Leftists demanded immediate American withdrawal.

Nor were disputes over which of these positions to support the only disagreements within the antiwar movement and local and national antiwar organizations. Many radical groups wanted local antiwar committees to endorse political candidates or take positions on a variety of other issues, including American racism and how to fight poverty. The Trotskyists, on the other hand, insisted that local antiwar groups should remain single-issue, broadly based organizations. They feared that efforts to expand their scope beyond the issue of Vietnam would destroy their unity. For that reason, the Trotskyists favored demonstrations as the only tactic that could unify the antiwar movement. The SDS was less enamored of demonstrations, believing that they diverted attention and resources from grass-roots political organizing, and was also scornful of political campaigns.

Such disputes could prove ruinous to efforts to build antiwar coalitions. For example, the Vietnam Day Committee (VDC) in Berkeley, California, voted to endorse the antiwar congressional candidacy of Robert Scheer in a 1966 Democratic primary, despite the bitter opposition of Trotskyists in the VDC. They insisted they would not encourage anyone to vote for a Democrat, argued that tying the antiwar movement to a political campaign would lead to pressure to water down antiwar demands, and complained that the VDC should stick to organizing demonstrations to end the war. Backed by antiwar liberals, New Leftists like Jerry Rubin, and the Communist-dominated Du Bois Clubs, Scheer won 45 percent of the primary vote. The VDC, however, was torn apart during the campaign. The Socialist Workers party gained organizational control, but the VDC soon faded away.[12]

From the beginning, conflict between its Communist and Trotskyist members deeply divided the National Coordinating Committee to End the War in Vietnam. By 1966 it was in disarray. Frustrated by its ineffectiveness, a group of radicals formed the National Mobilization Committee in the summer of 1966 to coordinate four days of local protests in November. Under the name of the Spring Mobilization Committee to End the War in Vietnam, it organized an April 1967 demonstration and became the preeminent national antiwar group. One of its offshoots, the Student Mobilization Committee (Student Mobe), set up to organize a student strike against the war, itself became a substantial antiwar organization.

Both the National Mobilization Committee and the Student Mobe were cauldrons of competing factions and radical parties. Once again, the issue of whether to focus exclusively on protests against the war proved divisive. The Communist party and the Du Bois Clubs tried to push the Student Mobe from an exclusively antiwar position to a "peace and freedom" platform in 1968, while Progressive Labor disliked the idea of student strikes. In May 1968 an effort to purge Young Socialist Alliance members from the Student Mobe backfired and the losers left, leaving the Trotskyists in effective control of the Student Mobe. National Mobe, meanwhile, fell into the hands of New Leftists such as Tom Hayden, Jerry Rubin, and David Dellinger who favored more militant confrontations with the authorities. By 1969, with most of its leaders under indictment for their role in the riots at the Democratic National Convention in Chicago, National Mobe was moribund.

Ironically, the Socialist Workers party and the Communist party, far from being on the militant extreme of the antiwar movement, were far more moderate than the SDS and the New Left. Transformed by the influx of Progressive Labor members and its own internal development, the SDS, which had begun its existence by calling for a humane, loving society, was angrily and vocally preaching violence and adopting both Marxist-Leninist language and goals. Its new theme was the transition from "protest to resistance." In Oakland, a "Stop the Draft Week" in October 1967 turned violent. On campuses efforts were underway to prevent recruiters from the military and Dow Chemical (a munitions manufacturer) from meeting with students. Demonstrators tried to block access to the Pentagon. SDS leaders talked about "insurrection." They visited and glamorized third-world revolutionaries, particularly the Vietnamese and Cubans.

The Collapse of the New Left

By 1967 the Students for a Democratic Society could boast of hundreds of chapters and tens of thousands of members. Despite such surface signs of prosperity, however, the SDS faced an ideological crisis. Many SDS members and leaders were confused about the organization's direction, unsure about the usefulness of peaceful protest and the likelihood of stopping the war or the draft, and increasingly intoxicated by apocalyptic rhetoric. They were looking for an all-embracing ideology to explain both what was happening in America and what to do about it. Marxism-Leninism was available as a tried and tested philosophy of revolution.

One version of Marxism-Leninism was put forth by Progressive Labor. By 1967 it had lost most of its small base of real workers as a result of a series of expulsions. In response it decided to focus on recruiting students. P.L. encouraged its members to attend to the more mundane and difficult jobs of organization and derided the more wild and reckless actions advocated by some SDS members as futile, dangerous, and counterproductive. It advocated a worker-student alliance as the only way to build a revolutionary movement in America. A growing number of people in the SDS, concerned that adventurism, wild cultural antics, and contempt for ordinary Americans—all increasingly in evidence in the student movement—would only delay the revolution, found P.L.'s message and discipline attractive.

The national leadership of the SDS, contemptuous of Progressive Labor, found itself unable to counter its arguments without itself reverting to Marxism-Leninism. As American campuses became battlegrounds over Dow Chemical recruiting, military research, draft resistance, and charges of racism, revolutionary language and fantasies escalated. In the spring of 1968 an SDS-led seizure of campus buildings, ostensibly to protest defense research on campus and the construction of a gymnasium in a public park in adjacent Harlem, paralyzed Columbia University. Both P.L. and anti-P.L. factions of SDS participated. A member of the anti-P.L. group, Mark Rudd, gained notoriety for such antics as informing Columbia president Grayson Kirk, "Up against the wall, motherfucker, this is a stick-up."[13] SDS leaders like Carl Davidson boasted of being Marxist-Leninists. Bernardine Dohrn, elected a leader of the SDS in 1968 just six months after joining the organization, announced: "I consider myself a revolutionary Communist." Tom Hayden called for "two, three, many Columbias."[14]

For a while in the spring and summer of 1968 the hopes of revolutionary Communists were bright. It seemed as if American society might be collapsing. Robert Kennedy and Martin Luther King, Jr., were assassinated. Rioting swept through scores of American cities as blacks went on a rampage. On numerous campuses angry students seized buildings and shut down classes. The Democratic party convention in Chicago turned into a debacle as police fought protesters in the streets and provoked charges of a police riot. America was not alone. In France student radicals, in alliance with Communist workers, came close to overthrowing President Charles de Gaulle's government in the streets.

That summer, Progressive Labor was a force to be reckoned with at the SDS convention, as Marxism-Leninism became de rigueur in the student movement. It controlled one-quarter of the delegates and was able to attract support from others on certain issues. It could point to France as an example of the power of a worker-student alliance. At the same time, P.L. denounced the demonstrations in Chicago as an example of adventurism that only alienated the workers who were absolutely essential for the success of an American revolution. In response, the national leadership of Students for a Democratic Society decided it had to become "more Marxist-Leninist than thou." It attacked P.L. openly for the first time as "external cadre" and insisted its adherents were the real Communists. In an effort to gain allies for its battle with P.L., the SDS leadership explored closer ties with the Black Panther party, itself committed to Marxism-Leninism, and even the Communist party. P.L., meanwhile, denounced the Panthers as reactionary nationalists because they were an all-black organization.

Neither side in the SDS's internal wars had an easy time formulating its version of Marxism-Leninism. The national leadership was handicapped by its lack of a coherent theory to answer Progressive Labor. Its reliance on students and young people as the revolutionary agents in American society ran up against the arguments that youth was not a permanent status and that students did not occupy essential positions in American society. P.L. also carried some heavy ideological baggage. American workers did not seem disposed to forming a revolutionary alliance with college students. In 1966 P.L. had denounced North Vietnam for accepting aid from the Soviet Union—which it regarded as a revisionist country. In the spring of 1969 Progressive Labor denounced Hanoi again, this time for selling out the revolution by agreeing to negotiations with the United States and castigated Cuba, where Castro "has taken the people into alliance with the most reactionary forces on earth," meaning the Soviet Union. Its revolutionary purity alienated many student radicals entranced by the youth culture of the 1960s.[15]

The national leadership of the SDS established the Revolutionary Youth Movement (RYM) in the fall of 1968 to oppose Progressive Labor. The RYM's program demanded that revolutionaries especially had to combat racism, which it believed had infected all of American society, including the white working class. It also saw the oppression of women as a special feature of American capitalism. P.L., on the other hand, insisted that the fundamental contradiction of this system was between the working class and all other classes. The RYM wanted students and American radicals to see themselves as allies of third-world revolutionaries and radical American blacks in the struggle against American society.

By the summer of 1968 the New Left, which had only recently advocated participatory democracy, had embraced the most rigid features of the Old Left it had once repudiated. Two dismayed SDS leaders lamented that "the anarchist style of earlier days had, by 1968, been replaced by rigid debates of organized factions who no longer talked about people's feelings and experiences but spoke in the pseudo-scientific language of Marxism-Leninism."[16] The last taboos fell rather easily. In the fall of 1969, Mike Klonsky, one of the leaders of the RYM and a red-diaper baby, cited Joseph Stalin favorably in internal debates. Several California SDS members, including Bob Avakian and Stanford English professor Bruce Franklin, insisted that "we should judge Stalin by Marxist (materialist) and (working) class standards, rather than by the bourgeois criteria of his imperialist, Trotskyite and revisionist assailants."[17] The implication was unmistakable that under the former standards Stalin did rather well.

The Students for a Democratic Society finally imploded at its June 1969 conference. Although Progressive Labor controlled only one-third of the delegates, it gained momentum and support when speakers from the Black Panther party, the RYM's ally, made lewd comments about the role of radical women in the revolutionary movement. As delegates shouted slogans at each other (P.L.'s chant was "Smash red-baiting"), avowed their support for Mao Zedong and the neo-Stalinist regimes of North Korea and Albania, and accused each other of deviating from true Marxist-Leninist ideology, the national leadership led a walkout and announced that since Progressive Labor was "objectively racist, anti-Communist and reactionary" it had expelled all P.L. members from the SDS.[18]

Students for a Democratic Society split into two irreconcilable parts, neither of which could ever capture even a fraction of the support the old SDS once had. Most of the old Marxist-Leninist sects, like the Spartacists, that had used SDS as a recruiting ground, remained in the P.L.-dominated SDS, which continued to focus on traditional Communist issues. Progressive Labor upheld the principle that class division was the most basic contradiction of American capitalism and remained true to the belief that it was necessary to organize the working class to make an American revolution. One of PL-SDS's major foci in the next year was building its Worker-Student Alliances on campus by seeking to organize university janitors. That effort sputtered, and by the spring of 1970 PL-SDS was down to some 3,000 members. It continued to decline and soon disappeared.

The other SDS had a more spectacular afterlife. Before the 1969 convention a group of leaders issued a statement entitled "You don't need a weatherman to know which way the wind blows," a line taken from a Bob Dylan song. The "Weatherman" group eschewed a traditional Marxist-Leninist emphasis on the working class. Nonetheless, it grandly proclaimed its commitment to communism: "The goal is the destruction of US imperialism and the achievement of a classless world; world communism." It announced that the task of young white revolutionaries was to aid those third-world forces fighting American imperialism, by armed struggle if necessary, and insisted that a vanguard, centralized cadre was required to launch the attack on imperialism. Since, Weatherman claimed, most white Americans were advantaged by their "white-skin privilege," it regarded them as enemies of the revolutionary movement. [19]

Not all, or even most, SDS members could accept this analysis or the activities to which it led. During the spring and summer of 1969 Weatherman squads, following the group's injunction to raise their level of militancy, invaded high schools to beat up teachers, thinking such actions would impress working-class youngsters. A group known as the Revolutionary Youth Movement II, led by Mike Klonsky, Noel Ignatin, and Bob Avakian, began to criticize Weatherman almost immediately for its scorn for the working class and its adventurism.

Other New Left forces began to disassociate themselves from Weatherman. At the 1969 SDS convention Weatherman had proclaimed the Black Panther party the vanguard of the revolution. The Panthers, however, were moving towards an alliance with the Communist party. In the summer of 1969 the C.P. and the Panthers cooperated to stage a United Front against Fascism conference. When Weatherman denounced the major concrete proposal coming out of the conference, community control of the police, on the grounds that it would lead to white vigilantism, Black Panther leaders denounced them as "a bunch of those jive bourgeois national socialists and national chauvinists" and warned that "the first motherfucker that gets out of order had better stand in line for some kind of disciplinary actions from the Black Panther Party." [20]

Such denunciations had little effect. The language used by radicals had become increasingly shrill, and revolutionary actions were now rushing to catch up with and match the rhetoric. A few hundred Weathermen organized in collectives during the summer of 1969. In addition to their efforts to appeal to working-class high school youth in order "to develop cadre, 16 year old Communist guerrillas . . . to smash the pig power structure," they took on the task of making real Communists out of their members. To overcome their middle-class upbringing and values—"to make ourselves into tools of the revolution" according to Bill Ayers—the collectives practiced karate and tried to root out the desire for privacy and individualism. Many sought to smash monogamy through enforced group sex, both homosexual and heterosexual.[21]

Bernardine Dohrn and several other Weathermen traveled to Cuba that summer and met with a Communist delegation from Vietnam, which urged them to begin armed struggle within the United States. This advice further fed the belief of the Weathermen that they had the obligation to fight "in the belly of the beast." American revolutionaries could contribute to the worldwide revolutionary struggle by bringing the war home. To the Weathermen the duty of a revolutionary was to make the revolution. Convinced that the United States was on the verge of defeat in Vietnam and that a revolutionary situation was imminent in this country, the group planned a Days of Rage campaign in Chicago for 8–11 October 1969. It was convinced that thousands of revolutionary youth would show up, ready to do battle with the police.

About 600 revolutionaries appeared in Chicago, but the only other organization to endorse the action was the Workers World party's Youth against War and Fascism. In a series of destructive rampages through the streets, the Weathermen managed to destroy a considerable amount of property, injure some police and law enforcement personnel, and get hundreds of their own members arrested. The Days of Rage succeeded in alienating virtually all of the radical Left, which denounced the Weathermen's behavior as "Custeristic." Weatherman's descent into guerrilla warfare and PL-SDS rigidity spelled the death knell for the Students for a Democratic Society. When school began again in the fall of 1969, campus groups disintegrated as students refused to follow either a rigid Marxism-Leninism or a violent Third Worldism.

Weatherman was not daunted. That Christmas 400 people gathered at a "War Council" in Flint, Michigan, and decided that Weatherman would go underground. Weatherman's isolation and extremism was so total that members discussed whether killing white babies was politically correct. Bernardine Dohrn praised Charles Manson, the cult figure whose band had committed a number of murders: "Dig it. First they killed those pigs, then they ate dinner in the same room with them, they even shoved a fork into a victim's stomach! Wild!"[22]

For the next several years Weatherman collectives carried out a series of bombings across the country, taking credit for more than two dozen (of the more than 800 nationwide) in a six-year period. Most were directed at police stations, military installations, and corporate headquarters, although one bomb went off in a women's bathroom at the Capitol.

The most spectacular and destructive explosion, however, took place in March 1970. A Greenwich Village townhouse being used as a bomb factory by one Weatherman Underground group accidentally blew up, killing three people, including Terry Robbins, a Weatherman leader.

Still another SDS offshoot had an equally bizarre afterlife. In the late 1960s a onetime Trotskyist, Lyndon LaRouche, became a guru to SDS members at Columbia University. LaRouche and his followers emerged out of the ruins of the SDS as the National Caucus of Labor Committees (NCLC). Never very large, in the early 1970s NCLC attempted to establish its hegemony on the left by physically assaulting Communist party members. The NCLC also used psychological terror to brainwash its own members and ensure unquestioning loyalty to LaRouche.

LaRouche abruptly shifted course in the mid-1970s, forming alliances with the anti-Semitic Liberty Lobby, castigating Jews and Judaism, and denouncing Great Britain's Queen Elizabeth as a drug pusher. During the 1980s the NCLC championed fusion energy and the Reagan administration's Strategic Defense Initiative, created an extensive private intelligence network, raised tens of millions of dollars, and sought to elect its members to public office as Democrats. By the end of the decade, LaRouche's conviction and imprisonment for fraud linked to his fund-raising techniques severely weakened his organization.

The SDS was not the only radical group to face serious problems as the 1960s ended. While the antiwar movement became more and more mainstream and respectable, sectarian squabbles increasingly dominated radical politics. In July 1969 many of the same people once associated with the now-defunct National Mobilization Committee to End the War in Vietnam formed the New Mobilization Committee. It too, however, was soon torn by the same disputes that had divided its predecessor— whether its focus should be organizing demonstrations or broadening its agenda to include other issues besides the Vietnam War. In the spring of 1970 it split apart. The Socialist Workers party took the lead in forming the National Peace Action Coalition, while Sidney Lens and Sidney Peck, cooperating with the Communist party and other radical forces, built the National Coalition against War, Racism, and Repression, which soon renamed itself the People's Coalition for Peace and Justice. While the two groups occasionally cooperated and did coordinate the largest antiwar demonstration in American history in April 1971, the end of large-scale American involvement in Vietnam and the growth of such liberal and moderate organizations as the Vietnam Moratorium reduced their effectiveness.

Trotskyists and Maoists

No Old Left group benefited as much from its antiwar work as the Socialist Workers party. Its leading role in the Student Mobilization Committee and activism in the National Mobilization enabled it to gain hundreds of new recruits. Many came to the SWP through its youth group, the Young Socialist Alliance. By the mid-1970s the SWP had perhaps 2,500 members, with a like number in the Young Socialist Alliance. In 1976 the Socialist Workers party presidential ticket drew 91,000 votes. SWP candidates ran for local and state offices across the country on explicitly Socialist platforms.

Virtually all of the SWP's members, however, were young, white, and middle class. Most had been attracted to the SWP because of its antiwar activities, but that source of recruitment began to dry up early in the 1970s. In an effort to become a more proletarian party, the SWP's National Committee decided in 1978 to initiate a turn toward industry. Party members were encouraged to find factory jobs. Party leader Jack Barnes insisted that "there are more workers developing anticapitalist sentiment or greater openness to anticapitalist conclusions and solutions today than at any other time in American history." Intended to root the party in the industrial working class, this decision, coming just as American politics swung sharply to the right, helped to weaken it. Membership began to decline, and few members were able to obtain secure jobs in the face of the recession of the early 1980s.[23]

Internal strife, a phenomenon not new to Trotskyism, contributed to the SWP's difficulties. While several small groups of dissidents had struggled against the dominant party line in the early and mid-1970s, in the early 1980s the SWP's abandonment of some of the traditional tenets of Trotskyism provoked an uprising that devastated the organization and set off its most severe schism in decades. The controversy was linked to the transfer of power within the SWP from one generation to another. Until the early 1970s the dominant leadership of the SWP could trace its revolutionary commitment back to the 1930s, if not earlier. Farrell Dobbs, several times the party's presidential candidate, had been a leader of the Minneapolis Teamsters strikes of 1934, and had succeeded Jim Cannon, the party's founder, who even in retirement remained an active presence. Dobbs stepped down as national secretary in 1972 and was succeeded by Jack Barnes. Within a few years, virtually all of the leadership was composed of college-educated people initially drawn to the SWP by the antiwar and civil rights struggles of the 1960s.

In 1981 party leaders launched an attack on such longtime staples of Trotskyism as the theory of permanent revolution and, indeed, on Trotsky himself. Jack Barnes castigated most Trotskyists around the world as "hopeless, irredeemable sectarians" isolated from the revolutionary struggle. He argued that a new center of the Communist world was emerging in Central America and the Caribbean and that the SWP had to give its full support to Fidel Castro, the leader of that new movement, in order "to be recognized as legitimate components of the worldwide Communist movement that must be built."[24]

A host of opponents to these views quickly emerged, despite draconian bans on dissent or factions within the SWP. Dissidents charged to no avail that the SWP's new policies ran counter to traditional Trotskyist views and violated norms of internal party debate. Longtime party members were summarily expelled for a variety of ideological and organizational sins, some real and others imagined. By 1984 virtually all of the party's founders and veterans had been ousted or had quit. Together with other SWP dissidents, they formed several small opposition groups. The Fourth Internationalist Tendency, North Star Network, and Socialist Action sought to uphold traditional Trotskyist principles or unite with other radical groups, but they remained tiny and little-noticed sects. The SWP itself continued to lose members. There were only around 1,300 in 1981; by the middle of the decade membership was probably down to 700 or 800.

Even that small number still made the SWP the largest of the horde of Trotskyist sects in the United States at the beginning of the 1990s. Others of some note included the Spartacist League, still led by James Robertson, probably the most doctrinaire radical group. It focused much of its effort on militant demonstrations against neo-Nazis and Klansmen. The Workers League, led by David North, carried out a long-running campaign alleging that the Socialist Workers party had for years been controlled by American intelligence agents. Most members of these small groups are students or former 1960s radicals. While they occasionally can organize rallies or marches of a few thousand people around such specific issues as combating the Ku Klux Klan, they have very little effect on American life.[25]

For a brief time in the 1970s Maoist organizations were the fastest-growing segment of the American Communist movement. Convinced that the Chinese Communists had avoided the bureaucratic conservatism that had afflicted the Soviet Union, attracted by the revolutionary élan of the Red Guards and the Cultural Revolution, excited by visions of a people's guerrilla war, and able to romanticize the poverty and backwardness of China as signs of revolutionary purity, a few thousand veterans of the SDS became Maoists. It was not, however, the Progressive Labor party, the first pro-Chinese grouping in this country, that benefited from the Maoist growth. P.L. had been left with part of the remnants of the Students for a Democratic Society in 1969. Its newspaper, *Challenge,* reached a circulation of 90,000 by the middle of the 1970s. But P.L. abandoned Maoism. Early in the decade it denounced the Chinese government for traveling down the same revisionist path as the Soviet Union. Its membership quickly shriveled up. For several years P.L.'s major public activities were the violent protests launched by one of its front groups, the International Committee against Racism (InCar), which specialized in disruptive "antiracist" actions directed against speakers deemed offensive. Among InCar's targets were opponents of affirmative action, sociobiologists, and Nazis and Klansmen. Although it had about 1,500 members in the late 1970s, InCar was never able to be more than an irritant.

The Maoist mantle was picked up in the early part of the 1970s by a number of other groups, most of which traced their origin back to one or another faction of the SDS. The two largest, the Revolutionary Union (later the Revolutionary Communist party) and the October League (later the Communist Party Marxist-Leninist) were both led by SDS veterans. Revolutionary Union's leader, Bob Avakian, was a Berkeley SDS activist. At the end of 1973 his group had almost 1,000 members in more than 25 cities. Its rival, the October League, was led by Mike Klonsky and Lyn Wells, both leaders of RYM II, the SDS faction that had refused to follow the Weathermen into the revolutionary underground. The October League was probably only slightly smaller than Revolutionary Union, with many more blacks and working-class members than the largely white, middle-class Revolutionary Union.

In 1973 the *Guardian,* an independent pro-Maoist newspaper, sponsored a symposium designed to unify the various Maoist tendencies in a new Communist party. The effort failed, and by the middle of the decade the Revolutionary Communist Party (RCP) and the Communist Party Marxist-Leninist (CPML) were bitter rivals, competing for the official Chinese franchise in the American revolutionary movement. China's arrest of the Gang of Four, a group of Mao Zedong's followers, its repudiation of the Cultural Revolution as a monstrous horror, and China's increasing rapprochement with the United States caused a crisis among Maoists. The CPML gave its support to the Chinese government and

Deng Xiaoping. The RCP temporized, but finally condemned Deng in 1978, charging that revisionists had taken power in Beijing.

The CPML found it exceedingly hard to maintain its revolutionary credentials while supporting China's foreign policy, which more and more involved a tacit alliance with the United States and opposition to Soviet-backed liberation movements and guerrilla forces. One split took place in 1979–80 when the editor of the party's newspaper quit. Shortly afterward, Klonsky resigned amid charges he had committed "crimes." One faction threatened violence against another. As membership declined, the Communist Party Marxist-Leninist merged with a breakaway group from the RCP, but the hemorrhaging continued until it disbanded in 1982.

The Revolutionary Communist party continued to function through the 1980s, even though its membership declined sharply from a high of 2,000 to less than 500. It increasingly emphasized spectacular and disruptive demonstrations and gestures, ranging from spray-painting bridge overpasses to burning flags. After being indicted on multiple charges stemming from a violent demonstration against Deng Xiaoping's visit to Washington in 1979, Bob Avakian fled to France. It was an RCP member whose prosecution for flag burning led to a Supreme Court decision in 1988 declaring state laws banning the practice a violation of the First Amendment. The RCP has attempted to recruit among high school students, dropouts, and punks.

Other smaller Maoist organizations also survived the 1970s. The League of Revolutionary Struggle, led by black poet Amiri Baraka, once known as Leroi Jones, continued to profess respect for Mao's ideas. Baraka had been close to Progressive Labor in the early 1960s, writing in its journal that "if America is not stopped in its tracks it will destroy the world. . . . The majority of American white men are evil."[26] The League of Revolutionary Struggle focused on recruiting blacks, Hispanics, and Asians particularly on the West Coast, where it was able to establish a presence in a variety of ethnic student organizations. In September 1990 the League voted to disband. The majority concluded that Marxist-Leninist principles were contrary to their beliefs, which had changed as a result of the crisis of communism.

One Maoist group, the Communist Workers party (CWP), founded in 1979, was involved in a bloody shoot-out with Klansmen and American Nazis that year in Greensboro, North Carolina, that left five party members dead. Largely composed of Asian Americans, the CWP also recruited blacks and white veterans of the New Left. After a brief flurry of publicity, it decided to infiltrate the Democratic party and created the

New Democratic Movement, which, by 1988, had elected several of its members to minor political offices, primarily in New York City, and been able to gain several million dollars in government grants. [27]

The handful of former student revolutionaries who had opted for terrorism became even more marginal in the late 1970s and 1980s. The few dozen Weather Underground Organization (WUO) members issued such manifestos as *Prairie Fire: The Politics of Revolutionary Anti-Imperialism,* in which they proclaimed that "we are Communist men and women," but no more than 1,000 people formed an aboveground support organization. In 1973 the Weather Underground came under the influence of Clayton Van Lydegraf, at one time a Communist party underground leader in Washington State. Van Lydegraf had joined Progressive Labor in the late 1950s but had found that organization too tame. He was expelled for ultraleftism. His hard-line Marxism-Leninism fit nicely with the WUO's extremism. In the late 1970s Van Lydegraf expelled Bernardine Dohrn and other WUO figures, who soon surrendered to authorities, generally serving brief prison terms. Van Lydegraf and several other members of his faction were arrested in 1977 on charges of conspiring to commit bombings.

A handful of WUO members took the step from revolutionary violence to criminal violence. Forming the May 19th Communist Organization, they joined with the Black Liberation Army (BLA) to commit armed robberies in the name of the revolution. One botched effort in 1981 to hold up a Brinks truck in Nyack, New York, left two policemen and a security guard dead. Authorities made a series of arrests, including onetime Weatherman leader Kathy Boudin, and virtually wiped out this terrorist wing of the Communist movement. [28]

The Black Liberation Army was one of the last remnants of the black Marxist-Leninist movement. Although several of the small Communist sects such as P.L. had briefly made inroads in the black community during the 1960s, the most significant Marxist-Leninist organizations among blacks were not interracial. One of the earliest inspirations for black Marxist-Leninists was Robert Williams, the head of an NAACP chapter in Monroe, North Carolina, who as early as 1960 was urging armed self-defense against racist attacks. In 1961 Williams fled to Cuba and then China after being charged with kidnapping an elderly white couple during a racial confrontation. From those countries he urged American blacks to engage in guerrilla warfare and gave instructions in the use of Molotov cocktails: "During the night hours, such weapons, thrown from roof tops, will make the streets impossible for racist cops to patrol." [29]

Williams was one of the inspirations for the Revolutionary Action Movement (RAM), a black nationalist movement influenced by Marxism-Leninism. Several of its members and leaders later turned up in the far more notorious Black Panther party, including Huey Newton and Bobby Seale of Oakland, who founded the party in 1966. Influenced by the writings of Mao Zedong and the Algerian Marxist Franz Fanon, Newton and Seale fashioned an eclectic ideology that anointed all blacks in American jails as political prisoners, called for armed self-defense for blacks, and glorified the lumpen proletariat—criminals, pimps, prostitutes, and street hustlers—as the revolutionary motor of history. While attracting some black intellectuals with their militancy, the Panthers' bravado and ideology also led to an influx of street criminals.

A number of hardened criminals joined the Panthers, including George Jackson, one of the Soledad brothers, a group of black California inmates charged with murdering a prison guard in 1970. Jackson's brother, Jonathan, attempted to seize hostages to free his brother that same year; when the episode ended he was dead along with two prisoners and a judge. In August 1971 George Jackson somehow procured a gun, led an abortive prison revolt that left several people dead, and was then killed by guards. For most of its brief history, the Black Panthers were locked in tense, often violent confrontations with police, whom they called pigs and accused of perpetuating genocide in the black community. Numerous BPP members were killed in shoot-outs with law enforcement agencies; others were killed in internecine warfare with rival groups. Newton spent several years in prison on a murder charge, and Seale was also accused of participating in the torture and murder of a Panther suspected of being an informer.

Throughout 1968 and 1969 the Black Panther party was wracked by conflict between forces loyal to Stokeley Carmichael, onetime leader of the Student Nonviolent Coordinating Committee, and supporters of Eldridge Cleaver, an ex-convict whose best-selling book, *Soul on Ice,* explained his rapes of white women as a political act. Carmichael wanted to subordinate the Panthers' Marxism-Leninism to a Pan-African racial unity, while Cleaver emphasized class struggle and alliances with white leftists. The most notable such event was a United Front against Fascism rally held in Oakland in the summer of 1969, largely financed by the Communist party.

Although Carmichael soon left the BPP to form the All-African People's Revolutionary party, the Panthers did not find internal peace. One faction loyal to Newton and Seale retained the Panther name and turned to community organizing. Another group, supportive of Cleaver, by then a fugitive in Algeria, renamed itself the Black Liberation Army and undertook a campaign of murder and robberies to raise money for revolutionary politics. Cleaver himself eventually left Algeria, denounced communism, experienced a religious conversion, and returned to the United States, where he supported conservative causes. BLA members were implicated in a variety of crimes, including a plot to blow up the Statue of Liberty. One BLA leader, Joanne Chesimard, also known as Assata Shakur, serving a life sentence for murder, was broken out of jail by the BLA and the May 19th Communist Organization and fled to Cuba. Newton also fled to Cuba to avoid prosecution but later returned to California; he was killed in a drug deal in 1989.

Other black revolutionary groups were less violent but just as unsuccessful as the Panthers in building lasting organizations. One that briefly flourished was the League of Revolutionary Black Workers, which developed from a 1968 wildcat strike at a Detroit Dodge assembly plant. With a strong core of black, working-class leaders, the league also attracted James Forman, another former SNCC leader, who wanted it to focus on gaining financial reparations for blacks from American whites. The league was eventually torn apart by a dispute over whether to focus on industrial organization or education and outreach; it split in the 1970s. One of its leaders, Ken Cockrell, was later elected to the Detroit City Council.

The Last Chapter of American Communism?

As all of the sects and grouplets that had come to life in the 1960s split apart, disintegrated, or withered, one Communist organization appeared as an island of stability in this sea of failure. Derided by the radicals of the 1960s as a staid, conservative dinosaur, the Communist Party USA had managed to avoid the apocalyptic visions and ruinous tactics that destroyed the New Left and most of its offspring. For former student radicals struggling to reconcile their political beliefs with the need to make a living and function in the real world, the C.P. provided a model.

The party had limped through the 1960s, critical of the extremism and freewheeling cultural radicalism of the New Left. In domestic politics it advocated alliances with liberal Democrats to counter right-wing Republicans, advocated peaceful coexistence with the Soviet Union, and insisted that the working-class and hence the union movement was a key element in any progressive coalition. None of these positions was calculated to appeal to the youthful radicals who despised liberalism and liberals, were far more excited by newer and more energetic Communist regimes than the Soviet Union, and believed that the union movement was racist and part of the status quo.

As the civil rights and antiwar movements gathered steam in the 1960s, Communists, ex-Communists, and fellow travelers of the Communist party were found all around them. Forced to lie low during the McCarthy era, they eagerly responded to new political opportunities even while the party itself barely crept along. As Irving Howe noted in 1965, "these people were present, ready and eager; they needed no directives from the Communist Party" to work for political causes in which they believed.[30]

During the 1960s some returned to the Communist party. Others did not, but remained sympathetic to the party's vision and respectful of its outlook. Stanley Levinson, a top adviser to Martin Luther King, Jr., and the Souther Christian Leadership Conference during the 1960s, had been involved in party financial affairs throughout the 1950s. The FBI had evidence that he had laundered Soviet funds used to support the C.P. Jack O'Dell, a former district organizer for the party, was a staff worker for King's Southern Christian Leadership Conference. Many of the early SDS leaders were red-diaper babies. Several leaders of the Free Speech Movement at Berkeley, including Bettina Aptheker, were Communists. Communists were active in the National Mobilization Committee and its various successors, which organized opposition to the war in Vietnam. The party itself also played a major role at several radical gatherings designed to build unity, including the National Conference for New Politics in the summer of 1967 and the Black Panthers' United Front against Fascism in 1970. By the end of the decade it had been accepted as a legitimate participant at radical gatherings, a far cry from its isolation of the early 1960s.

It took the Communist party several years to recover from the wounds inflicted on it during the late 1950s. In June 1964 the Du Bois Clubs held their organizational convention in San Francisco, marking the first effort to expand the party's youth work beyond the very narrow circle in which it had been circumscribed for more than a decade. Given wide publicity when Richard Nixon charged that the party had deliberately attempted to confuse its organization with the Boys Clubs, the Du Bois Clubs (named after W. E. B. Du Bois, the prominent black educator and activist who had become a Communist in the 1960s at the age of 90) included some non-Communists and managed to grow to some 1,500 members.

The more militant sections of the New Left, Progressive Labor, and Trotskyists scorned the clubs' refusal to emphasize socialism and condemn liberal politicians.

As the New Left waned, some of its disillusioned members joined the Communist party. The most prominent was Angela Davis, who had grown up in a black middle-class family in the Communist orbit in Birmingham, Alabama, and joined the party in the late 1960s. She became a national figure after Governor Ronald Reagan of California unsuccessfully tried to have her fired from a teaching position in the University of California system because of her party membership. Davis worked closely with the Black Panther party and the Soledad brothers, falling in love with George Jackson. After Jonathan Jackson's unsuccessful effort to free his brother, Davis was charged with murder when prosecutors linked her to the gun used in the affair. A fugitive for several years, she was tried and acquitted in 1972 after a massive defense effort led by the Communist party.[31]

Still, as late as the mid-1970s Communist party membership was well below 10,000. The decline of other radical groups, the continuing lessening of political and social strictures against communism, and the party's determination to step up its recruiting led to a modest but steady growth in membership for the next decade, reaching perhaps 15,000 by 1987. Well into the 1980s party leaders complained that "with the present size of the Party there are limitations on what we can do or contribute."[32]

The C.P. directed its recruiting efforts in the black and Hispanic communities, and these two groups have accounted for approximately 25 percent of the delegates at recent party conventions. The proportion of working-class members has apparently been declining, leading party leader Gus Hall to complain in 1983 that efforts on "industrial concentration have actually diminished." The Jewish presence in the party has also declined, in large measure due to intense party hostility to Israel and denial of Soviet anti-Semitism. On the other hand, party activities on college campuses, long invisible, began to flourish in the mid-1980s. An open leader of the Young Communist League, Jason Rabinowitz, was elected student body president at the University of Massachusetts, and YCL clubs were active at a number of other campuses.[33]

Party membership has never been the only determinant of Communist influence, however. One sign of the C.P.'s growing confidence that the political climate in America was shifting was its decision once again to run candidates for public office. Gus Hall, the nominee for president in all four elections from 1972 to 1984, received between 25,000 and 59,000 votes. After dropping to 35,000 in 1984, the C.P. decided that it would provide critical support for the Democratic candidates in the 1988 election rather than sponsoring its own ticket.

By the end of the decade the party had concluded that its best hope for political influence lay in a reconstituted Democratic party. It strongly supported efforts by Jesse Jackson and his Rainbow Coalition to gain strength in the Democratic party and transform its policies and objectives. Several Communists and party sympathizers worked in Jackson's campaigns. Jack O'Dell held a high position in the Rainbow Coalition. O'Dell, who has called anticommunism "a pathology," has actively supported a variety of party fronts in the past decade. Several black congressmen, most notably George Crockett of Detroit, had also long been associated with party causes. A growing number of political and labor figures, in fact, were no longer reluctant to associate themselves with Communist front groups. The United States Peace Council and the National Alliance against Racist and Political Repression, both controlled by the C.P., attracted such sponsors and officers as Gus Newport, then mayor of Berkeley, California, and representatives John Conyers, Charles Hayes, Ron Dellums, and George Crockett. Notable politicians and union leaders gave their names and presence to annual banquets of the Labor Research Association, another party-dominated organization.[34]

The revival of Popular Front attitudes and organizations was aided by the now-entrenched belief among custodians of American culture that any criticism of communism or Communists was a form of McCarthyism. A spate of academic studies sought to rehabilitate the reputation of the American Communist party, portraying it as an early harbinger of a more democratic, racially egalitarian, and humane America that had been thwarted by political repression.[35] Enough Marxist-Leninists had filtered into academic life that the Marxist Educational Press, headquartered at the University of Minnesota, was created to publish and distribute pseudo-academic works faithful to the party line. MEP also sponsored academic conferences at which participants combined panels on American imperialism and philosophical discussions of dialectical materialism. Films, novels, and works of nonfiction suggested not merely that American Communists had been victims of repression, but that they were, in the words of Victor Navasky, editor of the *Nation*, "moral exemplars."[36]

Following Watergate and revelations of abuses committed by intelligence agencies, academics and political activists alike advanced claims that the failure of American communism was linked to an obsessive American anticommunism that was a blot on American democracy. Joel

Kovel, the Alger Hiss Professor of Social Studies at Bard College, defined anticommunism as "an exploitation of the deep structures of racism for the purpose of managing threat to capitalist rule." At a conference devoted to anticommunism at Harvard in 1988, Kovel took solace in the fact that "the US is weakening and has less capacity to enforce a megalomaniacal ideology like anticommunism."[37]

But the 1980s ended with communism, not anticommunism, in disarray. The rejection of communism by those who had lived under "really existing socialism" (as Communists called the culture of the Soviet bloc) in Eastern Europe and the Soviet Union itself staggered the C.P. For a party that had always been in thrall to the Soviet Union, the admission by Soviet leaders that 70 years of Marxism-Leninism had led to economic, political, and moral bankruptcy was devastating. Gus Hall gamely praised Socialist renewal and insisted that those proclaiming the death of communism were engaging in "the big lie." Michael Parenti, a frequent intellectual commentator in the C.P. press, complaining that the state of Marxist studies in the Soviet Union was dismal, concluded, "Since the old Marxism was never tested by them in the crucible of capitalist and imperialist reality, where its explanatory power is so well demonstrated, but was usually ingested automatically like a catechism, it had no vibrancy or meaning."[38]

The Communist party's membership gains of the previous decade began to vanish, and signs mounted that another internal upheaval, not dissimilar from the one that had taken place late in the 1950s, was possible. The party's flagship newspaper, the *People's Daily World,* faced declining revenues and switched from daily to weekly publication. Open criticism and questioning of party policies began to appear, with some Communists attacking Soviet intellectuals, leaders, or journals as anti-Marxist. And some party members, particularly blacks, attacked Gus Hall and other longtime party leaders for the lack of democracy within the C.P. Hall, for his part, angrily complained that the "temporary ideological climate of 'anything goes'" in the Communist bloc seemed to have emboldened dissidents to "call for the removal or resignation of the national leadership and a change on these basic questions."[39]

In a speech to Party cadres in June, 1991, Hall accused Mikhail Gorbachev of "implicitly" endorsing the liquidation of the Communist Party and harshly criticized him for surrendering the USSR to capitalism. Although the CPUSA denounced the abortive coup against Gorbachev that took place in August, 1991, it also angrily condemned the attacks on the Communist Party that followed and rejected the notion that communism had failed or that the Soviet people had decided to abandon it. As communism collapsed in its historic heartland, the American Communists were left in a state of bewilderment and intellectual incoherence.[40]

Hall, by 1990, was one of the longest-serving Communist party leaders in the world. Born Arvo Halberg in 1910 into a working-class Finnish American Communist family on Minnesota's Mesabi iron range, he had grown up in the party. Educated at the Lenin School in Moscow, an organizer for the CIO's Steel Workers in the 1930s, and a Communist functionary for more than 50 years, he became party leader in 1959 by deftly pushing aside the ailing Gene Dennis. Under his guidance the Communist party barely profited from the largest upsurge in American radicalism since the Great Depression. Hall resisted even the modest efforts of Eurocommunist parties in the 1970s to distance themselves from Moscow. As the world Communist movement faces the worst ideological crisis in its history in the early 1990s, he has resisted change and tried to put the best face possible on the disaster. Hall has boasted that he has been in constant demand for interviews by the American media, as if the natural human fascination with a vanishing species was the same as serious attention to a viable political movement. The grandfatherly Hall, whose surface amiability masks an unyielding Stalinist core, may be destined to preside over the last chapter of American communism.

Chapter Six

American Communism after 70 Years

American Communists sought nothing less than the revolutionary transformation of society into a perfect egalitarian socialism that delivered
material and cultural abundance without oppression of any sort. Communist idealism, however, was not a gentle utopianism but a romantic
messianism that hated the existing world with its myriad imperfections
and looked forward to the apocalyptic coming of a collectivist utopia. In
1935 Lincoln Steffens assured Communists that they had the task "to
make and cross a bridge from one age to another, . . . from our old
Christian-Greek culture to the communist culture which will probably
prevail for the next two thousand years."[1] American Communists saw
themselves as agents of history whose doctrine was "omnipotent. . . .
True not only today, but for the whole of human history." They repeatedly proclaimed their victory "inevitable" and promised that under their
rule "society will literally remodel the planet to suit its own needs" and
"in a few years, all countries of the world would enjoy a wealth that would
make the present affluence of the United States look like the contents of
a bindle-stiff's bundle."[2]

   American Communists pursued their goals with remarkable energy.
They were ruthless and demanding not only with others but with themselves as well. One of the movement's founders appropriately entitled
his memoir of the party and its leaders *The Whole of Their Lives.*[3] The
movement made extraordinary demands on its members' time, energy,
economic resources, and willingness to accept the party's supremacy on
all matters of life. Most people, including those sympathetic to the move-

ment, could not live with those requirements. Turnover in party membership was so high that for most of the party's existence the typical member had been in the movement less than a year. For those who could deliver the devotion required, however, the movement constituted a close-knit band of brothers and sisters united in common fidelity to the revolutionary goal.

American Communists coupled their idealistic devotion to the movement with hatred of their opponents, a hatred of such fervor that it sometimes bordered on the maniacal. Communists habitually slandered and libeled those who opposed them as fascists, Nazis, racists, anti-Semites, and worse. Communists did not merely criticize the ideas of their opponents but denigrated their opponents as persons; in the world of American communism it was not possible for an opponent to possess integrity. One of the party's leading intellectuals in an unexceptional passage described some of the party's enemies as having "the morals of goats, the learning of gorillas and the ethics of—well, of what they are: racist, war-inciting, enemies of humanity, rotten to the core, parasitic, merciless—and doomed." As for the party's enemies on the left, the Trotskyists, Communists described them as "that putrid clique" that had been "vomited forth" from the movement. When the Soviet Union executed Trotskyists for treason, American Communists cheered them on, saying, "As for those who plotted the crippling of Soviet industry and Soviet farming and planned to have the only workers' country ruled by the lords of money again—to them *DEATH! THIS SHOULD BE THE MESSAGE OF EVERY YOUNG WORKER TO OUR ENEMY CLASS, THE BOSSES OF THE WORLD.*"[4]

American communism never forgave and never apologized. When its policies changed, the party expelled scores, sometimes hundreds, of its members for supporting the doctrines the party had just discarded. Even if a subsequent turn of strategy brought a return to doctrines for which those expelled had been anathematized, the party neither apologized to those it had expelled or asked them to return. In 1944 the party expelled Sam Darcy, an ally of William Foster, for his criticism of Earl Browder's doctrines; in 1945 the party expelled Browder, renounced Browderism, and elevated Foster to the party's leadership, but did not apologize to Darcy or ask him to return. The party never apologized to John Lautner for expelling him in 1950 although it later learned that the evidence against him had been false. Browder led the party for nearly 15 years, years that included its successful entry into the mainstream labor movement, its peak membership, and its rise to a position of significant, albeit limited, political influence. Even so, the party contemptuously expelled him, scorned his requests for readmission, and contemned him even in death, when its press failed to acknowledge him with an obituary.

A 1934 American Communist poem described the Soviet Union as "a heaven . . . brought to earth in Russia."[5] The description was not hyperbole but reflected the mental star around which the world of American communism turned. The fantasy that the Soviet Union had built or was building a society of material abundance while eliminating all oppression proved to American Communists that a Marxist utopia was attainable. To them it followed that the methods used by Soviet Communists would bring a heaven to earth in America as well. Within the limits of their knowledge, American Communists always strove to do what Moscow wanted, no more, no less. Along with intellectual guidance and some financial aid, the Soviet Union provided American communism with psychological support. Although Communists told themselves that the facade of American power hid a society wracked by internal contradictions that was tottering toward ruin, nonetheless, even they conceded that America was a colossus. The link to Soviet power gave American Communists the psychological strength to believe that they could overcome the American leviathan, to storm heaven itself.

Weakness as well as strength flowed from the Soviet link. Those policies that served Soviet interests often required American Communists to sacrifice their assets and forgo their ambitions to satisfy Moscow's foreign-policy needs. Public and governmental hostility to American Communists in part reflected hostility and fear of the Soviet Union. During the tensest years of the cold war, especially when American troops fought Communist soldiers in Korea, the American Communist party's support for the nation's enemies brought down on it the wrath of outraged American patriotism. But there is another dimension to the clash between communism and American nationalism: As an immigrant nation from the beginning, being American was in part an ideological act in a way being English, French, or German was not. The defining events in American history had strong ideological elements. The American Revolution was both a national war of independence and the political creation of a republican society based on individual liberty. The writing of the Constitution solidified the revolution's emphasis on republican liberty, and the document itself became a central symbol of American nationality. The vast and terrible agony of the American Civil War was both a war to preserve national union and a war over the definition and extent of human freedom. Out of this history a belief in personal freedom, individual liberty, and democracy became an integral part of American national identity.

From time to time currents have emerged in America that have defined American nationality in the more conventional way of birth and blood (the Know-Nothing movement of the 1850s and the Ku Klux Klan the 1920s, for example), but those currents always faded away or, as in the case of interning Japanese Americans in World War II, were later regretted. The ideological aspect of Americanism is reflected negatively in the belief in the existence of *un*-American activity. Any group or movement that seriously dissents from the principles of freedom, individual liberty, and democracy defines itself as being outside what most Americans regard as a central aspect of American patriotism. There have been many such groups in American history, from cultish religions to fanatical political movements. Most had limited constituencies and were tolerated or ignored because they did not threaten national institutions. Those movements perceived as serious dangers, however, became subject to fierce public and private attack. The American Communist party was among the latter and came to be perceived as a danger by reason of its profoundly antidemocratic ideology and link to the Soviet Union's power and threat to American national security.

The Communist role in the labor movement of the 1930s and 1940s, its greatest achievement, shows Communists' own sensitivity to their suspect status. Communists dominated the leadership of 18 CIO unions with a membership of 1,370,000 workers and were an influential presence in the leadership of CIO unions with as many or more members. Yet almost every major CIO Communist concealed his Communist allegiance. (Ben Gold, head of the Furriers, was one of the few exceptions.) CIO Communists feared, correctly, that public acknowledgement of their Communist loyalties would offend many workers. The Communist movement never developed a mass constituency of its own, not even during the Great Depression of the 1930s. The Communist party in the late 1930s and the 1940s achieved a significant role in the labor movement and the liberal wing of the Democratic party in a few states and cities, but not under its own banner. Its success rested with its ability to take a subordinate part in the emerging mass production unions and to follow in the slipstream of New Deal liberalism. When its own policies or those of the Soviet Union required it to lay aside the shelter of mainstream liberal and labor institutions, it faced annihilation as a significant force.

American communism was not a secret conspiracy or a clandestine arm of Soviet intelligence, although it had aspects of both. Espionage was a sideshow to the party's main activities, but the periodic surfacing of shadowy links between American Communists and Soviet intelligence served to confirm in the public mind the movement's anti-American character.[6] So, too, did its habits of semiconcealment. The government, with the enthusiastic support of large segments of the public, also harassed, prosecuted, and persecuted the movement in 1919–21 and again in 1949 and into the 1950s. In both periods public authorities abused the constitutional rights of Communists, and extremist private anti-Communist organizations engaged in oppressive vigilante activity. Although American Communists were the victims of abuse, the history of the movement is not a history of victimization. In both episodes constitutional protections and democratic habits restrained public authorities, limited the reach of anti-Communist laws, or forced authorities to retreat from abusive behavior. Even during the early 1950s, the high tide of McCarthyism, the Communist party functioned legally, its spokesmen publicly advocated its doctrines, its recruiters brought in new members, and its press published daily and weekly newspapers, journals, pamphlets, and books in the millions of copies.

The Communist movement's major setbacks were self-inflicted. By the end of the 1930s the Communist party's membership approached 100,000, and it had achieved a measure of influence in the burgeoning industrial union movement, acceptance in elite cultural circles, and a limited role in the New Deal wing of the Democratic party. Then, in response to the Nazi-Soviet Pact of 1939, American Communists ditched the Popular Front stance that had led to this success and virulently attacked Roosevelt's policy of aiding the anti-Nazi belligerents. By 1941 Communists were on the defensive in both the labor movement and the political arena. Only the Nazi attack on the Soviet Union in June 1941 saved American Communists from marginalization and loss of their major assets. In late 1941 Communists revived the Popular Front, regained their positions within liberal and labor institutions, and by the end of the war reached the peak of their power. Then, in response to Stalin's cold-war policies, American Communists dropped the wartime Popular Front and adopted confrontation with established liberal leaders and national policies. In 1948, however, no new Hitler appeared to save Communists and their allies from their folly. Voters overwhelmingly rejected Henry Wallace's Progressive party and assured the dominance of anti-Communist liberalism in the Democratic party and the labor movement.

The 1948 defeat swept away almost all of the party's gains since the mid-1930s. The governmental prosecution and public harassment of

Communists that followed in the 1950s, although damaging, were attacks on an already broken movement. Very nearly the final blow came in 1956, not from American authorities or McCarthyist fanatics, but from the Soviet Union. Khrushchev's announcement that the heaven brought to earth in Russia had been a Stalinist hell shattered the mental universe of American Communists. The party lost over three-quarters of its members in two years. The nearly moribund remnant showed some life in the 1980s when refugee radicals fleeing the collapse of the New Left injected some younger blood into the party. This modest growth, however, crumpled in 1989 and 1990 in the face of the collapse of Communist rule in Eastern Europe and the decay of communism in the Soviet Union. If communism survives in the Soviet Union, the American Communist party probably will survive as well. If communism dies in the Soviet Union, it likely will die in America as well.

In 1932 John Scott, an American Communist, went to Magnitogorsk in the Soviet Union to work as a welder for five years in the building of Stalin's premier steel-making city. In a memoir written on his return he recorded his personal observation of the astoundingly high human price of the hyperindustrialization program, the starving of peasants driven from the land in the collectivization program, and the murderous injustices of Stalin's purges. Although disconcerted, Scott's experiences did not disillusion him with communism. He stated that the Soviet people believed (and Scott clearly shared their belief) "it was worth while to shed blood, sweat, and tears" to lay "the foundations for a new society farther along the road of human progress than anything in the West; a society which would guarantee its people not only personal freedom but absolute economic security." Fifty years later Magnitogorsk, along with the rest of the Soviet Union, is in severe crisis, with an economy in grim disarray and a society crippled by the systemic failure of Soviet communism. The future that Scott assumed would justify the appalling cost in human life and suffering instead condemns it as a hideous waste. Scott's memoir, read in the 1990s, is a sad story of wasted commitment and wasted life. So, too, American communism is a sad tale of wasted commitment and wasted life.[7]

Chronology

1917   Lenin and the Communist party seize power in Russia.

1919   Two separate Communist parties founded in the United States. Red Scare raids drive American Communists underground.

1921   The Communist International forces squabbling American parties to unify. American Communists form a legal Workers party, controlled by the underground.

1922   The underground Bridgman Convention raided by police.

1923   Communist underground dissolved.

1924   Communists gain control of Farmer-Labor party, abandon support for Robert La Follette's presidential bid and nominate William Foster.

1925   Comintern intervenes in intraparty dispute and gives control to Charles Ruthenberg. C.P. leads Passaic textile strike.

1927   Ruthenberg dies, succeeded as party leader by Jay Lovestone.

1928   Sixth Comintern Congress proclaims new era of revolutionary upsurge. American C.P. sets up dual unions to supplant AFL. Comintern urges self-determination for black Americans in the Black Belt. Trotskyists expelled.

1929   Stalin removes Lovestone; C.P. expels him. Communists lead Gastonia textile strike.

1930   Communists lead raucous demonstrations of unemployed.

1931   Angelo Herndon and Scottsboro cases focus attention on plight of Southern blacks. Communist-led hunger marches.

1932   Presidential ticket of Foster and Ford gets over 100,000 votes, calls for a Soviet America.

1933   First new united fronts, such as American League against War and Fascism, formed.

1934   Earl Browder becomes general secretary of the Communist Party USA. Dual unions dissolved.

1935   Seventh Comintern Congress proclaims Popular Front policy. Formation of American Student Union with substantial Communist presence.

1936   Communists give indirect support for FDR's reelection. Communist organizers flock into the CIO. For first time majority of party is native-born. Party prominent in National Negro Congress, Workers Alliance, and League of American Writers.

1937   Several thousand American Communists fight in the International Brigades in Spain. C.P. embraces FDR after his Quarantine the Aggressors speech.

1939   Nazi-Soviet Pact leads to break with FDR and renunciation of Popular Front. Most fronts collapse.

1941   Nazi attack on Soviet Union spurs second Popular Front.

1942   C.P. calls for second front in Europe. Supports incentive pay schemes and no-strike pledge.

1943   Teheran meeting of FDR, Churchill, and Stalin. Comintern dissolved. Young Communist League replaced by American Youth for Democracy.

1944   Browder dissolves the Communist party and replaces it with the Communist Political Association. Communists and allies take control of American Labor party in New York.

1945   Article by French Communist Jacques Duclos criticizes abolition of the C.P. Browder refuses to recant and is expelled from the reconstituted party the following year.

1946   Eugene Dennis becomes general secretary of CPUSA.

1947   Soviet Union announces formation of Communist Information Bureau (Cominform). Truman sets up loyalty program for government employees. Top party leaders indicted for violating the Smith Act.

1948   Communists support Henry Wallace's Progressive party, fracturing alliances in the CIO and on the Left.

1950   CIO expels Communist-led unions. Passage of McCarran Act, setting up Subversives Activities Control Board.

1951 Party leaders convicted under Smith Act jump bail and go underground. Party creates elaborate underground apparatus.

1956 Khrushchev's secret speech on Stalin's crimes causes upheaval, exacerbated by Hungarian Revolution. Reform faction led by John Gates pushes for change in structure and policies.

1957 Prosecution of Communists using the Smith Act made virtually impossible by the Supreme Court's Yates decision. Party hardliners, led by William Foster, gain upper hand in the party as disillusioned Communists quit.

1958 John Gates resigns from CPUSA. *Daily Worker* shuts down. Membership reduced to 3,000.

1959 Gus Hall engineers Dennis's ouster as general secretary and becomes new party leader.

1961 Pro-Maoists expelled from the C.P., form the Progressive Labor Movement the following year.

1962 Students for a Democratic Society adopts Port Huron Statement.

1964 Free Speech Movement at the University of California, Berkeley. Progressive Labor Movement active in Harlem riots.

1965 Trotskyists and Communists active in anti–Vietnam War movement.

1966 Formation of Black Panther party.

1968 SDS activists lead seizure of buildings at Columbia University. Radicals disrupt Democratic National Convention. Progressive Labor and independent Marxist-Leninists compete for control of SDS.

1969 SDS splinters. Formation of Weatherman, dedicated to violent protests and guerrilla war in "Amerika."

1973 Various Maoist groups compete for influence among remnants of New Left.

1979 Five leaders of Communist Workers party, small Maoist sect, killed by Nazis and Klansmen in Greensboro, North Carolina.

1981 Remnants of Weather Underground and Black Liberation Army arrested after botched holdup of Brinks truck in Nyack, New York, leaves several dead.

1989 Signs of C.P. growth cut short by collapse of communism in Eastern Europe.

Notes and References

Chapter 2

1. C. E. Ruthenberg, "The Russian Revolution and the American Communist Movement," *The Worker,* 4 November 1922, 2.

2. Harry N. Scheiber, Harold G. Vatter, and Harold U. Faulkner, *American Economic History* (New York: Harper & Row, 1976), 229, 241, 243.

3. Aileen S. Kraditor, *The Radical Persuasion, 1890–1917: Aspects of the Intellectual History and the Historiography of Three American Radical Organizations* (Baton Rouge: Louisiana State University Press, 1981), 9–10.

4. *Proceedings of the First Convention of the Industrial Workers of the World* (New York: IWW, 1905), 1–2.

5. *International Socialist Review* 12 (February 1912): 467.

6. *New Times,* 18 July, 1, 8, 15, 22 August 1914.

7. Louis Fraina, "Unionism and Mass Action," *The Revolutionary Age,* 12 July 1919.

8. "War Proclamation and Program" of the S.P. at the St. Louis, Missouri, convention, April, 1917, quoted in New York Legislature, Joint Legislative Committee [Lusk Committee], *Revolutionary Radicalism: Its History, Purpose, and Tactics* (Albany, N.Y.: J. B. Lyon, 1920), 613–18.

9. *Rabochey—i—Krestyanin,* 8 November 1919, quoted in Lusk Committee, *Revolutionary Radicalism,* 1359–60. *Rabochey—i—Krestyanin* was published by the Union of Russian Workers.

10. Harry Hiltzik in "Report of the National Left Wing Conference," *The Revolutionary Age,* 9 August 1919, 13. "What Is Victory Anyway?," *The Ohio Socialist,* 1 January 1919, 3.

11. Lenin and Leon Trotsky, *The Proletarian Revolution in Russia,* ed. Louis C. Fraina (New York: Communist Press, 1918), xix. John Reed, "Red Russia: The Triumph of the Bolsheviki," *The Liberator,* March 1918.

12. C. E. Ruthenberg, "Austria Joins the Soviets," *The Ohio Socialist,* 23 April 1919, 4.

13. John Reed, *Ten Days That Shook the World* (New York: Boni and Liveright, 1919), xii.

14. *Luokkataistelu,* May 1919, quoted in Lusk Committee, *Revolutionary Radicalism,* 1191.

15. *The Revolutionary Age,* 31 May 1919; Alexander Stoklitsky, "Along the Descent to Disaster," *The Revolutionary Age,* 15 March 1919.

16. Julia Hill, "The Bolsheviks Will Catch You If You Don't Watch Out," *The Revolutionary Age,* 18 December 1919.

17. "Platform and Program: Communist Labor Party," reprinted in Lusk Committee, *Revolutionary Radicalism,* 809–17.

18. "The Communist Party Manifesto," reprinted in Lusk Committee, *Revolutionary Radicalism,* 776–98.

19. *The Communist,* 18 October 1919.

20. The membership numbers here and most of those used in this chapter are from Theodore Draper, *The Roots of American Communism* (New York: Viking Press, 1957). The language breakdown total is slightly above the number of recorded dues-paying members.

21. "Reds Ousted But Red Prevails," *The Ohio Socialist,* 22 January 1919, 1.

22. *The Communist,* 4 October 1919.

23. "Communist Party Manifesto," 782.

24. Quoted in William Leuchtenburg, *The Perils of Prosperity, 1914–32* (Chicago: University of Chicago Press, 1958), 81.

25. Quoted in Irving Howe and Lewis Coser, *The American Communist Party: A Critical History (1919–1957)* (Boston: Beacon Press, 1957), 67.

26. "Program of the United Communist Party," reprinted in Lusk Committee, *Revolutionary Radicalism,* 1882.

27. Quoted in Draper, *Roots of American Communism,* 262–63.

28. Quoted in ibid., 274.

29. Quoted in ibid., 277.

30. Quoted in Edward Johanningsmeier, "William Z. Foster and the Syndicalist League of North America," *Labor History* 30 (Summer 1989): 338.

31. *The Communist,* March 1922, quoted in Draper, *Roots of American Communism,* 354. There were once again two newspapers entitled *The Communist.* This quote is from the one published by the underground enthuiasts.

32. John Pepper column, *The Worker,* 25 August 1923, 3.

33. Roger B. Nelson [Lovestone], *The Communist,* 21 October 1921.

34. A. Raphael [Bittelman], *The Communist,* October 1921.

35. Lincoln Steffens, *The Autobiography of Lincoln Steffens* (New York: Harcourt, Brace, 1931), 799.

36. Quoted in Aileen Kraditor, *"Jimmy Higgins": The Mental World of the American Rank-and-File Communist, 1930–1958,* (New York: Greenwood Press, 1988), 221.

37. "Speech by Wm. Z. Foster at Y.W.L. Convention," *Daily Worker*, 9 October 1925, 4. The Young Workers League was the youth arm of the C.P.

38. Quoted in Harvey Klehr, "Leninism and Lovestoneism," *Studies in Comparative Communism* 8 (1974): 9.

39. Quoted in Theodore Draper, *American Communism and Soviet Russia* (New York: Viking Press, 1950), 298.

40. Joseph Stalin, "First Speech Delivered in the Presidium of the E.C.C.I. on the American Question, May 14, 1929," in *Stalin's Speeches on the American Communist Party* (Communist Party, U.S.A., [1931?]), 31.

41. Max Bedacht, "The Comintern Address to Our Party," *Daily Worker*, 3 July 1929, 4.

42. Whittaker Chambers, *Witness* (New York: Random House, 1952), 203–4.

43. Max Shachtman, "Memoirs and Interviews," Oral History Project, Columbia University, 1972, 432.

Chapter 3

1. Will Weinstone, "March 6th in the USA," *International Press Correspondence*, 20 March 1930, 257.

2. *Daily Worker*, 29 March 1930, 1, 5; 30 March 1930, 1, 3.

3. Earl Browder, "Next Tasks of the Communist Party of the USA," *Communist*, November-December 1930, 973.

4. "Resolution of the Political Secretariat of the ECCI [Executive Committee of the Communist International] on the Situation and Tasks of the CPUSA," Theodore Draper Papers, Emory University, box 1, folder 22, pp. 2, 4–6.

5. *New York Times*, 17 October 1930, 1, 3.

6. *Daily Worker*, 11 February 1931, 1; 13 February 1931, 3.

7. Ossip Piatnitsky, *Urgent Questions of the Day* (London: Modern Books, 1931), 5–6.

8. *Daily Worker*, 29 August 1931, 2.

9. Alex Baskin, "The Ford Hunger March—1932," *Labor History* 13, (Summer 1972): 331–60.

10. Roger Daniels, *The Bonus March* (Westport, Conn.: Greenwood Press, 1971), 174–75.

11. Malcolm Cowley, "King Mob and John Law," *New Republic*, 21 December 1932, 155.

12. *Labor Unity*, 29 March 1930, 2.

13. "Resolution of the Political Secretariat of the ECCI."

14. "Lessons of the Strike Struggles in the USA," *Communist*, May 1932, 410.

15. Ibid.

16. Theodore Draper, "The Communists and the Miners, 1928–1933," *Dissent* 19 (Spring 1972): 371–92; *Labor Unity,* May 1932, 16.

17. William Z. Foster, *Toward Soviet America* (New York: Coward-McCann, 1932), 271–317.

18. *Culture and the Crisis* (New York: Workers Library, 1932).

19. *Daily Worker,* 22 May 1933, 2; 3 June 1933, 3. Clarence Hathaway, "A Warning against Opportunistic Distortions of the United Front Tactic," *Communist,* June 1933, 534.

20. J. B. Matthews, *Odyssey of a Fellow-Traveller* (New York: privately printed, 1938).

21. Harvey Klehr, *The Heyday of American Communism: The Depression Decade* (New York: Basic Books, 1984), 114–17.

22. Jack Stachel, "Lessons of the Economic Struggles and the Work in the Trade Unions," *Communist,* March 1934, 286.

23. *Daily Worker,* 15 September 1934, 4.

24. *Daily Worker,* 1 October 1932, 3.

25. Klehr, *Heyday,* 161–66.

26. Gil Green, "The Open Letter and Tasks of the YCL," *Communist,* August 1933, 818.

27. James Wechsler, *Revolt on the Campus* (New York: Covici, Fried, 1935).

28. Harvey Klehr and William Tompson, "Self-Determination in the Black Belt: Origins of a Comintern Policy," *Labor History* 30 (Summer 1989): 354–66.

29. *New York Times,* 28 February 1931, 22; *Race Hatred on Trial* (New York: Workers Library, 1931).

30. *Daily Worker,* 30 August 1934, 6. Sinclair lost the general election.

31. *Daily Worker,* 16 February 1935, 7; 19 January 1935, 3. "On the Main Immediate Tasks of the CPUSA," *Communist,* February 1935, 126.

32. *VII Congress of the Communist International: Abridged Stenographic Report of Proceedings* (Moscow: Foreign Languages Publishing House, 1939), 361.

33. Institute of Marxism-Leninism, Central Committee of the CPSU, *Outline History of the Communist International* (Moscow: Progress, 1971), 403.

34. Earl Browder, "For a Common Front against the War-Makers," *Communist,* November 1937, 1043.

35. Melvyn Dubofsky and Warren Van Tine, *John L. Lewis* (New York: Quadrangle Books, 1977).

36. CPUSA Political Committee Minutes, 23 March 1939, in Draper Papers, box 1, folder 60.

37. Clarence Hathaway, "The 1938 Elections and Our Tasks," *Communist,* March 1938, 216.

38. Earl Browder, *Unity for Peace and Democracy* (New York: Workers Library, 1939), 24.

39. Israel Amter, "Work among National Groups: A Central Communist Task," *Communist,* May 1939, 462.

40. John Haynes, "The New History of the Communist Party in State Politics: The Implications for Mainstream Political History," *Labor History* 27 (Fall 1985): 549–63.

41. John Salmond, *A Southern Rebel: The Life and Times of Aubrey Willis Williams, 1890–1965* (Chapel Hill, University of North Carolina Press, 1983).

42. Joe Klein, *Woody Guthrie: A Life* (New York: Knopf, 1980).

43. Alan Wald, *The New York Intellectuals* (Chapel Hill: University of North Carolina Press, 1987).

44. Philip Jaffe, *The Rise and Fall of American Communism* (New York: Horizon Press, 1975), 38–49.

45. "Keep America Out of the Imperialist War," *Communist,* October 1939, 901.

46. Quoted in Maurice Isserman, *Which Side Were You On?: The American Communist Party during the Second World War* (Middletown, Conn.: Wesleyan University Press, 1982), 63, 65.

Chapter 4

1. Earl Browder, "Teheran: History's Greatest Turning Point," *The Communist,* January 1944, 3, 7.

2. Earl Browder, *Teheran and America* (New York: 1944).

3. Robert Thompson, "Reply to Letter to the editor," *Spotlight,* February 1944. Claudia Jones "From the Editor" *Spotlight,* April 1944, quoted in Kraditor, *"Jimmy Higgins,"* 67 *Spotlight* was published by the C.P.'s youth arm.

4. Joseph E. Davies, *Mission to Moscow* (New York: Simon & Schuster, 1941), 357.

5. Jacques Duclos, "On the Dissolution of the American Communist Party," translated in *Political Affairs,* July 1945.

6. "CP Raps Press Hubbub on Browder," *Daily Worker,* 30 April 1946, 2.

7. Quoted in Howe and Coser, *American Communist Party,* 455.

8. William Z. Foster, "American Imperialism, Leader of World Reaction," *Political Affairs,* August 1946, 694–95.

9. William Z. Foster, "Leninism and Postwar Problems," *Political Affairs,* February 1946, 102.

10. Alexander Bittelman, "Stalin: On His Seventieth Birthday," *Political Affairs,* December 1949, 1. Elizabeth Gurley Flynn, "He Loved the People," *Political Affairs,* April 1953, 43.

11. Alexander Bittelman, "How Shall We Fight for Full Employment," *Political Affairs,* January 1946, 57–58.

12. Eugene Dennis, *America at the Crossroads: Postwar Problems and Communist Policy* (New York: New Century, 1945).

13. Eugene Dennis, "Defeat the Imperialist Drive toward Fascism and War," *Political Affairs,* September 1946, 798, 802.

14. Quoted in Bert Cochran, *Labor and Communism: The Conflict That Shaped American Unions* (Princeton, N.J.: Princeton University Press, 1977), 267.

15. Eugene Dennis, "The Communists and 1948," *The Worker,* 28 September 1947.

16. Joseph Starobin, *American Communism in Crisis, 1943–1957* (Cambridge: Harvard University Press, 1972), 232.

17. Quoted in Cochran, *Labor and Communism,* 300.

18. For a detailed discussion of the struggle between Popular Front and anti-Communist liberals in Minnesota, see John Earl Haynes, *Dubious Alliance: The Making of Minnesota's DFL Party* (Minneapolis: University of Minnesota Press, 1984).

19. Quoted in Curtis MacDougall, *Gideon's Army* (New York: Marzani & Munsell, 1965), 1:191.

20. Quoted in Starobin, *American Communism in Crisis,* 199.

21. "Special Study: 'How to Spot a Communist'," Joseph Rauh Papers, Manuscript Division, Library of Congress, box 72. The Mosinee incident and similar matters are discussed in Richard M. Fried, *Nightmare in Red: The McCarthy Era in Perspective* (New York: Oxford University Press, 1990), 98–99.

22. The nomenclature and description of the C.P. underground are from Starobin, *American Communism in Crisis,* 214–223.

23. Fried, *Nightmare in Red,* 131.

24. Eugene Dennis, *The Communists Take a New Look* (New York: New Century, 1956).

25. Quotations from Kraditor, *"Jimmy Higgins,"* 85; *Mainstream,* March 1957; and American Jewish Committee, *Memorandum on the American Communists.* The view advanced here follows that of Kraditor.

26. Peggy Dennis, *The Autobiography of an American Communist: A Personal View of a Political Life, 1925–1975* (Westport, Conn.: Lawrence Hill, 1977), 225.

27. "For Creative Marxism," *The Worker,* 23 September 1956, 7.

28. Eugene Dennis, letter to the editor, *Daily Worker,* 12 Nov. 1956, 4.

29. *International Affairs* (USSR), March 1957.

30. *The Worker,* 9 March 1958. "On the Resignation of John Gates," *Political Affairs,* March 1958, 7–9.

Chapter 5

1. Walter Goodman, *The Committee* (New York: Farrar, Strauss & Giroux, 1968), 422–34.

2. C. Wright Mills, "Letter to the New Left," in *The New Left: A Collection of Essays,* ed. P. Long, (Boston: Porter Sargent, 1969), 25.

3. Maurice Isserman, *If I Had a Hammer . . . The Death of the Old Left and the Birth of the New Left* (New York: Basic Books, 1987), 167–70. Guenter Lewy, *The Cause That Failed: Communism in American Political Life* (New York: Oxford University Press, 1990), 226–35.

4. Goodman, *The Committee,* 441.

5. David Garrow, *The FBI and Martin Luther King, Jr.* (New York: Norton, 1981), 21–78.

6. Todd Gitlin, *The Sixties: Years of Hope, Days of Rage* (New York: Bantam Books, 1987), 109–26.

7. Jack Newfield, *A Prophetic Minority* (New York: New American Library, 1966), 144.

8. Ibid., 119.

9. House of Representatives, Committee on Un-American Activities, *Violations of State Department Travel Regulations and Pro-Castro Propaganda Activities in the US,* 88th Congress, September 13, 1963, 3:698.

10. Kirkpatrick Sale, *SDS* (New York: Vintage Books, 1974), 237.

11. Fred Halstead, *Out Now* (New York: Monad Press, 1978), 37–38.

12. Ibid., 154–65.

13. Gitlin, *The Sixties,* 307.

14. Sale, *SDS,* 451; Gitlin, *The Sixties,* 308.

15. Sale, *SDS,* 535.

16. Ibid., 489.

17. Ibid., 521.

18. Ibid., 563–74.

19. Harold Jacobs, ed., *Weatherman* (San Francisco: Ramparts Press, 1970), 53.

20. Sale, *SDS,* 590.

21. Ibid., 582, 583.

22. Peter Collier and David Horowitz, "Doing It: The Inside Story of the Rise and Fall of the Weather Underground," *Rolling Stone,* 10 September 1982, 30.

23. "The Revolutionary Perspective and Leninist Continuity in the United States," *New International,* Spring 1985. *Militant,* September 1, 1978, 1.

24. Jack Barnes, "Their Trotsky and Ours," *New International,* Fall 1983.

25. For more extensive discussions of these groups, see Harvey Klehr, *Far Left of Center: The American Radical Left Today* (New Brunswick, N.J.: Transaction Books, 1988).

26. Leroi Jones, "The Black Man Has No Other Choice," *Progressive Labor,* November–December 1964, 26, 27.

27. Harvey Klehr, "Maoists Move In on Manhattan Dems," *Our Town,* 2 August 1987.

28. John Castellucci, *The Big Dance* (New York: Dodd, Mead, 1986).

29. *Crusader,* May–June 1964.

30. *Dissent,* Summer 1965.

31. Angela Davis, *An Autobiography* (New York: Random House, 1974).

32. *Daily World,* 5 May 1983.

33. *Daily World,* 10 May 1985.

34. Jack O'Dell, "The Mass Movement and Electoral Politics," *CALC Report,* December 1984.

35. See, for example, Fraser Ottanelli, *The Communist Party of the United States: From the Depression to World War II* (New Brunswick: Rutgers University Press, 1991), David Leviatin, *Followers of the Trail: Jewish Working Class Radicals in America* (New Haven: Yale University Press, 1989), Robbie Lieberman, *My Song Is My Weapon: People's Songs, American Communism, and the Politics of Culture* (Urbana: University of Illinois Press, 1989), Roger Keeran, *The Communist Party and the Auto Workers Unions* (Bloomington: Indiana University Press, 1980), Robin Kelley, *Hammer and Hoe: Alabama Communists During the Great Depression* (Chapel Hill: University of North Carolina Press, 1990), Christopher Johnson, *Maurice Sugar: Law, Labor, and the Left in Detroit, 1912–1950* (Detroit: Wayne State University Press, 1988), Gerald Horne, *Black and Red: W.E.B. Du Bois and the Afro-American Response to the Cold War, 1944–1963* (Albany: State University of New York Press, 1986), and Franklin Folsom, *Impatient Armies of the Poor* (Niwot, Colorado: University Press of Colorado, 1991). A vigorous and spirited attack on this new history of the CPUSA is Theodore Draper, "American Communism Revisited," *New York Review of Books* 32, 8 (May 9, 1985) and "The Popular Front Revisited," *New York Review of Books* 32, 9 (May 30, 1985).

36. Victor Navasky, *Naming Names* (New York: Viking Press, 1980), 423.

37. Harvey Klehr and David Evanier, "Anticommunism and Mental Health," *American Spectator,* February 1989, 28–30.

38. *People's Daily World,* 16 June 1990.

39. *Workers Vanguard,* 15 June 1990.

40. *People's Weekly World,* 3 August 1991, p. 4; 24 August 1991, p. 18.

Chapter 6

1. Anna Louise Strong, *I Change Worlds: The Remaking of an American* (New York: Holt, 1935), v.

2. A. B. Magil, "Scientist of Socialism," *New Masses,* 22 January 1946. William Foster, *The Twilight of World Capitalism* (New York: International, 1949), 149. "Just a Minute," *New Masses,* 10 December 1946.

3. Benjamin Gitlow, *The Whole of Their Lives: Communism in America: A Personal History and Intimate Portrayal of Its Leaders* (New York: Scribner, 1948).

4. Quoted in Kraditor, *"Jimmy Higgins,"* 62–63.

5. Tillie Olsen, "I Want You Women Up North to Know," *Partisan,* March 1934.

6. The relationship of the C.P. with Soviet intelligence is discussed in Herbert Romerstein and Stanislav Levchenko, *The KGB against the "Main Enemy"* (Lexington, Mass.: Lexington Books, 1989).

7. John Scott, *Behind the Urals: An American Worker in Russia's City of Steel.* (Boston: Houghton Mifflin, 1942), 248. Scott later turned against communism.

Bibliographic Essay

Although the authors have done original research on aspects of Communist history and take responsibility for the interpretation advanced in this volume, in preparing this comprehensive history of the movement they wish to acknowledge their reliance upon and heavy debt to other researchers, some noted below, who have written on the movement's history.

Among the leading books on the history of American communism are Theodore Draper's *The Roots of American Communism* (New York: Viking Press, 1957) and *American Communism and Soviet Russia: The Formative Period* (New York: Viking Press, 1960); both are superb scholarly studies of the origins of American communism and take the history of the party up to 1929. Draper emphasizes the power of Soviet bolshevism in shaping American communism and the rapid subordination of American communism to Soviet leadership. Harvey Klehr's *The Heyday of American Communism: The Depression Decade* (New York: Basic Books, 1984) carries the story to the beginning of World War II. Whereas Draper's books looked almost exclusively at the party's inner life, *The Heyday of American Communism* reflects communism's spread into broader arenas, with material on Communist work in the labor movement and among farmers, ethnic groups, blacks, intellectuals, the unemployed, and youth. Although the authors are not convinced by Maurice Isserman's argument in *Which Side Were You On? The American Communist Party during the Second World War* (Middletown: Wesleyan University Press, 1982) that in the Popular Front period the party recruited a generation of Communists who sought a democratic form of communism, Isserman's scholarship makes his book an excellent history of the party during the war. Philip J. Jaffe's *The Rise and Fall of American Communism* (New York: Horizon Press, 1975) is partly a biography of Earl Browder, partly a history of the party from 1939 to 1945, and partly a compilation of C.P. documents. Joseph Starobin's *American Communism in Crisis, 1943–1957* (Cambridge: Harvard University Press, 1972) carries the party's history from Browder's ouster in 1945 to the near disintegration of the movement in 1956–58. Starobin was a party official who became a historian after he left the movement. His involvement in the movement gives his narrative considerable emotional power. He sees the party's tragic and fatal flaw in its attachment to the model of Soviet communism and its voluntary subordination to Soviet foreign policy goals. Irving Howe and Lewis Coser's *The American Communist Party: A Critical History* (Boston: Beacon Press, 1957) was for many years the only comprehensive one-volume history of American communism. Although polemical in tone and growing dated, its excellent scholarship makes it still a useful work. Guenter Lewy's *The Cause That Failed: Communism in American Political Life* (New York: Oxford University Press, 1990) combines a summary of party history with an examination of post–World War II liberal anticommunism and of the relationship of major civil liberties, peace, and disarmament groups and the New Left of the late 1960s and early 1970s with communism. Aileen S. Kraditor in *"Jimmy Higgins": The Mental World of the American Rank-and-File Communist, 1930–1958* (Westport Conn.: Greenwood Press, 1988) provides an analysis of the attitudes and ideology of ordinary Communists.

A number of books treat the Communist role in the labor movement. Bert Cochran's *Labor and Communism: The Conflict That Shaped American Unions* (Princeton, N.J.: Princeton University Press, 1977) emphasizes the struggle between Communists and anti-Communists in the United Auto Workers and several other key CIO unions. Cochran emphasizes the totalitarian and pro-Soviet character of American communism but is also highly critical of anti-Communists for supporting America's cold-war stance. Harvey A. Levenstein's *Communism, Anticommunism, and the CIO* (Westport, Conn.: Greenwood Press, 1981) surveys the Communist role in the CIO. Although mildly critical of American communism's undemocratic character and Soviet links, Levenstein largely treats CIO Communists in a sympathetic fashion while seeing opposition to communism as inherently morally suspect. In sharp contrast, Max Kampelman in *The Communist Party vs. the C.I.O.: A Study in Power Politics* (New York: Praeger, 1957) sees the Communist role as negative, conspiratorial, and manipulative and shares the position of anti-Communist union leaders such as Walter Reuther and Philip Murray. The Communist role in several key unions is discussed in Ronald Schatz's *The Electrical Workers* (Urbana: University of Illinois Press, 1983), Joshua Freeman's *In Transit: The Transport Workers Union in New York City, 1933–1966* (New York: Oxford University Press, 1989) and Roger Keeran's *The Communist Party and the Auto Workers Unions* (Bloomington: Indiana University Press, 1980). The party's pioneering work in organizing agricultural workers is discussed in Cletus Daniel's *Bitter Harvest: A History of California Farmworkers, 1870–1941* (Ithaca, N.Y.: Cornell University Press, 1981) and Robin Kelley, *Hammer and Hoe: Alabama Communists During the Great Depression* (Chapel Hill: University of North Carolina Press, 1990). Lowell Dyson's *Red Harvest: The Communist Party and American Farmers* (Lincoln: University of Nebraska Press, 1982) is an admirable scholarly examination of the activity of American Communists among farmers from the early 1920s until the late 1930s.

Nathan Glazer in *The Social Basis of American Communism* (New York: Harcourt, Brace & World, 1961) examines the socioeconomic background of Communist party members. Harvey Klehr in *Communist Cadre: The Social Background of the American Communist Party Elite* (Stanford, Calif.: Hoover Institution Press, 1978) looks at the ethnic and social background of members of the party's central committees. The role of Finnish Americans in American communism is discussed in Auvo Kostiainen's *The Forging of Finnish-American Communism, 1917–1924: A Study In Ethnic Radicalism*, Annales Universitatis Turkuensis, Series B, no. 147 (Turku, Finland: University of Turku, 1978). Mark Naison in *Communists in Harlem during the Depression* (Urbana: University of Illinois Press, 1983) provides a scholarly and generally positive appraisal of Communist work among New York blacks. Charles Martin's *The Angelo Herndon Case and Southern Justice* (Baton Rouge: Louisiana State University Press, 1976) and Dan Carter's *Scottsboro: A Tragedy of the American South* (Baton Rouge: Louisiana State University Press, 1969) discuss two key episodes of the C.P. work among black Americans.

Daniel Aaron's *Writers on the Left: Episodes in American Literary Communism* (New York: Harcourt, Brace & World, 1959) discusses the influence of communism on writers in the 1930s and 1940s. Larry Ceplair and Steven Englund in *The Inquisition in Hollywood: Politics in the Film Community, 1930–1960* (Garden City, N.Y.: Anchor Press, 1980) looks at Communist and other radical political activity in Hollywood in the late 1930s from a sympathetic perspective. Robert Rosenstone in *Crusade on the Left: The Lincoln Battalion in the Spanish Civil War* (New York: Pegasus, 1969) examines the role of American Communists in the Spanish conflict. Two leading Communist splinter groups are examined in Constance Myers's *The Prophet's Army: Trotskyists in America, 1929–1941* (Westport, Conn.: Greenwood Press, 1977) and Robert Alexander's *The Right Opposition: The Lovestoneites and the International Communist Opposition of the 1930s* (Westport, Conn.: Greenwood Press, 1981). The role of communism and Communists in the New Left of the 1960s and 1970s is discussed critically by Peter Collier and David Horowitz, two former New Left journalists turned anti-Communists, in *Destructive Generation: Second Thoughts About the Sixties* (New York: Summit Books, 1989). Sympathetic accounts of the New Left include *SDS* (New York: Vintage Books, 1974) by Kirkpatrick Sale, *The Sixties: Years of Hope, Days of Rage* (New York: Bantam Books, 1987) by Todd Gitlin, president of SDS in 1963, and *"Democracy is in the Streets": From Port Huron to the Siege of Chicago* (New York: Simon & Schuster, 1987) by James Miller, an SDS activist in the late 1960s. Harvey Klehr's *Far Left of Center: The American Radical Left Today* (New Brunswick, N.J.: Transaction Books, 1988) surveys New Left and Marxist-Leninist radicals active in the 1970s and 1980s.

Two key espionage cases that in the public mind linked American Communists with Soviet espionage are definitively discussed in Allen Weinstein's *Perjury: The Hiss-Chambers Case* (New York: Knopf, 1978) and in *The Rosenberg File: A*

Search for the Truth (New York: Holt, Rinehart & Wilson, 1983) by Ronald Radosh and Joyce Milton. Earl Latham's *The Communist Controversy in Washington* (Cambridge: Harvard University Press, 1966) provides a reliable history for anyone needing an introduction to the House Un-American Activities Committee, the Smith Act, the controversy over loyalty programs, the Hiss-Chambers Case, the Amerasia affair, and the saga of Senator Joseph McCarthy. Richard M. Fried's *Nightmare in Red: The McCarthy Era in Perspective* (New York: Oxford University Press, 1990) is also a useful survey. The two best books on McCarthy himself are David M. Oshinsky's *A Conspiracy So Immense: The World of Joe McCarthy* (New York: Free Press, 1983) and Thomas C. Reeves's *The Life and Times of Joe McCarthy* (New York: Stein and Day, 1982).

Readers wishing to examine the history of American communism in more detail have available a large body of literature. John Earl Haynes's *Communism and Anti-Communism in the United States: An Annotated Guide to Historical Writings* (New York: Garland, 1987) lists more than 2,000 books, journal articles, and dissertations. The production of new studies is high, and more recent publications are listed in the quarterly bibliographic articles carried in the *Newsletter of the Historians of American Communism*.

Index

The Authors

Harvey Klehr, Samuel Candler Dobbs Professor of Politics at Emory University, is the author of *The Heyday of American Communism: The Depression Decade* (New York: Basic Books, 1984), *Communist Cadre: The Social Background of the American Communist Party Elite* (Stanford, Calif.: Hoover Institution Press, 1978), *Far Left of Center: The American Radical Left Today* (New Brunswick, N.J.: Transaction, 1988), and, with Bernard K. Johnpoll, the *Bibliographical Dictionary of the American Left* (Westport, Conn.: Greenwood Press, 1986) and numerous essays on the American Communist movement.

John Earl Haynes has edited the *Newsletter of the Historians of American Communism* for 10 years and is the author of *Communism and Anti-Communism in the United States: An Annotated Guide to Historical Writings* (New York: Garland, 1987), *Dubious Alliance: The Making of Minnesota's DFL Party* (Minneapolis: University of Minnesota Press, 1984), and many articles on American communism and anticommunism.